T0159360

The Perennial Philosophy

Series

World Wisdom
The Library of Perennial Philosophy

The Library of Perennial Philosophy is dedicated to the exposition of the timeless Truth underlying the diverse religions. This Truth, often referred to as the *Sophia Perennis*—or Perennial Wisdom—finds its expression in the revealed Scriptures as well as the writings of the great sages and the artistic creations of the traditional worlds.

Of the Land and the Spirit: The Essential Lord Northbourne on Ecology and Religion appears as one of our selections in the Perennial Philosophy series.

The Perennial Philosophy Series

In the beginning of the twentieth century, a school of thought arose which has focused on the enunciation and explanation of the Perennial Philosophy. Deeply rooted in the sense of the sacred, the writings of its leading exponents establish an indispensable foundation for understanding the timeless Truth and spiritual practices which live in the heart of all religions. Some of these titles are companion volumes to the Treasures of the World's Religions series, which allows a comparison of the writings of the great sages of the past with the perennialist authors of our time.

Cover: All Saint's Church, Bakewell (part of the
Peak District National Park), in Derbyshire, England

OF THE LAND &
THE SPIRIT

The Essential Lord Northbourne
on Ecology & Religion

Including Correspondence with
Thomas Merton

Edited by
Christopher James,
the 5th Lord Northbourne
&
Joseph A. Fitzgerald

Foreword by
Wendell Berry

World Wisdom

Of the Land and the Spirit:
The Essential Lord Northbourne
on Ecology and Religion
© 2008 World Wisdom, Inc.

Library of Congress Cataloging-in-Publication Data

Northbourne, Lord, 1896-1982.
Of the land & the spirit : the essential Lord Northbourne on ecology & religion :
including correspondence with Thomas Merton / edited by Christopher James, the
5th Lord Northbourne & Joseph A. Fitzgerald ; foreword by Wendell Berry.
    p. cm. -- (The library of perennial philosophy)
Includes bibliographical references and index.
ISBN 978-1-933316-61-1 (pbk. : alk. paper) 1. Religion--Philosophy. 2. Tradition
(Philosophy) 3. Agricultural ecology. I. Merton, Thomas, 1915-1968. II. James,
Christopher, Lord Northbourne, 1926- III. Fitzgerald, Joseph A., 1977- IV. Title. V.
Title: Of the land and the spirit.
  BL51.N83 2008
  201'.77--dc22

                                                                2008026351

Printed on acid-free paper in United States of America.

For information address World Wisdom, Inc.
P.O. Box 2682, Bloomington, Indiana 47402-2682
www.worldwisdom.com

CONTENTS

* Indicates material previously unpublished in book form.

FOREWORD

From the beginning it was always possible to find farmers who were intuitively suspicious of the industrialization of agriculture. Perhaps they objected to the increased authority of suppliers and experts. Perhaps they felt the discord between machinery and living creatures. Perhaps they had a rational fear of toxic chemicals. Perhaps they disliked paying cash for energy and fertility that they had previously received in kind from their farms and their good work. Among at least a few, for whatever reasons, there was a persistent distrust. Had it been otherwise, the growth of criticism and finally of resistance over the last sixty or seventy years could not have happened.

And so Lord Northbourne's *Look to the Land*, written late in the 1930s and published in 1940, is not an anomaly. It came certainly from its author's heritage and character as a countryman. His intuition, his *sense* of what made for good farming and healthy soil, must have told him, as it told others, that something was badly wrong with a view of agriculture that was reductively scientific, materialist, and mechanical. What is remarkable, even astonishing, is that he was capable so early of a criticism that still is sufficiently complex and coherent.

As a critic of agriculture, Lord Northbourne's qualifications went far beyond what we think of as intelligence and education. He was intelligent and educated, of course, but he was also experienced, observant, and passionately affectionate toward the land and the farmers. It is affection, I think, that sets him apart from the "objective" proponents of industrialization who, if they have affection, cannot admit it. And it is affection that undoubtedly gives to his criticism its indispensable breadth.

The criteria of industrial agriculture have been strictly limited to productivity, mechanical efficiency, and profitability (to the industrial suppliers of technology, fuel, and credit). Anyone experienced in good farming will recognize intuitively that those three measures, in isolation, can lead only to the impoverishment of everything involved (except, temporarily, the industrial suppliers). By contrast, Lord Northbourne rejected the simplifications by which productivity, for instance, could be divided from fertility and fertility from the life cycle and the life cycle from health. His purpose, as he understood, had to be wholeness. Agriculture partakes of the wholeness of life, which it inescapably must either preserve or destroy. In confronting industrial agriculture, he saw that he was confronting a "sickness" that was at once spiritual, economic, and biological.

Agriculture, as he saw it, is an order of perhaps infinite complexity, involving perhaps everything, from the microorganisms of the soil to the human cultures that can be founded only upon the soil. It involves the interdependence of all living creatures and of all living creatures with the non-living. And so it can be evaluated only by a complex set of standards that are separable only as a convenience of thought. The standards necessarily are *both* qualitative and quantitative, biologic, economic (in the usual sense of provisioning, but also in the senses of frugality and caretaking), social, cultural, and aesthetic. Farming involves intelligence, wisdom, devotion, love, compassion, freedom, wildness, harmony, health. It raises urgently questions about economic justice, propriety of scale, harmony between nature and human economy or wildness and cultivation. And all these concerns and considerations, to the limited extent that they can be thought about, can be resolved only in the art of farming a particular farm.

Lord Northbourne's writing on agriculture can thus be seen as an early, and an immensely capable, reaction against scientific reductionism and the partitioned structure of modern intellectual life. To say this is to give the reason for his continuing usefulness. As a critic of agriculture, he aimed at wholeness of vision, and nobody has come closer to achieving it.

⇥◆※◆⇤

From the complexity of his agricultural standards, and his perception that the problems of industrial agriculture have a "spiritual aspect", it is not surprising that much of Lord Northbourne's thought and writing was devoted to religion. Religion is a far more difficult subject than agriculture, and yet it is a subject that cannot be ignored, simply because it is not ignorable. Those who take agriculture seriously enough and study it long enough will come to issues that will have to be recognized as religious.

They must start, where Lord Northbourne starts, with the contempt for the material creation that, in our utter estrangement from reality, we call "materialism". Farmers, as some might say, are the primary materialists, for they are preoccupied with the insistent materiality of the world. But this very insistence drives them beyond materialism into the presence of mysteries and wonders. They do not control the weather or the seasons. They deal directly with powers, cycles, and lives that they did not make and do not entirely know. They know firsthand that "except a corn of wheat fall into the ground and die, it abideth alone: but if it die, it bringeth forth much fruit". They are well-positioned to doubt that the quality of human life can be rendered in a materialist or a merely quantitative accounting. As Jesus evidently knew, the connection of farming to religion is direct.

Lord Northbourne deals with this connection in Chapter 5, "Agriculture and Human Destiny",[1] published in 1970. This, to my mind, is one of the two paramount essays gathered here, both because of the importance of the subject and because of the intelligence with which it is treated. We need only to notice that, in the four decades since this chapter was written, the human economy—by means of toxic chemicals, nuclear technology, earth-moving machinery, and explosives—has grown fearfully as a geographic and even a geologic force; that the phenomenon of "peak oil" has placed us in a crisis of unprecedented extent and gravity; and that, therefore, the survival of proper methods and standards of land use has greatly increased in urgency.

"Agriculture", Lord Northbourne writes, "is the foundation of human life". This, though still and forever undeniable, may seem shockingly radical in a time when many experts believe agriculture has been superseded by manufacturing or "service" or "information". But agriculture is not just an economy. It is also (especially if we include forestry) the principal way we humans determine our place in nature, and therefore the principal way we practice, directly or by proxy, our religion, or our lack thereof. Now, as Lord Northbourne clearly saw, we are working out and suffering the implications of our divorce from Nature. But that divorce, so nearly perfect as it now is, is fairly recent:

> Formerly, man lived more or less in harmony with Nature, and played his part in maintaining what we call "a balance of Nature".

---

[1] Originally titled "A Glance at Agriculture". —Editors

> That natural balance, if we could but see it so, represents a fulfill-
> ment of the divine ordinances whereby all living things are related
> one to another through their common origin in God. . . .

Because we are at once natural creatures and created in God's
image, we necessarily mediate "between God and Nature". This is a
tough spot to be in, as the great teachers of religion have told us, and
as we are proving for ourselves. It is a tough spot because, in it, we
cannot be "neutral" and we cannot escape. We have great power, for
which the biblical term is "dominion", and we cannot use it except
well or poorly. If we use it poorly, which is to say selfishly, our
dominion itself is turned against us—as we are seeing in the reduc-
tions, distortions, and injustices of industrial agriculture and its sub-
serving sciences.

If an out-of-control agri-industrialism has thrown us profoundly
out of harmony with Nature and therefore with God, then it seems
that good farming would be just as validly and as fully a practice of
religion as any other vocation or kind of work. But here we encounter
what may be the greatest fault of our civilization. And here I appear
to be at odds with Lord Northbourne, who insists on the compat-
ibility of "orthodoxy" and the "true charity" of traditional religion
with "traditional laws" that "serve to maintain the social hierarchy".
Jesus undoubtedly was not a "social reformer" in our sense of that
term, and yet his teachings grant a decided precedence to fishermen,
shepherds, plowmen, sowers of seed, servants, and "the least of these
my brethren". My immediate point is that we have inherited an idea
of social hierarchy that depreciates bodily work as menial or servile or
low, and that this depreciation has been disastrous for (among other
arts) agriculture.

We obviously must deal, as Lord Northbourne does, with the
example of Mary who, in Luke 10:38-42, chose the "one thing [that]
is needful". And I can deal with this passage only by confessing that I
don't understand it. Though here, as elsewhere in the Gospels, I will-
ingly accept my failure of insight and my need for patience, maybe I
can usefully explain my bewilderment. Mary's sister, Martha, com-
plained that Mary wasn't helping her. Jesus evidently having come
to dinner without forewarning, Martha had a lot of housework on
her hands. She "was cumbered about much serving", like the Good
Samaritan and others whom Jesus praises, and like every good farmer.

If her work "was blameless and even necessary", as Lord Northbourne admits it was, I can't see why Jesus doesn't classify it as "needful". Nor can I see why Mary and Martha must be thought to represent mutually exclusive alternatives. Why, on the *next* day, couldn't Martha have sat at Jesus' feet while Mary did the housework? If we take this passage alone as indicating a divinely recommended hierarchy of occupations, then it seems to me that we come by mere logic to the modern structure of "mind over matter", in which good farmers are thought to be performing "mind-numbing", merely necessary work, while philosopher-kings sit clean-handed in universities performing the elitist and reductionist work of genetic modification—which I think is not what Lord Northbourne had in mind.

It may be objected that the most important human occupation is prayer, and that (as Lord Northbourne is careful to remind us) Jesus said for us to "take no thought, saying, What shall we eat? or, What shall we drink? or, Wherewithal shall we be clothed? . . . But seek ye first the kingdom of God, and his righteousness; and all these things shall be added unto you." But Jesus says this, nevertheless, in the material and practical circumstances of our earthly life, which are unforebearing and absolute and which he seems to take for granted. His instruction to seek first the kingdom of God does not imply that if we adopt that priority we will be nourished and clothed automatically or miraculously. Those benefits, though they are owed ultimately to God, will not come to us if we have not mastered and if we do not practice the arts of agriculture, viticulture, animal husbandry, cooking, food-preserving, sheep-shearing, spinning, weaving, and sewing. Might not these practices, properly performed, be ways of seeking the kingdom of God, as work (good work, I assume) *has* been said to be a way of prayer? At any rate, Jesus did not advise the hungry to pray for food or the sick to pray for health. He fed them, and he healed them.

When we get to questions of practice, it appears to me that the things of time and the things of eternity are not readily separable, and that sometimes they may be the same things.

→‣●✦✦●‣←

In his later writings Lord Northbourne aligns himself with a company of writers known as Traditionalists or Perennialists. The writers so designated, who were his associates and influences, are listed in the Introduction to this book: René Guénon, Frithjof Schuon, Marco Pallis, Ananda Coomaraswamy, Titus Burckhardt, and Martin Lings. I have read the four last-named at length and have been strongly affected and influenced by them. And so I find in Lord Northbourne's writings on art much to sympathize or agree with. But in reading him, as in reading other Traditionalists, I am sometimes bewildered. Here again it may be useful if, without disagreeing necessarily, I attempt to explain my bewilderment.

In Chapter 15, "Art Ancient and Modern", one never knows exactly what is meant by the adjectives "ancient" and "modern". Most people, I suppose, know vaguely what is meant by "ancient", but when does "ancient" leave off and "modern" begin? And what are we to make of twentieth century writers such as T. S. Eliot or David Jones or James Joyce who have ancient preoccupations but are modern in manner? If you are saying that "ancient art" is categorically better than "modern art", you have to get down to cases. You have to talk about specific artists and specific works of art. It is necessary "to compare things that possess a quality with things that do not", as Lord Northbourne himself suggests in Chapter 5. This is our only way of making qualitative sense either of art or of agriculture.

That this is true is demonstrated immediately in Chapter 16, "The Beauty of Flowers", which in my opinion is the second of this book's paramount essays. Maybe it is not possible to make a *winning* argument about beauty, but the argument here is precisely detailed and therefore persuasive. It has the authority and exuberance of exact knowledge and of long and ardent thought. It is a splendid essay, a masterwork, and it is exemplary.

Wendell Berry
Lanes Landing Farm
Port Royal, Kentucky

PREFACE

Lord Northbourne was a farmer who sought to fulfill a deeply felt responsibility towards the land he worked (he was, in fact, the first writer to describe his approach as one of "organic farming"), but he was also a man of faith who strived to see all things by the light of God's glorious and timeless Truth. This combination of concern for ecology and religion—for the earth which houses and sustains our life, and for God who gives purpose and meaning to our life—characterized Lord Northbourne both as a man and writer. In a manner that is simultaneously lofty and well-grounded, Lord Northbourne inquires into diverse aspects of the human situation. He begins with an examination of our necessary connection to the land, and thence proceeds to explore the broad fields of tradition, metaphysics, art, and life, each of which is seen in the light of the Spirit. The present anthology is intended to illustrate the uncommon breadth and depth that characterizes the written work of Lord Northbourne.

Of the Land and the Spirit: The Essential Lord Northbourne on Ecology and Religion is jointly edited[1] by Christopher James, the 5th Lord Northbourne and son of the author of these writings, and myself. Nearly half of the twenty articles presented herein have never before been published in book form. The remaining articles are gathered from the three books Lord Northbourne published during his life, *Look to the Land* (1940), *Religion in the Modern World* (1963), and *Looking Back on Progress* (1970).[2] We have arranged the selected articles in five topical sections that represent the recurring themes of

---

[1] The majority of articles are included in their entirety with only minor editorial changes, such as alterations to the punctuation and form of some sentences in order to enhance readability. In the interest of maintaining the succinctness of this anthology, we have abridged five of Lord Northbourne's more lengthy articles: "Soil and Growth"; "Health and Food"; "Farms and Farmers"; "Look to the Land: Sustainability"; and "The Ineluctable Alternative: A Letter to My Descendants". We believe that these changes do not alter the meaning or fundamental integrity of the text.

[2] Lord Northbourne's previously published books are available through Sophia Perennis (Ghent, NY). Each contains fascinating and valuable articles which for reasons of space cannot be included in the present volume.

Lord Northbourne's work. In brief these sections can be described as follows:

Farming: An Ecology in Practice

In four chapters taken from *Look to the Land*—his prescient first book written before the outbreak of the Second World War—Lord Northbourne diagnoses the causes of the linked biological and spiritual sickness affecting nearly the entire world. We are, however, left with a sense of hope as he offers a holistic prescription for a return to well-being. Lord Northbourne's "Agriculture and Human Destiny" further specifies the connection between the troubled state of modern agriculture and our disturbed relationship with God; as a sign of the times and a warning for our future, he points to a series of changes that have made it almost impossible for us to conceive "that agriculture—in common with all other human activities, social, artistic, military and so forth—can ever have been sacred". In his brief and intensely personal "Compassion in World Farming", Lord Northbourne gives voice to his frustration and disappointment after fifty years of a life in agriculture with the ever-increasing intensity of the forces pressing in the direction of "factory farming"—a concern that is coupled with his stubborn determination that "It is not all drugs and chemicals, nor ever will be."

On the Value of Tradition

In his articles "Religion and Tradition" and "Looking Back on Progress", Lord Northbourne, a man of the 20th century, attempts to stand back from the conditioning of his own time in order to assess without prejudice what we have gained and what we have lost through modern "progress". Lord Northbourne further seeks to define the merits as well as the limits of scientific inquiry, which is now so deeply embedded into nearly every field of human endeavor. In "Decadence and Idolatry", "Intellectual Freedom", and "Change in the Church" Lord Northbourne describes, with characteristically unsentimental realism, the present-day enfeeblement of religious institutions—a condition which, he also points out, must be partially reversible through a spiritual renewal that begins with the individual.

Metaphysical Principles

Lord Northbourne writes about traditional metaphysical principles with refreshing directness, paying careful attention to the practical consequences of the principles he discusses. His article "With God All Things Are Possible" uses this biblical pronouncement (Matt. 19:26; Mark 10:27) as a key to unlock the implications of the metaphysical notion of "all-possibility", including how this concept helps us to understand the cause of evil, the existence of which all must face in life's journey. In "What Am I?" Lord Northbourne attempts to answer this fundamental human question, along with its corollary, "What is my neighbor?", the answer to which, he suggests, forms the basis of true and realistic charity. In "On Truth, Goodness, and Beauty", Lord Northbourne attempts to show how—despite possible appearances to the contrary—truth, goodness, and beauty are fundamentally more important in this world, and more real, than their contraries of error, evil, and ugliness, which ultimately are mere shadows.

Art and Symbolism

In "Art Ancient and Modern", Lord Northbourne, himself a painter and lover of the arts, explores formal and functional differences between traditional and modern art. In his delightful article, "The Beauty of Flowers", we hear a lifelong gardener and keen lover of flowers reflect on what flowers themselves can tell us about the nature of beauty and joy. In both "A Cross Awry" and "A Reflection on Christmas", we hear a concerned defender of the Christian message lament certain contemporary abuses while nonetheless offering homage to the undying, pure spirit of the revelation of Christ.

Lessons from Life

One of Lord Northbourne's greatest gifts as a writer lies in his ability to help make sense of universal human life experiences. In "Old Age" we hear him as an old man speaking in a compelling and affecting way on the symbolism and practical realities of old age. In "The Problem of Pain", we see a man attempting to step back from the universal human experience of pain and speak to us of its possible meanings. In "The Ineluctable Alternative: A Letter to My Descendants", we listen to a father and grandfather speak from his heart and offer his life's wisdom to his children, grandchildren, and their children yet to come.

Appendix

We are privileged, through the letters they exchanged, to listen in on an extended conversation that took place between Lord Northbourne and Thomas Merton, the well-known Trappist monk and author. One senses the deep mutual respect these individuals had for one another as each attempts to explain his point of view on important contemporary issues of Christian and world religious life.

There is a Chinese proverb that Lord Northbourne liked very much, and which, one may rightfully say, he put into practice: "It is better to light one candle than to curse the darkness." Our hope is that the accumulated wisdom expressed in these writings of Lord Northbourne may help to shed some light on important life issues that affect us all. And lest we believe that we must or may force an answer to our problems, we would do well to remember Lord Northbourne's affirmation that:

> As humans we cannot command the heavenly influences; all we can do is to lay ourselves open to them without struggle or thought and without preconception; we can but listen for the "still small voice" which Elijah heard on Mount Horeb when the wind and the earthquake and the fire had passed by; the heavenly voice which is always waiting to be heard when the din and confusion of the world are stilled. (from "A Reflection on Christmas")

Joseph A. Fitzgerald

INTRODUCTION

Where there is no vision the people perish.
Proverbs 29:18

Not often does an Olympic sportsman become an organic farmer, educationalist, and monetary reformer, and then go on to become a philosopher who also translated some of the most important metaphysical texts of the modern age.

My father was a man of exceptional and comprehensive vision. He saw that our western society is in danger of destroying itself. In his writings he draws attention to the dangers we face as we abandon traditional values, and seeks to outline how human society could function more in harmony with nature and with traditional wisdom.

Most of us, at one time or another, ask ourselves the key questions "Who am I?", "Why am I here?" Do the answers to these questions lie within the realm of scientific discovery and logical deduction alone? Must they remain mysteries, comprehended, if at all, through spiritual inspiration, artistic vision, or divine revelation? The search for an answer to these questions led my father, in his fifties, to an understanding which changed his life.

Born in 1896 my father, Walter Edward Christopher James (later 4th Baron Northbourne[1]), was heir to a long line of country landowners distinguished for their public service in Parliament and the arts. His great grandfather was a Member of Parliament and a friend and supporter of Gladstone. His father was trained at the Slade Art School, had a house and studio in London, and became a Trustee of the National Gallery, but was also a keen cricketer and enjoyed

---

[1] The British peerage, which continues to exist after several centuries, consists of the following grades: duke, marquess (marquis), earl, viscount, and baron. Like all hereditary barons my father was in common usage known and addressed as Lord Northbourne. The word Baron was mainly reserved for legal and more formal documents. Until 1999 all peers had a right to "a seat and a voice" in the House of Lords, the Second Chamber of Parliament (similar to the U.S. Senate). My father chose not to take his seat, preferring to serve his country in Local Government and in other ways.

country life. He described himself in *Who's Who* as "an artist and sportsman, but principally artist".

As a boy my father lived with his family in London but spent most of his holidays with his parents in his grandfather's house in Kent, or in Northumberland where they had an estate on the moors, a paradise for a young boy. Educated at Eton, at the age of 18 he went straight from school into the Northumberland Fusiliers during the opening months of the First World War. He served in Salonika and then, under General Allenby, led Indian Muslim troops in Palestine. He joined a machine-gun regiment and was Mentioned in Despatches. Though spared the worst slaughter and destruction of the Western Front, he was marked for life by the horrors of that war.

In 1919 he went up to Oxford to read agriculture but spent much of his time rowing. He became President of the Oxford University Boat Club (O.U.B.C.), rowed twice in the Oxford and Cambridge Boat Race and once for England in the 1921 Olympic Games. Thereafter, he and a rowing friend bought a small farm near Oxford and settled down to learn the craft and the hard work of farming. Harvesting and haymaking were easily handled by inviting a group of Oxford rowing friends, and providing a cask of beer.

When the recession struck they sold out at a loss and he returned home to run the Home Farm on his family estate near Dover in Kent. He was elected a member of the Kent County Council and took on the responsibility of chairing its education committee. This voluntary job fired his interest in education and was the beginning of fifty years of public service to the county of Kent.

In 1924 he married my mother, Katherine Nickerson, daughter of George Nickerson of Boston, Massachusetts, a successful businessman who had played a major role in the development of the Burlington and Ohio Railway as it pushed out to the West in the latter part of the nineteenth century. In 1926 I was born, the oldest, and the only boy of his five children. We lived at Northbourne Court, a house on the family estate which dates back to the sixteenth century and is set among the walls of a ruined Elizabethan garden. It became one my father's greatest loves to plant and to tend this garden for the next fifty years. He made it into one of the most beautiful in England.

His lifelong pastimes were painting and gardening. An amateur botanist as well as an artist, the beauty of flowers fascinated him. His garden at Northbourne Court (and the flowers he cut from it, which he always arranged in the house himself) was a continuing source of fulfillment and pleasure to him all his life.

It is often recognized that poets and musicians can develop and pass on intimations of the divine which are not accessible to us through rational understanding. Beauty, along with love, can speak to us of truths which cannot be understood or expressed through science or logic alone. Many recognize the same quality in painting or singing, but few realize that designing and planting and tending a garden can also be an intimation of immortality, a modest reflection of Paradise. For my father his garden, and I believe in a lesser way his pictures— mainly of flowers, but also of landscapes and his children—were a reflection of Paradise.

In a letter written in perfect French to the wife of the French Ambassador, Martine de Courcel, who had suggested to him that his garden was like "a corner of paradise", he replied:

> God allows us to do our best to imitate His Paradise, however incompletely, provided that we never forget that all beauty comes from Him alone and remains always in Him, without any loss and for ever.

His painting was an additional source of fulfillment as well as of pleasure and relaxation. Between the wars he painted mainly in oils and pastels. Later, during the Second World War his only relaxation was, every Sunday afternoon, to listen to a concert on the radio and paint a watercolor, usually of flowers. After the war he held several successful exhibitions of his pictures in London.

He was a devoted family man and loved his wife and his five children. When we were young he spent hours playing with us, teaching us to draw, and reading aloud to us. He had a charming and infectious sense of humor. Many of the things he read to us he enjoyed as much as we did—*Three Men in a Boat*, *The Bridge of San Luis Rey*, and the writings of Saki were among them. As I got older he would take me with him on long walks around the Estate, teaching me about farming and about the importance of man's relationship with the land.

Although his painting and gardening were important to him throughout his life, between the wars my father's chief interest was organic farming. He ran both his garden at Northbourne Court and the Home Farm according to the biodynamic precepts for organic farming laid down by Rudolf Steiner (although he never followed Rudolf Steiner in his other ideas). He was one of the very first organic farmers in England and has, indeed, been credited with coining the term "organic farming" to describe a method of farming which avoids the use of all chemical fertilizers, pesticides, and weed-killers.[2] In organic farming fertility is maintained by composting and returning all organic wastes to the soil. I don't know whether the mysterious additions to the compost heaps recommended by Steiner did indeed make them ferment better, but I do remember that the compost they produced was black and juicy and contained a surprising number of earthworms. Amongst my happiest memories as a small boy is my father's enthusiasm as we visited the compost heaps together!

In the late thirties he held a conference on organic farming at Northbourne Court and during 1938-39 wrote a book, *Look to the Land*,[3] about the importance of wholeness in food and the damage to people and communities caused by "factory farming" and the "mining" of the world's top soils.[4] At that time, twenty-five years before Rachel Carson's book *Silent Spring* warned the world of the dangers of the unsustainable exploitation of the earth's resources, he foresaw the problems which would be created by man's irresponsible destruction of the world's top soil, the often thin and fragile layer of living surface soil which supports human communities, makes possible the production of the world's food, and sustains the natural environment as we know it.

At this stage of his life he was deeply concerned by the sickness of modern society, especially the increasing breakdown of traditional rural communities. He diagnosed this as stemming from the severance of man from his organic links with the land and with the wholeness of life. He was impressed by the work of Dr. G.T. Wrench, who studied the Hunza tribesmen in northern India, showing them to be an exceptionally healthy people, living in an isolated and traditional rural

[2] See Philip Conford, *The Origins of the Organic Movement* (Edinburgh: Floris Books, 2001).

[3] It was published to wide acclaim, with the review by *The New English Weekly* stating that: "The amount of knowledge packed between the covers of this book is formidable; the amount of wisdom inestimable."

[4] *Look to the Land* also contained proposals for a thoroughgoing monetary reform.

society based on self-sufficiency and the twin principles of wholeness (eating as far as possible the whole of the plants they grew), and the rule of return (returning all organic wastes to the soil after careful composting). He nonetheless saw that "man does not live by bread alone" and that the fullness of life and the prosperity which should be integral to its nature demands obedience to a sacred law. This was a vision of life that embraced the inter-relationship of God, man, and the soil in a unity that is in stark contrast to that materialistic, mechanistic way of life instituted by the philosophy of "progress", which has molded our society in the twentieth century.

In September 1939, my father was offered an opportunity to contribute to the war effort as Chairman of the "War Agricultural Committee", which was formed to organize and revitalize the agriculture of East Kent in order to provide food to replace the imported supplies that were being lost in ships sunk by German U-boats in the Atlantic. He rose to this challenge with enthusiasm and worked at it seven days a week almost without a break for the duration of the war years. He did occasionally find time to meet with a small group of like-minded farmers and writers who called themselves "The Kinship in Husbandry", which included such notable figures as Harold Massingham, Adrian Bell, Lord Portsmouth, and Rolf Gardiner. Their objective was to think about and to plan for the future of the countryside and of agriculture after the war.[5] Several members of "The Kinship in Husbandry" played major roles in the founding of the "Soil Association", an important contemporary organization in the United Kingdom for the promotion and certification of organic food and farming.

With the coming of the peace in 1945 my father continued to run the Home Farm and took on a new responsibility as Provost and Chairman of the Governors of Wye Agricultural College in Kent, which became the Agricultural College of London University. He held this post for 25 years, a period of substantial development for the College.

---

[5] A selection of their views was published in part in *The Natural Order: Essays in "The Return to Husbandry" by Fourteen Writers*, edited by H. J. Massingham (London: J.M Dent & Sons, 1945). An article by my father is included.

He did not return to the fully organic farming that he had been forced to abandon during the war when, as Chairman of the War Agricultural Committee, he had had to tell others to use fertilizers and sprays in order to increase production. However he never abandoned his understanding of the importance of wholeness, sanity, and sustainability in the way we treat the natural world. Jointly with E.F. Schumacher, the renowned author of *Small is Beautiful*, he held a Conference based at Northbourne Court to explore the possibility of reviving the small self-sufficient family farm in England. He continued to observe with some concern the way in which man was destroying his environment, his quality of life, and even himself, but he began to doubt whether the organic movement was the key to changing this trend. His attention was turned to a more directly spiritual analysis of the state of the modern world. This seemed to him to offer a new and radically different way in which he could help his fellow men and fulfill the purpose of his own life.

The event which changed his life was the discovery of traditional and universal metaphysics in the writings of René Guénon and Frithjof Schuon. Through his book *Look to the Land*, he had met Marco Pallis, who in turn had introduced him to the "Traditionalist" (or "Perennialist") writers René Guénon, Frithjof Schuon, Ananda K. Coomaraswamy, Titus Burckhardt, and Martin Lings. He thereafter undertook to translate several books by Guénon, Schuon, and Burckhardt from French into English.

It was this work, and the friendship of those writers, which taught him that the roots of the world's problems are first and foremost spiritual. They confirmed his intuitive understanding of the importance of tradition and enabled him to find a credible answer to those challenging questions that had so far eluded him. They showed him a way of living his life which drew together its diverse strands and gave them meaning. This he was able to do in a context that engaged his intuitive sense of beauty, love and truth, and his understanding of the importance of man's relationship to the land. He had found the "way", which for him fulfilled the needs he sets out so clearly in the chapter in this anthology entitled "Religion and Tradition".

Through the Traditionalist writers he came to understand the reasons for the apparently irreconcilable differences between the teachings of the great revealed religions, and to realize that there is a "perennial philosophy", a "transcendent unity", which runs through them all. Like different routes to the summit of the same mountain, the starting points may be far apart but the paths get closer and closer as they approach the top. Whichever path is taken, the view from the top is the same; but on the way up the paths must not be confused.

His writings over the last 30 years of his life were driven by his urgent wish to help those capable of doing so to understand the traditional teachings so that they could make more informed decisions about how to live their own lives. In his writings he looks at the traditional point of view in a variety of contexts and contrasts its values with those of our "progressive" society today. He shows that secular materialism—based as it is on scientific observation and on deduction from that observation—can never be authoritative or even useful in understanding matters outside its own domain, which is restricted to the material world. In particular it can never validly address the ultimate cause or meaning of the Universe, nor can it speak with authority on man's role in it.

In the message to his descendants, part of which is included in this anthology, he shows that although organized religion is not the only way to a deeper consciousness of spiritual truth, for most people, to follow one of the great revealed religions provides the safest path, if it is lived faithfully and with understanding.

My father died in 1982 at the age of 86. He always retained his love for his garden and for the beauty of flowers. He continued to work in his garden until a few months before his last illness. I remember that only a few days before his death he insisted on being carried downstairs to supervise one more time the arrangement of the great bunch of flowers that always stood in front of a mirror at the end of the drawing room. This simple act expressed the truth of which he had written: that the "evanescence of flowers is not a matter for regret. It is an ever-present reminder of what we are".

My father was fortunate and happy in the spiritual path which he chose for himself. I hope that this anthology of his writings may help others to find the spiritual way which they are seeking.

The Kingdom of Heaven is like a merchant in search of fine pearls; on finding one pearl of great value, he went and sold all that he had and bought it. (Matthew 13:45-46)

Christopher James,
the 5th Lord Northbourne

Walter James, the 4th Baron Northbourne

I

FARMING

An Ecology in Practice

The best can only spring from that kind of biological completeness which has been called wholeness. If it is to be attained, the farm itself must have a biological completeness; it must be a living entity, it must be a unit which has within itself a balanced organic life. Every branch of the work is interlocked with all others.

From "Farms and Farmers"

1. Soil and Growth[1]

The Interdependence of Living Creatures

Every detail of the life of every person is in some way related to the lives of innumerable other people, and is dependent on them; the people concerned are mostly quite unknown to him, and may be living almost anywhere on the surface of the earth. Though this be a truism, it must be stated in order to emphasize the uselessness of considering the situation of any man or association of men or geographical unit as if it were isolated from all others. It must also be stated in order to be extended.

Besides being bound up with the lives of his fellow men, every man's life is bound up with the lives of innumerable non-human creatures which constitute his food, which provide him with clothing, shelter, material to work with, or pleasure; and to whose lives he in turn consciously or unconsciously contributes. Thus there is a very real economic and biological linkage, comprehensive and of infinite complexity, between all living creatures in the world. This linkage really constitutes the lives of those creatures. With the improvement in communications accompanying the progress of the mechanical age, this linkage has become more comprehensive, more rapid, and more direct than it ever was before between parts of the world physically remote from each other. This fact is clearly recognized as an important feature of the economic situation. But the economic aspect of things, being largely concerned with the production of food and raw materials from animals and plants, is clearly a function of biological states. Economics have been discussed *ad nauseam*. The biological state of the world has, in its broader aspects, received relatively little attention, though it conditions the economic state.

Above all these matters is the spiritual aspect of the relationships which constitute the life of man. It is said that man is a spiritual being. He may not always be so, but at least his existence is valuable only in

---

[1] Excerpted from *Look to the Land*, Chapter 1 (1940). In this seminal book, written before World War II, Lord Northbourne became the first writer to use the term "organic farming". —Editors

proportion to its spirituality. He can achieve spirituality only if earthly things are not his masters: only if he can control the earthly side of his being, thereby achieving that perfect balance which alone permits of higher development. That which is sick is out of control, and is upsetting the balance. The spiritual sickness of the world is, like the economic sickness, very rightly a matter of profound concern. These, together with the biological sickness which is the subject of this book, are almost certainly only different aspects of one phenomenon. But that is no reason to ignore the biological view of the situation, which must always for us, while we are alive, be a very relevant point of view. In considering it we can and must try to relate it to other concerns—economic, intellectual, and spiritual.

The Organism Not a Machine
Biology is the study of the mechanism of life, and this mechanism is a continuous flow of matter through the architectural forms we know as organisms. The form alone has any life or any organic identity, just as a whirlpool has identity, though it has no continuity of substance. So there can be no true analogy between even the simplest living creature and any conceivable machine. The said flow of matter is the process of nutrition in its widest aspects. Each kind of organism obtains the continuous supply of material which it needs for its nutrition in its own characteristic way. Most of the higher forms of life can only use material which has been previously taken up by other (not necessarily lower) forms of life, and which at the time of use retains the architecture of those other forms. Man is, of course, absolutely dependent on the availability of material of that kind for his nutrition, and, as is the case with other creatures, only a limited category of such material is suited to his particular needs. Man, being omnivorous, has a wider range of choice than most.

Ever since the growth of population outstripped the food-producing potentialities of virgin nature, farming (including for the sake of brevity now and hereafter every kind of cultivation of crops or animals) became man's only possible way of maintaining life: it became not only necessarily his main occupation, but also the critical link in that flow of material which is himself, and a link dependent for its soundness on his own efforts.

That which links together all the phases and processes of farming, and which is therefore its foundation, is the soil in all its infinite variety. If the soil is the foundation of farming, the soil is also the foundation of the physical life of man. It is the background of his life. The importance of farming in the national life is now receiving wider recognition. But that recognition mostly takes the form of a vague realization that the most is not being made of a national asset, one valuable in peace and indispensable in war, and that the six per cent or so of the population of Britain which is actively engaged in farming is in a very difficult position. Most of the consideration given to farming in this country is based upon that very limited point of view. It is assumed that farming is one of the many activities which are of importance in the national life, and that we are only interested in farming in other countries insofar as they may be able to produce food more cheaply than we can. Such agitation as is directed to the improvement of farming in Britain mostly comes from the six per cent who work on the land, and thus from so small a minority that it could not be effective even if it were wisely directed and free from suspicion of sectional prejudice.

Few people realize as yet that the agricultural problem is by its very nature every bit as much a townsman's problem as it is a farmer's problem: and that there is far more in it than a question of cheap and abundant supplies of food. This book is an attempt by a layman, writing for laymen, to set forth how much more there is in it.[2] It is an attempt at a biological and economic conspectus of our present situation. As such, it must start from the soil.

The Soil a Living Entity
First, as to the nature of soil. Each of the innumerable kinds of soil can be looked at as a complex of variables, living and non-living, quite staggering in the number and variety of its factors. Many of these factors have been the objects of scientific study, both separately and in combination. . . . The soil is a whole world to itself. But as a world it is also an entity: a variable entity and a living entity, and one with which, as an entity, every farmer and gardener is intimately concerned. Most people in the world are still farmers or gardeners, and they,

---

[2] *Look to the Land* contains a total of five chapters; included in the present anthology are excerpts from four: "Soil and Growth" (the present chapter), "Health and Food", "Farms and Farmers", and "Look to the Land: Sustainability". —Editors

who handle the soil, must look upon it and treat it as a living whole. For it is as a living thing, not as a dead medium, that the soil is most important to us.

[Lord Northbourne discusses the use of "dead" mineral fertilizers in cultivation; also the then new process of "hydroponics".]

The Importance of Humus

It is the top layer of the soil which is alive; that layer which may be from an inch or two to a foot or two in depth, and which is, in general, darker in color and more friable than any of the layers lower down which constitute the subsoil. There is no need to tell farmers or gardeners that plants grow readily in the top soil, and will only grow very badly, if at all, in subsoil; though the subsoil is often richer in minerals. The top layer is darker and more friable because it contains "humus". Humus is a product of the decay of once living material. Decay is of course a biological process—it does not occur in the absence of organisms—and humus itself exhibits varying degrees of biological activity. It is the great controlling and balancing factor in the soil. The suitability of a soil for cultivation depends to some extent on the nature and conditions of its mineral constituents, but more on the humus it contains: both as to the amount of that humus, which can vary from zero to nearly one hundred per cent, and still more as to the state of activity of the humus. A pure peat is nearly one hundred per cent humus; but most of it is inactive, so it is infertile. The depth and activity of the living layer is the measure of the fertility of a soil.

This layer has other characteristics besides color and relative crumbliness. Humus, the balancer, can not only make sticky soils crumbly, it can also give cohesion to soils which would otherwise be too friable, for instance to sandy soil. It improves the "tilth" of all soils. A soil in good tilth absorbs and retains water, yet it allows any surplus to pass through it. Unless the passage of such water is obstructed lower down, such a soil never becomes waterlogged; yet it suffers less from drought than a similar soil not in good tilth. It acts like a sponge: greedy for all it can comfortably carry, and retentive of it, but allowing any surplus to escape. If the humus in a soil is lost or becomes inactive, the soil will gradually lose these characteristics and revert to its inherent faults: stickiness, dryness, or whatever they may be.

The Nutritional Needs of Plants
These facts are well established and easily verified. The other main characteristic of the living layer is the basis of most sound practice, but is much less easy to test scientifically. Therefore these days its importance is underestimated. It is so inconvenient when things will not submit to exact measurement that we prefer to ignore them even if, as in this case, they are vital. The characteristic is that of acting upon the minerals in the soil and rendering them available to plants; or, to put the point in a more obscure yet probably not less valid way, the conferring on plants of the power to make use of minerals in the soil, even though these be present only in excessively minute quantities. There is no doubt that in practice when the biological activity of the soil falls, plants growing in it begin to show symptoms of specific deficiencies; sometimes even when chemical analysis reveals no lack of the particular constituent concerned. That constituent is then said to be present in a form in which it is not available to plants, and is added to the soil in chemical form. The extreme case is that of the hydroponics already mentioned, in which the plant is growing on a non-living medium, and all requirements have to be supplied artificially in exactly the right form and proportions. How many so-called soil deficiencies are really due to non-activity of the living layer of the soil? To attempt an answer now would be to anticipate unduly.

So when the living layer loses activity—but let us not prevaricate any longer and start that sentence again. When the living layer is sickly or dying the soil loses its tilth or texture, its control of water, and its powers of digestion. That is to say, it loses its fertility. So loss of fertility is the ill health of the soil. The soil becomes unhealthy when the living layer is not supplied with the right food. That food is, broadly speaking, organic matter in the right state of decay, or in condition to undergo such decay.

In the later stages of ill health, the top layer of the soil changes in accordance with the nature of its mineral constituents. It may become hard, so that not only can roots not penetrate it, but rain runs off the surface without sinking in. Such hard soil tends to crack. The rain runs in the cracks, which widen into gullies. These gullies finally coalesce and the whole surface may be washed away. That is one kind of erosion, or death of the soil. Alternatively, the surface may become very loose. In that condition it can be washed away; but it is also liable to be caught and blown away by the wind. Thus can a once fertile soil

7

not only be totally lost, but converted to an instrument of destruction: silting up rivers and causing floods, or choking living creatures with dust. Erosion can be slow or rapid. Soil can be washed slowly downhill on sloping land, gradually impoverishing the higher or more sloping ground—so-called sheet erosion. But, fast or slow, the end is the same: the sea, whence geological upheavals alone can recover the lost soil.

[Lord Northbourne discusses the contemporary problems of erosion in the U.S.A., Canada, South America, Africa, China, India, Russia, and Europe; also the economic causes of erosion, including international debt, and the urge to speed.]

2. Health and Food[1]

[Lord Northbourne discusses evidence of the contemporary state of ill health in Britain.]

Health and Farming

Health is more than the absence of disease. The absence of disease is only one of the signs of health; it may not even be the most important. Health is a state of balance internal and external, a unity, a wholeness, a power. It is not something physical or mental or spiritual, but must include all three aspects or it is not whole. We lack a standard. Whatever that standard may be, it is unlikely to be one susceptible of exact measurement. It is certainly not that of mere physical exuberance. Perhaps the best indication of health may be a deep satisfaction with life, accompanied by a command of self which permits of the dominance of the highest faculties.

The health of man and the health of his land are not two distinct matters which can properly be considered separately and apart. Farming is the external mechanism of human biology; it is an essential part of the process of nutrition, which constitutes man's physical life and conditions his health. So if farming were unsound it would be strange if man's physical life remained perfectly adjusted. And if his physical life is maladjusted—that is to say, out of control—the other aspects of his life must suffer. If it is true that man cannot live by bread alone, it is also true that he cannot live without bread; and if his bread is defective he cannot be expected to live well. His life is interlocked with the lives of many other creatures, so if he cannot live well neither can those creatures which live in close relationship with him. If his nutrition is wrong, so will theirs be, and vice versa.

Health depends on nutrition, but nutrition, being a cyclical process, also depends on health. Supposing any creature to be supplied with all its nutritional needs in the proper form; suppose then that for some reason unspecified that creature's powers of assimilation are impaired; then everything which that creature supplies to its fellow

---

[1] Excerpted from *Look to the Land*, Chapter 2 (1940). —Editors

creatures is also impaired, and their nutrition suffers. So, if at any point in the ever-moving cyclical flow which represents the nutritional interdependence of all living things a serious fault develops, a vicious circle may be set up, from the ill effects of which no creature may be exempt. The original fault will then itself tend to get worse. In their efforts to escape from such a situation and to get what they need many organisms will be compelled to adopt a way of life which is destructive of the whole scheme rather than contributory to it; which is predatory rather than symbiotic. The fact that the destruction of the whole scheme must in the end be their destruction too may not at the time be perceived at all, or if it is perceived it may not impress itself strongly enough to outweigh what appears to be the need of the moment, and so will not be sufficient to induce a more reasonable course of action. Something of that kind seems to have happened to us.

Our relation to our fellow creatures has become predatory rather than symbiotic. Some of our fellow creatures are very small and live in the soil. We have perhaps been hardest of all on them. At least the signs of our victimization of them, which are loss of fertility and erosion, are particularly obvious. But if the part which these organisms in particular play in our lives is as important as it seems to be, then we must suffer if they do. That seems to be exactly what is happening. Such an idea becomes more than a plausible hypothesis if it can be reinforced by comparisons between ourselves and peoples who do not live as we do. Fortunately such comparisons are possible.

Comparative Studies of Health
There are still places in the world where something approaching perfect health in man can be found. And there are instances of what appears to be true symbiotic living. These instances have by no means received the study they deserve, and there is some danger that, unless such study is set on foot intensively forthwith, the conditions of the people concerned may alter so much as to make investigation more difficult and less profitable. A very few pioneers have seen the importance of investigations of this kind, notably Major General Sir Robert McCarrison. The story of his studies of the Hunza people in north-western India has been vividly told by Dr. G.T. Wrench in his book

The Wheel of Health.[2] The reader—the lay reader especially—must be referred to that book for the thrilling details of this investigation, and for a full estimate of its significance. Suffice it to say here that the Hunza peoples enjoyed remarkable health and vitality; that they were not aggressive; that their farming was self-contained and an example of the perfection of care, nothing whatever being wasted; that their crops were as healthy as themselves.

There are, or have been, at least three other peoples to whom we may refer as examples of symbiotic living. The perfect teeth of the inhabitants of the island of Tristan da Cunha first attracted attention. These islanders are Europeans, few in number, and have often been without communication with the outer world for as much as three years on end. They must of necessity practice a self-contained waste-less farming, for the island is inhospitable. Their general health appears to be remarkably good.

Certain tribes of Eskimos have been found to be (or in some cases, alas, to have been) singularly free from disease, active, and contented. These tribes had not come into contact with what we call civilization, and their lives were by civilized standards hard, limited, and unhygienic. Their food was monotonous and largely of animal origin, especially in winter. . . .

Each according to his kind, these peoples in particular have approached perfection, and there are doubtless others who have done so. They may not have been endowed with the highest potentialities of the human race. That is a question of standards and is outside the present discussion. Within the limits of their potentialities it is clear that they have attained a state of balance, of harmony with their environment and with each other, of physical development and endurance, of freedom from disease, and of true civilization each according to their kind, quite unknown among peoples whose basic rule of life is different; and in strong contrast with the state in which, for instance, we in England now find ourselves. We may flatter ourselves that our potentialities are higher than theirs: that is poor consolation if we allow ourselves to degenerate in peace or to be annihilated in war.

[2] London: The C.W. Daniel Company, 1938; New York: Dover, 2006. —Editors

The Whole Diet

What is the common rule of life of these peoples? It seems to be a nutritional rule, for no other common factor is discernible in the lives of these very varied peoples. And it is not a rule of diet in the ordinary sense, for between them they ate almost everything under the sun, both cooked and raw, and in very varying proportions. The Eskimos were mainly carnivorous, the other three peoples had mixed diets varying greatly in their constituents, but with vegetable foods as the staple. It does not seem that food faddism of any kind can find support from a comparative study of the relative health and diets of these peoples, for so far as the kind of food eaten is concerned there seems to be no factor common to the four. There are, however, two common factors of a different kind.

The first is that the food was either natural (that is to say, not cultivated) or it was so cultivated as to preserve the nutrition cycle complete at all stages; the cycle which may be represented diagrammatically in this way:

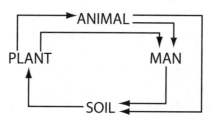

That is to say that the "Rule of Return" was faithfully observed, so that not only was every scrap of available organic material returned to the soil, but it was returned after careful treatment by methods handed down from generation to generation: methods designed to bring it into a form in which it is at once seized upon by organisms in the soil which retain it and eventually yield it up again to plants.

The other nutritional factor common to these peoples is that so far as possible they ate the whole of each plant or animal which furnished them with food. They showed in fact a general preference for parts which we often discard, notably the internal organs of animals, and the outer skin of plants, seeds, and animals.

It seems that if either or both of these two rules—the rule of return and the rule of wholeness—are broken, a vicious circle is established.

For example, the teeth may deteriorate and it may therefore become less easy to eat skins and bones; failure to do so may accentuate the deterioration of the teeth, and so on. The two rules are really the same: the rule of wholeness means no waste in the upward half of the cycle, from soil to animal or man; the rule of return means wholeness in the downward half, in which all goes back to the soil. The cyclical flow must be quantitatively and qualitatively balanced throughout.

[Lord Northbourne discusses the experimental evidence of the good health of rats fed on Hunza food versus the poor health of rats fed on English food.]

Quality and Price of Food
The typical food of most of us today is white bread. It forms the basis of our diet. It is interesting to consider a loaf of white bread in the light of what has been said about food in general. The chances are that the wheat has been grown abroad, most probably under a system of continuous wheat-growing, very likely on land the fertility of which is in some degree exhausted. After a period of storage, during which it may be chemically treated against insects, it is put through a modern roller mill. These mills are most ingeniously contrived so as to separate out the skin (as bran, middlings, etc.) which contains the vitamin B and most of the minerals, and the germ which contains vitamin A and other vitamins, and the oil which is the "life" of the wheat. The skin and germ are largely sold for feeding animals. That which remains is nearly all starch, and even that may be artificially bleached. So that, even if wheat is healthily grown, most of the life-giving and so-called protective constituents are removed, and what is perhaps even more important—the completeness or wholeness or structure of the wheat berry as a living unit is destroyed. White bread is mere filling. It is probably no exaggeration to say that it generally does not nourish at all. Further comment on the subject of bread for energy seems superfluous. Brown bread varies greatly. It may contain only a proportion of bran, or both bran and germ. But in the latter case the germ is usually cooked before being added to the flour to ensure keeping, so that when it has been baked it is twice cooked. It is well known that twice cooking has a most deleterious effect on nutritive value, especially where proteins or vitamins are concerned. Some brown breads are made of whole wheat, untreated except by grinding. The standard price applies only to white bread.

The things that really matter in food, those which make it effective as a vehicle of life and which constitute its quality in the fullest sense of the word, are seldom taken into account, either when scientists are discussing nutrition, or when the housewife is buying her food. The housewife has nothing to guide her in the right direction and much to guide her in the wrong one, even when she is not under the necessity of buying the cheapest filling food available. Anyhow, the food that ought to be obtainable is for practical purposes unobtainable by a vast majority, even at an exorbitant price. We have got into the habit of accepting price as to some extent a measure of quality. But the price which the farmer receives, or which the consumer pays, is nowadays usually a result of factors which have no relation to quality in the true sense: such as adaptability to standardization, suitability for canning, storage, transport over long distances, and generally ease of marketing or manufacture. Quality in the true sense relates only to excellence from the consumers' point of view, that is, the effect on his health or pleasure or both.

One of the most important factors in quality, except perhaps for cereals and certain limited classes of preserved foods, is absolute freshness at the time of consumption. The price of foods, together with many other criteria which determine the proportions in which foods are actually bought, bears little relation to this vital factor of freshness—vital in the true sense of the word. But much ingenuity is expended in devising means for substituting for real freshness the appearance or illusion of freshness. Such means include methods of preservation, chemical and physical, and additions of coloring matter or of substances designed to stimulate the organs of taste or of smell. Just as we aim at an imitation of health in ourselves, our animals and plants, so we aim at an imitation of health in our food. Most of our food is in fact so ill-grown and stale and unhealthy that it has lost its characteristic and stimulating savor. That state of affairs can by no means be compensated by any development of the culinary art, still less by supplementary titillators of the palate bought in bottles or tins. Such things cannot make up even for the lack of true savor in food, let alone for the lack of real nourishment.

Civilization and Farming
The history of food is the history of farming, and the history of farming is the history of civilization. We are often told that there are

symptoms of decadence in Western civilization. There is at least strong reason to suppose that many symptoms which are in evidence today have accompanied the periods of decline of former civilizations, such as urbanization and commercialism, with a decay of farming and the importation of food; the growth of a class distinguished purely by its wealth, with its concomitant dependent class; and the appearance of certain diseases of civilization, notably bad teeth and rheumatism (which are easily diagnosed from skeletal remains). Egypt and Rome are clear cases in point. *Latifundia perdidere Italiam*—"They have destroyed Italy by large-scale farming"[3]—is a significant contemporary comment.

It seems that civilization springs from the land. In due course wealth increases, and the temptation to adopt a way of life based on money, and one at variance with true biological law, becomes too great. Then follows the exhaustion of the land, and the decline of the farming population, out of which the nation's vitality was raised and maintained. We realize vaguely the importance of a strong rural population as a source of vitality to a nation. But we do not seem to see precisely why this should be the case, and so of course our efforts to restore the life of the country are feeble, and misdirected.

[Lord Northbourne discusses quality versus cheapness; also the danger that the pasteurization of milk may become compulsory.]

Purity

Purity is the advertiser's watchword. But in practice it has come to be almost synonymous with sterilization. Sterilization means killing, in order to remove the likelihood of unwanted change. It is the very opposite of freshness. The excellence of freshness consists in the existence of susceptibility to change. It implies liveliness. But we avoid, or are compelled or persuaded to avoid, all that is changeable and lively in favor of that which is as inert as possible. As a matter of fact it is practically certain that nothing which is chemically pure is of any use at all. Even chemically pure water is no good to drink. The subtleties which really count are all of the nature of impurities. Our efforts to remove them are fairly successful. Of course impurities in food can be noxious, or even fatal, but a dangerous excess of deleterious matter

---

[3] Pliny, *Historia Naturalis* XVIII.vii. —Editors

can be excluded in more ways than one; and what is a dangerous excess to an unhealthy creature can be harmless or beneficial to a healthy one. Hygiene is all very well, but it is no substitute for health. We have got into the habit of thinking that health can come from the mere avoidance of germs or dirt, while we neglect the foundations of health and so get more and more into a state in which we cannot withstand bacteria or dirt, and so we get more and more terrified of them. Yet neither ought to matter in the least, neither does matter to healthy people, and neither is in fact escapable by any one, or ever will be. As always, negative policy directed solely to the avoidance of evil is useless in the absence of constructive work for good.

Probably also, in addition to the constituents of food, its structure is important, and perhaps more than important. Not only its chemical structure, but its vital structure, which is in the nature of things not analyzable, because any process of analysis, however refined, must destroy it. Here we come back to ideas related to that of "wholeness", which are so unscientific and so desperately important. Of such is the quality of food.

Perversion of Taste

One strange consequence of the prevailing loss of any real quality in food is that a great many people, even relatively poor people, eat habitually far too much. And this is the case in spite of the fact that malnutrition is known to be almost unbelievably prevalent. Malnutrition is rarely nowadays a quantitative phenomenon. The organism can never be satisfied with the tainted, bleached, washed out, and long dead material with which it is supplied, and being unsatisfied calls out for more. In vain does man distend his stomach with an excess of such things—what he must have is not there. In the end, power of assimilation fails, and that which could give strength becomes too strong to be taken.

An inevitable accompaniment of this state of affairs is a deterioration or perversion of taste. When this takes place a vicious circle is established which is very difficult to break. For taste is the sense on which we rely in fact for the final decision as to what is good for us or not, and when it is perverted that which is good may become unacceptable.

Qualitative Deterioration

It is not only in food that deterioration of quality and a simultaneous deterioration in taste are evident. Most people have to put up with inferior stuff in all departments of life; it is all they can get. Much ingenuity is devoted to making it presentable and even attractive when new, and still more to selling it. But it lacks that combination of refinement and solidity, within and without, which is quality. Quality in the commercial sense is merely that which people can be persuaded to buy, or fooled into buying. We of this generation have largely forgotten what real quality means. It means individuality as much as anything else. It cannot be produced in a hurry. It is always the result of the application of human thought and care, ungrudgingly bestowed. It is never cheap.

After all, the only thing that really matters is the quality of human life. Anything which contributes to the quality of human life is true wealth. Judged by that standard, much of the vaunted wealth of today is rubbish, or if it is not by nature rubbish, it is rendered valueless by the lack of something in man that could give it value to man. Good housing, for instance, is of no use to inhabitants who have not access to the means of establishing a right relationship to life itself. We consider wealth mainly in terms of quantitative production per man, with a proviso that by some means or other a market must be found or created for that which is produced. In other words we imagine that the problem of production has been solved, and that the present problem is mainly one of distribution. That sort of idea is responsible for the outcry against the existence of "Poverty in the midst of potential Plenty".

The Illusion of Plenty

The real situation is one of poverty in essentials amid plenty of non-essentials. Expressed in financial terms only, poverty has been very greatly reduced in the past few decades. The "standard of living" has greatly improved. But what you mean by the phrase "the standard of living" depends on what you mean by "living". We have plenty, actual and potential: but plenty of what? That is the real question. We have plenty of manufactured goods and more if we want them; we can have plenty of money as soon as we care to allow money to be equated to production; we have plenty—in the quantitative sense only—of food; but in the kind of food which is the absolutely indispensable basis for satisfactory living we are miserably poor, and must of necessity remain so for a very long time. We are equally poor in almost everything else that really contributes to the quality of human life. It is the greatest possible mistake to assume that all we have to do is to get the machinery going at full blast and to distribute its products by a different kind of machinery called either money or communism or the State or anything else. What we really have to do is to go right back to the very beginning and start afresh. The beginning is of course the soil. And when we have the sense to do so we shall find that doing so is intensely satisfying, and that the other things will in due course "be added unto us", provided that we are not again deceived into sacrificing vital quality to mere cheapness.

Waste
We seem, however, at present to be very deeply involved in trying to make a so-called economy work, of which the overriding principle is the calculation of financial profitableness. Economy is supposed to mean, among other things, avoidance of waste. Insofar as we avoid wasting money we are successful. But we waste almost everything else with a prodigality which is fantastic; especially those things which contribute to the quality of human life. We waste not only the foundations of the health of all, but also most of the human vigor, creativeness, and power that remains to us, either in war or in futile activities pursued in the name of business. Here, however, we are more concerned with the wastage of the foundation of life, which is soil fertility. The more modern the economy of a country the more rapid is that wastage. We have seen how the influence of a so-called highly developed economy can bring destruction to the soil of distant countries over which that economy extends its influence, so that their fertility is directly swept into the sea or into the air or buried under sand or silt. We have seen, too, how the fertility of the highly developed country is maintained precariously if at all by means of foods and manures imported from the distant countries. It now remains to see how that imported fertility is finally wasted. It is in fact consigned to the sea through sewers, or to the air or the subsoil through the burning or burying of so-called refuse. These are the most important sources of waste, but there are others, including the careless handling of manure, and the discarding or burning of potentially valuable organic matter

by farmers and gardeners. Even food which might be good is wasted if the power to assimilate it properly fails.

[Lord Northbourne discusses how sewage and other refuse should be seen as valuable organic fertilizer.]

Everything that has had life can have life again, and in regaining life it can draw into the sphere of life some fragment of that which has been hitherto lifeless. If you burn your old trousers, presumably made largely of wool, you are destroying potential life, committing a sort of murder. Properly composted (for the quality of the life you renew in them is of primary importance) they can give power to a living plant to seize upon hitherto non-living material in the soil and bring it into the living world. But be careful of newspapers. There are few things so contaminating as printers' ink. There is probably a moral somewhere in that fact.

The Rule of Return

Life can only win over that which is inanimate if, within the cycle of life, the rule of return is faithfully observed. If it is not observed, life lives wastefully on itself—on its own capital, so to speak, and loses power over its environment, becoming weak, unhappy, and ugly. Then nature no longer seems bountiful, as she can be when her rules are kept. All this question of observing the rule of return is no mere economic question, nor is it a purely scientific one. It is part of the wonder and beauty and poetry of living. There is poetry in the ever-recurring process of the conversion of ordure and decay into utility and beauty. If we would understand these matters we must go to the poets rather than to the scientists and economists. That is not to say that a scientist cannot be a poet as well, though it seems more difficult for an economist to be one.

There is no place for beauty in our economy, unless you count what we teach to our young people as "commercial art". We waste almost everything that really matters most, and fanatically conserve two things which have no intrinsic virtue, which are useful only insofar as they are subject to the laws of life and serve the needs of life. As masters, and still more as gods, they are infinitely destructive. They are mechanical energy, and money.

However, when we want to be severely practical, we still say: "Let us get back to earth." But we don't usually take ourselves literally enough. If we are to rise up again towards spiritual power we must first get back to earth. So we must try to revalue those activities by which we maintain contact with the earth, and which we know as farming. We have got to reconsider all our ideas about the place of the land in our lives, and therefore of all our activities which affect the land in any way, of which farming is the chief. It is not a case of enabling the farmers to serve the public better. It is a case of the public, and especially the urban public, serving the land better. Only so can the land serve them. Not until the people as individuals understand the position and act accordingly can farmers or governments do what is necessary.

3. Farms and Farmers[1]

[Lord Northbourne discusses the unique importance of land to human nutrition; also the fact that farming is only incidentally an industry.]

The True Status of Farming

Farming stands quite alone. Its status is unique. But it has lost its status and become one of the many industries which cater for the wants and needs of man; and by no means a favored one at that. Urban and industrial theories and values have supplanted the truer ones of the country. These true ones survive mainly as a sentimental attachment to country life and gardening. Is the romance of country life really only a poetic survival of a bygone age, not very practical because there is no money in it, or is that romance something to which we must cling and on which we must build? Is farming merely a necessary drudgery, to be mechanized so as to employ a minimum of people, to be standardized and run in ever bigger units, to be judged by cost accounting only? Or is the only alternative to national decay to make farming something real for every man and near to him in his life, and something in which personal care, and possibly even poetic fancy, counts for more than mechanical efficiency? Mechanical efficiency is all very well—it is good, but life can be sacrificed to it.

Mechanical efficiency is the ideal of materialism, but unless it is subservient to and disciplined by the spirit it can take charge and destroy the spirit. In life, though not in mechanics, the things of the spirit are more real than material things. They include religion, poetry, and all the arts. They are the mainsprings of that culture which can make life worthwhile. Farming is concerned primarily with life, so if ever in farming the material aspect conflicts with the spiritual or cultural, the latter must prevail, or that which matters most in life will be lost. As in life the things of the spirit count for more than material things, so it must be in farming, which is a part of life. Farming must be on the side of religion, poetry, and the arts rather than on the side of business, if ever the two sides conflict. In these days they do indeed

---

[1] Excerpted from *Look to the Land*, Chapter 3 (1940). —Editors

conflict, and we see the results of that conflict and of the temporary victory of materialism around us today. The calculation of profitableness has brought us to the very brink of disaster; a disaster of which an obvious aspect is a risk of the death of the body, but of which the more serious aspect is a risk of the death of the soul.

Things which are true on the spiritual plane are also true on the material plane. As surely as that which is material is valueless unless it is built upon a sure spiritual foundation, so industry is valueless unless it is built upon a sound biological substructure: in other words, on a sound agriculture. (It will be noticed that the good Anglo-Saxon word "farming" is used throughout in this book in preference to the Latin word "agriculture". The only justification for the use of the rather ugly word "agriculture" might be its association with the word "culture". But the word "culture" has been much abused and has come to have a slightly artificial and even sometimes a sinister significance in the mouths of high-brows and dictators respectively. There can anyhow be no possible justification for calling a farmer an agriculturist.)

Industry is a superstructure on farming. This is an obvious truism, for we could live without the one, but not without the other. But we behave as if farming were an appendage—a necessary one of course—to industry. Yet industry dominates farming, and so of course dominates the life of man, of which farming is a part, not an adjunct. Industry was made for man; yet men are now looked on as being creatures useful to industry—either as machine minders, salesmen, or, most important today, as buyers of the products of industry. This outlook prevails among many modern reformers, especially monetary reformers, whose main idea seems to be to make men more efficient purchasers, so as to relieve the machine of its present chronic constipation. Forgive the crudity. Analogy between the social organism and the human may not be altogether misleading. Periodical stimulation by injections of money may be no less habit-forming and so no less injurious in the end than periodical injections of drugs. Both have to stop some time, and it is the stopping which is painful. . . .

The Farm as a Living Whole

The chief characteristic of real farming is that it is a way of life rather than a business, and it is inevitably the way of life of all, not only of those immediately engaged in it. It requires a completely different approach from that made to industry. It need not—in fact must not—be unbusinesslike; but business must serve and not override man's vital needs. Unless it is the chosen way of life as well as the business of those engaged in it, their hobby and their first love, it will degenerate. And this must apply to all engaged in it, not only to the farmer-employer or owner but to every worker. A right relationship to the land brings with it right human relationships. Though the former is in part lost, these human relationships survive on many farms in spite of the wage-and-profit system which prevails. There is a mutual understanding and respect and a sense of responsibility which is rare in industry. It is the natural relationship of people engaged in the same job, when they know their job and have a job worth knowing. In such living there is wisdom and contentment.

Conservatism of Farmers
There is also wisdom and contentment in the unhurried rhythm of country life, which is mistaken by the smart townsman for slowness in the uptake. Farmers know from experience that "the mills of God grind slowly, but they grind exceeding small". Hence their very real conservatism, their suspicion of change, and reluctance to submit to regimentation or rationalization. This mental conservatism is wholly natural, and fundamentally sound. It proceeds from an attitude to life which is absorbed rather than consciously acquired by people who live in contact with living things. They know that the behavior of living things does not necessarily conform itself to the formulas of theorists, and that nature will not be speeded up. They know that the complexity of the problems with which they have to deal becomes fantastic if an attempt be made to arrive at a complete analysis of these problems; that the balances of the innumerable factors concerned is of infinite delicacy, and that the ultimate result of any disturbance of them can rarely be foreseen; and that for these reasons empirical knowledge is not to be despised or lightly discarded. . . .

A farmer must think ahead, not a month or a year, but at least a complete rotation, which may be from two to ten years or more; all the time balancing every factor—pasture, arable, livestock, manuring, manpower; watching growth and longing for improvement as a mother with her child. Yet not only thinking and watching, but working hard and making quick decisions all the time. Truly a man's job, and one inevitably spoilt by flurry, or by constant changes of policy. . . .

Individualism and Independence of Farmers

Farmers have a reputation for individualism and independence. These are sound qualities, but they are not appreciated in a modern large-scale business. (But then that is a debased form of organization.) They are not incompatible with the highest forms of social organization—indeed they give it value; for they improve the quality of the smallest units, from which any such organization must grow. Nothing can grow downwards from the top. "The master's foot fats the soil" is a true saying. The farmer must be master of his plot, however small. He then really cares personally for it, more than for what he can get out of it, which is the first condition for the building up of a sound biological unit.

Various kinds of centralization, rationalization, and standardization may be good in the manufacturing industry, or they may not. They are certainly almost always bad when applied to farming, whether that application is made by governmental authority or under any kind of oligarchical private enterprise, or by farmers themselves acting individually or in concert under financial pressure. Financial pressure appears in many different forms: as compulsion and as temptation; as mortgage interest or as offers of credit made under seemingly harmless conditions; as indebtedness to dealers and threats of the withholding of markets, or as alluring advertisements of cure-alls and infallible profit makers.

Hard Work

Farming demands hard work and it demands devotion, like everything which is worthwhile for its own sake, and if it is not found worthwhile for its own sake by those engaged in it, it will not be good farming. It is the greatest of crafts, and the excellence of a craft depends on the unsparingness of the work bestowed on it by the craftsman. Craftsmanship decays where machinery plays too big a part. Machinery can do more and more things, but it has no taste or judgment, nor can it exercise wisdom. Therefore no work done by machinery can be done under the immediate influence of those qualities. This fact matters less when standardized materials are being dealt with, as in a factory, than when the ever changing qualities of natural and living things are being dealt with, as on a farm. And the quality of the product of farms is vastly more important to us than the quality of the product of factories.

Mechanized farming can therefore be very unlike what farming ought to be, especially when it tempts the farmer to work on too big a scale and too quickly. This does not mean that mechanical aids should be dispensed with altogether; it does mean that mechanization can be a terrible snare. It often is so, for so far manufacturers' attention has largely been devoted to producing machinery intended to increase the scale and speed of operations, machinery which makes possible the kind of soil exploitation which has led to desert-making on a scale hitherto unparalleled, and which is forcing the application of similar methods to our own soil. Machinery for small-scale work is however improving, and may be very valuable if used with judgment, so as to reduce drudgery where to do so is possible without loss in the quality of the work. But still, the very best in farming as in all other crafts can only be produced by hand, and less than the best will not do.

It is true that physical toil can overwhelm a man if it dominates his life unduly. It can keep him in a more or less brutal or apathetic state. To the extent that it does so, release from toil is a good thing. But that does not mean that all toil is bad. Probably a certain minimum amount of it is necessary both for his health and for his mental balance and for his fullest development. Hard healthy outdoor work can be the finest recreation in the world; only when carried to excess does it become deadening, and when it has to be done without understanding, purpose, or inspiration. It is certain that in real farming there can be no escape from hard work, even laborious work. But, even apart from its great variety, it is curiously satisfying work. All of it is skilled work; much of it demands the exercise of the highest craftsmanship, and of real sympathy and understanding in dealing with living creatures. It is capable of fulfilling many of our deepest spiritual needs. But it is only so when cheapening is not the first aim. In these days to do things properly usually costs too much, and that has taken the joy out of farm labor.

Nor is the labor necessary all that of the hand and muscle alone; there must be hard thinking too. On a farm there is a best moment for everything as well as a best way to do it, a moment settled not by calendar or clock or the state of prices, but by weather and growth, ripening and reproduction. The most constant attention and awareness are demanded, in small things as well as in great, and awareness means intense application of the mind to the farm itself, and not merely or even mainly to the market.

Organic Versus Chemical Farming

The best can only spring from that kind of biological completeness which has been called wholeness. If it is to be attained, the farm itself must have a biological completeness; it must be a living entity, it must be a unit which has within itself a balanced organic life. Every branch of the work is interlocked with all others. The cycle of conversion of vegetable products through the animal into manure and back to vegetable is of great complexity and highly sensitive, especially over long periods, to any disturbance of its proper balance. The penalty for failure to maintain this balance is, in the long run, a progressive impoverishment of the soil. Real fertility can only be built up gradually under a system appropriate to the conditions on each particular farm, and by adherence to the essentials of that system, whatever they may be in each case, over long periods. Such building up of a coherent living unity is utterly incompatible with frequent changes of system and with specialization. Yet the modern farmer is continually up against the temptation to make changes in order to secure a quick return where it appears there may be a chance of a profit for a few years in some particular line and to specialize in that line. In doing so he is tempted to use up accumulated fertility and trust to luck for the future. It is chiefly for these reasons that mixed farming is right, for it is only on the principle of constant exchange of living material, which is the basis of such farming, that real fertility (as against forced, artificial, or imported productivity) can be built up. Mixed farming is real farming. Unduly specialized "farming" is something else; it must depend on imported fertility, it cannot be self-sufficient nor an organic whole.

[Lord Northbourne discusses the use of artificial versus natural manures; also the use of poisonous chemical sprays.]

In the long run, the results of attempting to substitute chemical farming for organic farming will very probably prove far more deleterious than has yet become clear. And it is perhaps worth pointing out that the artificial manure industry is very large and well organized. Its propaganda is subtle, and artificials will die hard. But we may have to relearn how to treat the land before we can manage entirely without them, or without poison sprays. . . .

Self-sufficiency, Trade, and Art

There is, however, a much more fundamental aspect of the whole question of self-sufficiency. The vitality of an organization, a nation, or a world depends on the vitality of its constituent parts; and any entity which is unduly dispersed must lose the connection between its constituent parts and so become less alive. So if the smaller units which constitute a nation or a world have their separate internal relationships too loosely knit, they will become less alive as units; they will lose character and individuality. The higher the degree of biological self-sufficiency achieved by a farm, a district, or a nation, the more alive, the more vigorous, and the more creative it will be, and the more it will have to exchange with its neighbors, not the less. And the more individual any unit is the more such exchange will be refreshing to its neighbors. The livelier each of us is within himself the more he can contribute to the lives of others; real liveliness comes from within, not from without; it is the sign of that internal self-sufficiency which is vitality.

So trade is only good when it is a symptom of vitality. It can never of itself produce vitality; indeed it does not create anything. It is the craftsman who creates, and craftsmanship languishes when it becomes the servant of trade. Farming is—or should be—the greatest of all crafts. A craft does not approach perfection until it merges into art. So it is with farming, in which perfection for its own sake must be the aim, though it be approached but gradually. Perfection means beauty; beauty in art is the flowering of the urge to perfection which exists somewhere in all of us. In our feverish search for mere financial efficiency in farming we have suppressed that urge. It is no longer worthwhile to put beautiful finishings on a stack or elegant curves into a farm cart. Such things are the flowerings of true vitality; they cannot enter into the calculation of profitableness, so they have dropped out, and farming has become more and more a dying science and less and less a living art.

Beauty and the "Spirit of Place"

Every artist must be first a craftsman. Farming is the craft side of the art of living; that which we seem to have lost. With it has gone what Sir George Stapledon calls "The Spirit of Place"; that which has made England the lovable land she is. We feebly protest at the loss of England's rural charm, and form societies for the preservation of rural England. Good luck to them and may they succeed. But they will not and cannot succeed until they get back to the beginning and realize that charm comes from vitality, and that nothing can preserve it except vitality. We do not want only the imitation of health in our country any more than in ourselves. In neither case is it enough that we should only avoid or suppress that which gives obvious pain and offence; we must create that which is good; we must replace that which is lost with something better. To attempt to replace it by encouraging an attachment to the countryside which is purely recreational and sentimental is mere futility. It is perhaps worse than that, for it wastes time and energy in turning people's thoughts towards a totally false attitude in which first things are last and last things first.

It has been characteristic of English farming in the past that it has been full of the spirit of place. Our instinctive longing for some restoration of that state, and our appreciation of the artistic aspect of country life, show themselves in much sounder form in our national love of gardening than in the formation of societies to preserve country life. In gardening many of our finest traditions are enshrined, and they survive in spite of the drag of the towns and the spread of ugliness. Our love of gardening can blossom into something far greater. Its prevalence is a source of great hope.

4. Look to the Land: Sustainability[1]

The Future of Farming

When the forces of life have found out how to use mechanical forces for the ends of life rather than for the ends of death, then farming will be relieved of that load which now prevents its developing along the right lines. Any such development must come naturally and must not be imposed from above or it will not be on the right lines. Bearing in mind, however, the characteristics of real farming as distinct from that farming which is mere trading in, or processing of, stolen fertility, we can try to see what the farming of the future might be like, particularly as far as Britain is concerned.

Farms should be much smaller than they generally are today, especially on the more fertile lands. This does not mean that they would not be very variable in size, but that the labor and thought now bestowed on any given area needs to be concentrated on a much smaller area. An obvious corollary to this is that far more people would be wanted on the land. It would take a long time for these people to develop the qualities needed, though they are probably latent in most of us, and that is one reason for which hurry might be disastrous. To get these people on to the land without increase in the number of holdings would merely be to increase the labor force on farms as at present organized and to gain nothing, but rather to lose a good deal, insofar as individual care and responsibility are desirable. The point is that those who are willing and able to exercise individual care and responsibility and originality should have the opportunity to do so on their own land. Such people are of inestimable value and importance. The extent to which such desire for independence might develop under conditions different from those of the present day cannot be estimated. Let us hope it would develop to a very great extent. Even so, there will probably always be plenty of people who like a job without too much responsibility, and that not always because they are lazy-minded; it may on the contrary be because they wish to exercise their powers in

---

[1] Excerpted from *Look to the Land*, Chapter 5 (1940). —Editors

other directions, among which may be the pursuit of spiritual strength and activity. Such pursuit is entirely compatible with the performance of a steady job without too much worldly responsibility.

[Lord Northbourne discusses a 1935 report on the difficulty, under present conditions, of achieving success in small holdings.]

Specialization and Exhaustive Processes

. . . Unduly specialized farming is not compatible with the proper treatment of the soil. Carried out on a large scale, it is in part responsible for the present state of the soil of this unhappy world. In specialized farming, even when carried out on a relatively small scale, it is rarely possible to maintain fertility; for fertility depends on the balance of nutritional factors, on the completeness or wholeness of the "diet" of the plants and animals concerned and of the soil itself. It is (once more) not the same thing as productivity.

It is only possible to farm truly economically when this balance is preserved. It is necessarily upset when only a very limited variety of plants are grown, or when only one kind of livestock is kept. There may be a partial exception to this rule in the case of cattle. True fertility can be reasonably well maintained with cattle alone; nevertheless a mixture of livestock ensures a much better use of everything that is available on the farm. For instance, sheep graze particularly well after cattle, and poultry turn harmful insects to good use; both can be kept on a cattle farm without the reduction of the head of bovine stock, and each has a characteristic and beneficial effect on herbage which is supplementary to the effect of cattle. Apart from cattle, no other class of livestock is satisfactory alone. None can graze economically alone, each produces a characteristic and to some extent unbalanced manure, and all become liable to specific parasitic diseases and weaknesses if they are the only livestock on the ground. This is true even where stocking is very light, as on some of our hill sheep-runs, where the keeping of sheep alone is becoming very difficult even at the rate of one sheep to three acres, because disease still spreads while the land deteriorates. Exactly the same is true of plants. It is impossible to use to the full the resources of the soil except with a mixture of plants (either grown together as in pasture or mixed crops or grown in succession as in a proper rotation of crops). In monoculture it is impossible to keep disease at bay for long, and in addition it is impossible to feed animals properly except on a varied mixture. Grazing animals positively need "weeds" such as dandelion, yarrow, plantain, burnet, and all the charming variety of our native pastures. It has even been found to be worthwhile sowing them specially on reclaimed heath lands where they are not naturally present. . . .

So, whatever else it is, farming must be mixed farming—as mixed as possible. At least in some countries and some districts farmers cling obstinately today to mixed farming, and though they incur sometimes the criticism of economists for doing so, they are fundamentally right. For it is on the principles of mixed farming that the building up of fertility depends; on the mutual reactions and interdependence of crops and livestock, and on the entire avoidance of waste which only varied crops and varied livestock can provide for. Mixed farming is economical farming, for only by its practice can the earth be made to yield a genuine increase. Other kinds of farming are wholly or mainly trading in the elements of fertility, whether these elements be stolen from distant lands or obtained by means of honest biological exchange; which is not necessarily the same thing as a commercially honest purchase. A low price for wheat, for instance, may be commercially honest, but if it is made possible by the robbing of soil fertility, it is biologically dishonest. The penalties of biological dishonesty are more severe than those of commercial dishonesty.

[Lord Northbourne discusses the use, ultimately exhaustive, of mined or manufactured nitrogen, phosphorus, and potash (NPK) in creating fertility.]

The Biological Economics of Farming[2]

The fundamental economics of farming can only be expressed in terms of total effect on the fertility of the world. The relatively specialized farmer of today, with his complex requirements for his farm and himself, can with difficulty, if at all, escape from the predominance of the financial aspect of all that he does. It certainly does not pay him to impair the productivity of his farm—he who does so is and always has been a bad farmer. But the successful farmer of today is usually one who is successful in maintaining the productivity of his soil by the purchase of materials—feeding-stuffs or manures—which are cheap

---

[2] "Sustainability" is a term used today which closely resembles Lord Northbourne's concept of "biological economics". —Editors

because they are produced at the expense of fertility elsewhere. But that kind of successful farmer may not be a better farmer than another less "successful"; he may be only a more successful business man.

Therefore either the financial and economic complex in which we live must be so altered that the direction of the pressure which it exercises is changed, or alternatively at least some farmers or communities must insulate themselves from it. It may be that the alterations required in the economic complex can only be brought about by the building up from its biological elements of a new kind of community which is biologically self-supporting. And it is worth pointing out again that in the case of a completely self-contained farm or community, one which supplies all its own needs for men, animals, crops, and soil, any surplus that can be disposed of is clear gain to that community, however small the amount and however low the price. Only such a farm or community can be independent of money. But, more important, the said surplus represents not only a gain to the producers of it, but also to the world at large. It is a true profit; measurable no doubt in terms of money, but not primarily financial. The making of a financial profit conveys no information one way or the other as to whether the process by which it was made was exhaustive or the reverse. Yet it is that information which is important. It will of course be argued that by the use of imported chemicals and feeding-stuffs production per acre has been increased. That is true, but what has been the cost?

It will be further argued that it is impossible to maintain production at a level sufficient to maintain the inhabitants of populous countries if such importations are dispensed with. How can a farm be self-supporting when produce is constantly being taken off it, containing elements (especially nitrogen, phosphorus, and potash) which must be replaced? The answer is that of course they must be replaced; the real question at issue is: "How?"

We have seen that soil has been and is being maintained in wonderful condition by certain peoples, without apparent loss of fertility through the centuries. Obviously, no biological unit, however small or great, need necessarily suffer any loss of its elementary constituents, as matter is indestructible; provided only that, after passing through the phase of being part of an animal or plant, they all be returned to the soil in such a way that plants can recover them from the soil.

In that proviso we have the key to the search for the true bio-logical economics of farming. The problem is not one of finance nor of the supply of elements. There must necessarily exist enough elements in soil, plants, and animals to maintain life at its present standards on any area, however big or small. The problem is that of keeping them in circulation, of preventing them from reverting to forms in which they are inaccessible to life. It is not sufficient to obey the rule of return in its quantitative implications only. . . .

Diversification and Decentralization

Specialization in the modern sense is the division of labor carried to a more or less extreme point. Division of labor is the source of that material advantage which we call the "increment of association". But division of labor is only good when it is not carried so far as to react adversely on the minds of the individuals who are supposed to benefit materially from it, so as to deny them a whole life. So we must not be carried away by the possibilities of developing the "increment of association" through specialization, to the extent that the quality of our mental life is impaired, nor to the extent that the quality of our physical life, carried on as it is through farming, is also impaired. Even the immediate advantages supposed to be associated with most kinds of specialization in farming are mainly illusory. Though it be true that certain soils in an unimproved state may be best suited to limited cate-gories of crops or treatment, it is also true that good cultivation equal-izes soils. And it is true that the variety of systems of farming which are in the full sense mixed farming is infinite. There is ample room for adaptation to local conditions without abandoning the principle, which is that of working towards the greatest possible diversification so as to produce as complete an organic whole as possible.

That diversification is incomplete without the presence on a farm of such seeming superfluities as trees, bushes, hedges, and hedgerow weeds—or wildflowers as you may call them if your temperament is romantic. All these have their qualitative importance and value, both individually and collectively. Good cultivation is always beautiful, but most of us have a taste for wildness as well. It is pleasant that the best cultivation of all should be that which is not without its touch of wild-ness, so that it should present that picture of wildness and intimacy in association which is the most attractive picture of all; and which is, above all, the picture of England. . . .

33

As the farm itself, though small, must be internally diversified, so must the larger unit: the valley, the district, the county, the country. A sensitive adaptation of individual farms to the small variation in soil, aspect, moisture, and so on will in part ensure this wider diversification. Doubtless, however, in addition, some higher authority must see to it that woods are not injudiciously destroyed, that shelter is planted, or that other major works for the benefit of a big area are undertaken where necessary. Insofar as that authority derives its functions directly from the people working the land to be benefited, it will work well. Only common consent and the greatest possible degree of decentralization can do all that is necessary, and at the same time preserve the "Spirit of Place", without which character, individuality, and liveliness will be lost.

The adoption of true mixed farming is the first step towards the perfection of the individual farm, and after it of the countryside in all its aspects, as a healthy organic whole yielding a true profit rather than only a financial profit. The next step is the proper conservation, preparation, and return to the soil of all organic matter severed from the soil. Much of this is destined for consumption by men or animals. As to how that consumed by men can in practice be returned, without abandoning elementary hygienic principles, something has already been said. It is very unlikely that either the best method of preparation or the best way of using such material has yet been evolved. We feel an instinctive repugnance to its use for the growing of crops intended directly for human consumption. That repugnance may be mere prejudice, but it may also be soundly based, quite apart from any questions of the conveyance of infection. So we may just as well give way to it and use organic material prepared from sewage on pasture or on other crops intended for consumption by animals. If we look after our animal manure and vegetable wastes properly there need be no lack of organic feeding for the soil on which corn, vegetables, and fruit are grown for human consumption. . . .

Diversified Organic Farming: A Practical Proposition

Various methods of composting or preparation of farmyard manure and miscellaneous organic matter have come into prominence lately. Their widespread adoption obviously threatens the sales of commercially prepared fertilizers, organic or inorganic. Many attempts have been and are being made to discredit such methods, or alternatively to persuade people that compost is best prepared with the help of chemicals. In fact, some of the purely organic methods have proved very successful, particularly as regards the quality of the produce grown by them and its resistance to disease, and it has become clear that chemicals can economically be dispensed with, apart from the question as to whether they are or are not actually harmful. The best processes of organic fermentation are purely biological and are qualitatively changed, if not actually impeded, by the substitution of a chemical breakdown for a biological one. Apart from chemical processes, those best known in this country are the "Indore" process, developed from ancient Indian practices and introduced into this country by Sir Albert Howard, and the "biodynamic" method, evolved in accordance with the recommendations of the late Dr Rudolf Steiner. The latter method has been highly developed in the course of some fifteen years' work on the Continent, and its effectiveness may be said to be proved, though its supporters would be the last to claim that there is no more to be learned about it.

The fact remains that in any ordinary garden and on any reasonably well-balanced mixed farm, a quantity of organic manure can be produced amply sufficient to supply the needs of the soil. The ultimate benefit to soil, crops, and stock is not calculable, because non-measurable factors of a purely qualitative kind are involved such as health, palatability, and others more subtle; but the farmer or gardener can be confident that even from the start the extra labor involved will be at least balanced by the saving in purchased fertilizers. As always in farming, a change of method must not be adopted in a hurry, and the full benefits cannot be realized for a long time. But we have now sufficient experience to be able to say that a self-contained organic farm is no mere theoretical dream, practicable only for the "gentleman farmer" who farms for fun and can afford to lose money, but is an economical proposition for any farmer whose farm is not grossly over-weighted in any particular direction. . . .

This advocacy of small self-contained farms, relatively independent of outside purchases, seems to be very contrary to modern tendencies in the world of trade and commerce, with its ever-increasing specialization and centralization, reflected in the modern industrial town. It is indeed here categorically stated that those tendencies, whatever be their merits or demerits for manufacturing industry and trade, are, as they affect farming, diametrically opposed to the satisfaction of the essential biological needs of mankind, which are of course identical with those of the soil on which he lives and of all the other creatures of that soil.

The Problem of Distribution

But if we put these first things first, shall we really have to sacrifice anything worthwhile? A little leisure perhaps, which we today do not seem to know what to do with anyhow. Provided that growth in the right direction is spontaneous and not forced, which it can only be if it proceeds from the desire of the people concerned, there need be no dislocation, but only adaptation. It is a kind of dislocation from which we are suffering now; the changeover should rather take the form of a reallocation on a sounder basis. For instance, the whole "problem of distribution" as we know it is merely a result of dislocation, in the full derivative sense of the word. It is the maldistribution of production and of population which makes the distribution of goods so complicated, and which puts the country at the mercy of the distributor, especially when perishable goods are concerned. But even now much could be done, given a change of desires in the people. For example, a real demand for more fresh vegetables would soon bring market gardeners to a neighborhood. So long as people go on being fooled by advertisement (blatant or concealed) of processed foods, so long will they and the farmers be at the mercy of vast distributing concerns, whose every interest seems to be opposed to the people's real nutritional necessities. How can it be otherwise in a world of specialization and urbanization? Effective distribution seems to necessitate sterilization, which means killing, for failure to sterilize may mean infection in bulk. Hence the outcry for the pasteurizing of milk. But sterilization reduces the resistance to infection and the power of assimilation of the consumer of that which is sterilized. So yet more sterilizing seems to be necessary. A vicious circle again, of a type which should by now be familiar. . . .

There can be no real solution of the problem of distribution other than a rebuilding of society on a sound organic basis, which must involve a better distribution of the population, both within most countries and in the world as a whole. To attempt to look at the problem of distribution in isolation is to be led into the snare of "planned economy", equally a snare whether the planning be done by the State or by private interests holding quasi-monopolistic powers.

The only possible foundation for a sound organic life within any community is a close association of the people with the land.

Back to the Land?
The simplest and most direct way in which a closer association of the people with the land could come about is that as many people as possible should be living on the land, for at least some part of their lives. Farming as an occupation should be at least part of the normal way of life for a considerable proportion of the people of Britain, unless all that has been said about it hitherto is pure fancy. What that proportion should be is a matter for speculation at present, and can never be settled except by experience. It is essential that the people fortunate enough to be so placed should be able to make a living at least as easily as people otherwise occupied, and that they should be able to do so under conditions of the greatest possible individual, economic, political, and social freedom. Such conditions are not impossible of attainment, and will probably come about of themselves if the main obstacles to the evolution of a free and natural economy are removed, and if circumstances force upon people a clearer realization of where their true interests lie. It is doubtful if any one ever really learns otherwise than by force of circumstances. It looks as if circumstances were changing in a way that may impress the truth on people very forcibly.

[Lord Northbourne discusses the possibility of ruralization, or a movement back to the land; also the necessity of societal and governmental decentralization.]

The Curse of Adam
The nature of living things is that they are not mere machines. The fact that from one point of view they are machines has largely deceived us. But they are something more. That something more does not respond to mechanical or statistical treatment. It responds only to that for which we have no other word but love. Love can express itself in many ways, but if it is genuine it means giving—not of gifts but of self. We have tried to get without giving more than we could help. "Give and you shall receive" is not sentimental idealism, it is a simple, practical rule. That which we can and must give to the land is work, and if that work is given in love it will not be drudgery. But it will and must be work. The so-called "curse of Adam" is upon us:

"By the sweat of your brow you shall eat bread." Has it not become obvious that if we try to avoid it we die? But why call it a curse? Why not welcome it as a clue to our rejuvenation in terms of natural life? That kind of rejuvenation seems to be a necessary part of the rejuvenation of the life of the spirit for which every human being worthy of the name so ardently longs.

The Conquest of Nature

If we are to succeed in the great task before us we must adopt a humbler attitude towards the elementary things of life than that which is implied in our frequent boasting about our so-called "Conquest of Nature". We have put ourselves on a pinnacle in the pride of an imagined conquest. But we cannot separate ourselves from nature if we would. The idea of conquering nature is as sensible as if a man should try to cut off his own head so as to isolate his superior faculties. There can be no quarrel between ourselves and nature any more than there can be a quarrel between a man's head and his feet. If such a quarrel is invented it is the man who suffers, including both his head and his feet. We have invented or imagined a fight between ourselves and nature; so of course the whole of nature, which includes ourselves as well as the soil, suffers. We have even come to regard nature as something primitive, terrible, and squalid. If she is so, it is we who have made her so.

Nature is only terrible or squalid to those who do not understand her, and when misunderstanding has upset her balance. She is imbued above all with the power of love; by love she can after all be conquered, but in no other way. That has not been our way. We have attempted a less excellent way, and have upset the "balance of nature", so that she no longer appears to us in pleasant guise but in a guise in which the appearance of an opposition of forces—a "struggle for existence"—predominates over the appearance of a balance of forces. So we have come to believe in a struggle for existence as the only possibility, and we infer that any such struggle is necessarily painful. It is painful now, and not only to ourselves. But it was not always so and need not always be so. We are the head and have the responsibility. We have tried to conquer nature by force and by intellect. It now remains for us to try the way of love.

5. Agriculture and Human Destiny[1]

The crust of this earth periodically undergoes upheavals of various kinds and on various scales. In the course of the bigger ones, continents are submerged and new continents are raised up. In between there may be ice-ages, and ages of rain and of warmth affecting the whole surface of the globe, or parts of it only. All such occurrences, gigantic and overwhelming as they are from our point of view, are trivial incidents in a continuous series of changes occurring on a cosmic scale, staggering our imagination by their immensity and their duration, and reducing all terrestrial phenomena to a quantitative insignificance. Quantitatively speaking, human life is doubly insignificant, for it plays so small a part even in the geophysical history of this planet, and this planet cannot be considered as if it were isolated from the solar system, nor as if the solar system were isolated from the rest of the universe.

Therefore, if human life has any significance at all, it is not in the domain of quantity but in the domain of quality. It can only be worth preserving in virtue of its qualitative content or potentiality, although it does have an inherent quantitative aspect, and this cannot be preserved unless its quantitative requirements are met. The satisfaction of those requirements is justified only insofar as it is necessary for the development of the qualitative potentialities of mankind.

The main difficulty that arises in following up this statement is that the nature of those qualitative potentialities cannot be precisely defined. Quantity alone is measurable, quality as such is nameable but not measurable. Quality is forever what it is, and it is either perceived for what it is or not perceived at all. Nothing can convey its nature to anyone who cannot perceive it directly. Yet one must talk about quality, for it is the key to everything; without it there is nothing but the chaos of indistinction, the abstractness of pure number. In discussing quality, the most that one can do is to compare things that possess a quality with things that do not. Even then the comparison

---

[1] From *Looking Back on Progress* (1970). This article was originally titled "A Glance at Agriculture". —Editors

is meaningful only to someone who knows from experience what the quality in question is.

Of no quality is this more true than of the quality, or qualities, that can be called "spiritual". The word spiritual is inevitably misapplied or misunderstood by anyone for whom the limits of reality coincide with the limits of the measurable. The measurable is in the last analysis everything that can be brought within the analytical and descriptive powers of the human brain. If there were nothing that transcends those powers, all quality could be in principle reduced to quantity. The essential qualitative distinctiveness of man resides in his spiritual potentialities.

Terrestrial upheavals involve the periodical destruction of lives, human and other. This is apt to strike us as very terrible, and to make it difficult for us to understand how an all-merciful God can have ordered matters so. We forget that the law of birth and death is applicable, not to individual living creatures alone, but to everything on which an association with quantity confers a form, from universes downwards. All must perish; the Spirit, which is pure quality, alone is imperishable and always wholly itself. Both as individuals and as human societies we are perishable. Man has always known this, but at the same time he has always seen that there must, so to speak, be something behind it all, something imperishable and greater than himself.[2] To accept the perishability and dependence of ourselves and of the entire universe of forms, with all the humility that this acceptance implies, is a necessary prelude to the understanding of our situation, and such an understanding is indispensable to effective action. It seems that for the present our achievements in the domain of the quantitative and perishable have obscured from us our dependence on the qualitative and imperishable, thus confusing our sense of direction and frustrating much well-intentioned action.

[2] If that were not so, both he himself and the perishable world of forms would be wholly unreal, a mere fleeting illusion, causeless and aimless. Not only is any such conception contradicted by our own consciousness of existence, but it is also probably in the last analysis devoid of meaning.

What has all this to do with agriculture? Everything really; for the double reason that the soil, which is a product of terrestrial upheavals, provides its physical foundation, and that the relation of quality to quantity, not only in the final products of agriculture, but also in our approach to its problems, touches every one of us more closely than most people realize.

From the point of view of biology and economics alone, agriculture is the foundation of human life on this planet, and it has been so ever since the growth of population outstripped the food-producing potentialities of virgin Nature. Once established, it becomes the main expression of the relationship between man and Nature. All other human activities are as it were outgrowths arising from it and are dependent on it. We could get on without them, but not without agriculture. It therefore affects us more directly and more nearly than any other activity; the quality of our lives and our outlook is reflected in it, and its quality is in turn reflected back on them.

This self-evident truth has tended to become overshadowed by the attractions and disturbances of industrial development, but it is now being forced on us again in its quantitative aspect by the rapid increase in world population. Such an increase always seems to accompany an industrial revolution.[3] In an incredibly short time, industrial progress has become the aim of almost all nations, and an aim once established is not readily abandoned, especially when wealth is its target and seems within its grasp. Although we are faced with a danger of world starvation within a few decades, we continue to devote an ever-growing proportion of our money and energies to developments in the industrial field, the demands of which are insatiable. Industry is continually putting out fresh outgrowths which create new opportunities but with them new desires and new needs.[4]

[3] A population explosion is not necessarily or solely a result of more or better food, housing, or medical attention, all of which were for instance conspicuously lacking in the earlier stage of the British industrial revolution. They can no doubt help to keep it going once it has started, but they are not its cause.

[4] Curiously enough—or perhaps it is not curious at all—the newest desires are at the same time the most expensive and the most absurd, for instance, color television, ever faster travel, and putting men on the moon. Expansion for its own sake is the watchword; it can be achieved most quickly only at someone else's expense; when everyone is aiming at it, rivalry between sectional interests, national or otherwise, is

The dominant consideration in industry, the very principle on which it is founded, the consideration to which all others must give way, is the progressive reduction in the financial cost of producing and selling any given article. The purpose of that reduction is to free resources, both human and physical, for the production of a yet wider range of articles. The process is inherently cumulative and accelerative. It implies continual change of a kind that would nowadays be called a "redeployment of resources". It also necessitates an unremitting stimulation of the demand for goods, in other words, of desire. It is a case of continually persuading people to want what they did not know they wanted. It would be difficult to invent an economic background less well adapted than this to the fulfillment of the vital functions of agriculture.

As the industrial outlook becomes ever more universal, it becomes increasingly difficult, and eventually impossible, for agriculture to retain an outlook and methods incompatible with those of industry. Agriculture is affected above all by the unceasing worldwide pressure to reduce unit costs by adopting new methods, showing only marginal financial advantages, and continually being superseded by yet newer methods. The resulting instability does nothing but harm. Agriculture adopts the industrial outlook as nearly as its circumstances permit. It resisted for a long time, but is now thoroughly involved.

The typical organization of settled agriculture has been until recently of the kind known as a peasantry; it disappeared perhaps sooner in Britain than in most other countries. Its essential features are relatively small economic units, usually worked by families who derive most of their sustenance from their own holdings and sell or exchange only their surplus. Each unit or group of units is more or less self-contained and self-supporting both economically and biologically. The techniques of cultivation and care of animals are handed down with little alteration from generation to generation. Within this type of framework many variations can be found and have been studied; some

everywhere exacerbated, and preparations for war, whether "cold" or "hot", become the biggest drain on the resources of all.

of them have survived here and there to the present day, though not without modification. The way of life of a peasantry is above all traditional; its resistance to change has in the past been perhaps the main stabilizing factor in human civilization, while at the same time it has been a breeding ground of fine human qualities. Even today, among the few survivors of the ancient peasantries, it is possible to find outstanding examples of dignity, poise, and pride of function joined to real craftsmanship, no doubt related to a real sense of the place of man in Nature, and therewith of his relation to God. These qualities can make up for many faults. They are not sufficiently appreciated in these days, for they are not money-spinners; but civilization is nevertheless seriously impoverished when they are rare. The peasant has always been the butt of the smart townsman, although his way of life has also been romanticized. There is no justification for disparagement of the function of the peasant which is indispensable in a settled people.

Insofar as a peasantry retains some vestiges of the Edenic state from which it sprang, that function is much more than simple food-production, since it is the function through which man is integrated with his environment. Its romantic aspect is closely associated with that origin. In its decadence very little of that origin remains.

The peasant way of life has by now almost been wiped off the map of the world. It is true enough that it cannot meet what people perceive as the needs of our times, but then the people of our times do not know what their real needs are. If a peasantry can preserve something that conforms to the most profound human needs, that would at least explain why, of all the forms of human society, it is the most tenacious of life. But even where it has hung on up to the present day, it seems to be doomed. The tractor is replacing the draft animal, electricity is everywhere, television is in the living room, and a motor car is in the stall of the beast of burden. In many places where, in spite of all, something of the ancient spirit might survive a little longer, tourism is swamping it with artificiality.

The European and Asian peasant, who is evidently in mind here, is taken as the typical representative of a traditional agriculture. The way of life of the hunting nomad is by definition minimally agricultural, and is therefore excluded from the present discussion, except in order to mention that the true nomad may in many respects often be even nearer to the Edenic state than the peasant, and that the advent of modernism has destroyed his way of life even more quickly and more completely.

It may be worthwhile to summarize the nature of the outward changes brought about in agriculture by the rise to dominance of the modern industrial outlook.

Firstly: a progressive reduction in the number of persons directly engaged in agriculture, both in relation to the volume of its products and to the non-agricultural population. This tendency has gone further in Great Britain and the United States than elsewhere and the proportion of agricultural to total population is still falling. This has been made possible by the mechanization of an ever increasing number of agricultural processes and tasks, including the care of animals. Mechanization is the most typical feature of industrialization in all its forms. It is usually accompanied by the substitution of the wage-earner for the worker having a proprietary interest.

Secondly: and arising directly from the above: progressive increase in the average size of farms and of fields, so that the cost of elaborate and expensive machinery and equipment may be spread over a large area, and so that its use to full capacity may be as far as possible unrestricted. Consequential changes related to systems of tenure, finance, etc., need not be considered here, important though they be.

Thirdly: the substitution of chemical methods for older methods, both for the maintenance of the productivity of the soil and for combating diseases, weeds, and pests.

Fourthly: and arising directly out of the three changes already outlined: a progressive loss of economic independence, both in the individual agricultural unit and in agriculture as a whole. Agriculture is already very much dependent on industry for the fulfillment of its functions, and even, particularly in England, on the industry and products of distant lands. Herein lurks a risk of famine so far largely unrecognized.[5]

---

[5] For instance, British agriculture today is absolutely dependent on machinery, together with supplies of the necessary spare parts, fuel oils, lubricants, electricity, and other requirements, many of which come from abroad. Intensive stock farming

Fifthly: a growing demand for the standardization of agricultural and horticultural products, to meet the requirements of a mainly urban population, and of the distributors who not only serve it but also persuade it to want what it suits them to offer, namely products that are uniform, well packed in standard quantities, and as nearly as possible imperishable. A consequence of all this is the widespread practice of adding preservatives to a growing range of foods.[6] Once again, cheapness is the supposed justification of such practices, but even that advantage can be more than neutralized by costs of processing, packing, and distribution. There is an ever-growing gap between primary producer and ultimate consumer, conspicuous in its financial aspect although less so in its more important biological aspect. This, of course, is a very big question, covering as it does the whole field of human nutrition.

Sixthly: a growing instability arising out of the increasing rapidity with which the new ideas produced by research, together with economic and political changes, necessitate the adjustment or alteration of methods and of the approach to current problems. Agriculture ceases to be the main stabilizing factor, either economic or social, in a civilization, and finds itself involved willy-nilly in what is commonly called the "rat-race".[7] It is perhaps not too wild a guess to say that there has been more change in the past hundred years than in the previous thousand, and more in the last twenty than in the previous two hundred. This acceleration shows no sign of slackening.

All these changes mark the abandonment of a traditional approach in favor of an industrial approach. Industrial progress is founded on modern science, and so it is not surprising that agriculture claims to be more and more scientific, and to a large extent lives up to its claim.

---

on modern lines would be impossible without protective and curative drugs and supplements to natural foods; and, for so long as existing economic pressures continue present-day standards of crop production could not be approached without a liberal use of chemical fertilizers and weed-killers. It has been calculated that to keep one man employed full-time in agriculture in Britain, two men must be employed full-time in industry.

[6] The materials used have usually been shown by short-term experiments to be harmless, but, to say the least of it, we are entitled to expect from our food something better than harmless.

[7] It has been described as "doing unto others before they do unto you".

Most farmers accept this situation and many even welcome it, for they are far from being immune to infection by the ideology of industrial progress. By them as by others every step in this progress is hailed as an advance, and so it is from the purely industrial point of view. Every innovation brings at least a potential financial gain, but it is necessarily obtained at a price. The only motivation of industry is gain that can be measured in financial terms, but in agriculture the price may have to be paid in a less measurable currency, one that is qualitative rather than quantitative. No instance could be more self-evident than that of the sacrifice of beauty associated with industrial development, including the development of agriculture on industrial lines; a loss not only of natural beauty, but also of beauty in the things man makes for his use or pleasure. This is one of the qualitative losses that has not passed unnoticed. It is regretted, and many attempts are made to minimize it, but little is done to attack or even to understand its cause.

There are other problems. For instance, there has been a considerable outcry raised against what is called "factory farming" as applied to animals, mainly on the grounds that it is cruel, and there has been much argument on both sides. Without going into that argument, it can be asserted with confidence that so long as any producer who can cut his costs while still producing a saleable article can squeeze a producer who cannot do so out of business, there will be "factory farming" or something very like it, with all its inevitable effects on the quality of its products and on the animals involved.

There is also a controversy about the quality of food grown by "natural" as against "artificial" methods. It is really a question, not of natural against artificial, but of the degree of artificiality, the only natural foods being those that are produced in nature without human assistance; but questions of degree can be crucial. The subject can be argued *ad nauseam* and any answer arrived at is sure to be liable to criticism as being a result of prejudice, since no scientific proof is ever likely to be possible. Nothing less than experiments with whole communities prolonged over several generations could provide anything that could be called scientific proof, and by then it would be too late to be of much use.[8]

---

[8] Studies of living populations can however be informative. See, for example, *The Wheel of Health* by Dr. G.T. Wrench (New York: Schoken Books, 1972), a study of the

A return to older methods of cultivation and fertilization does not by itself touch the root of the matter. This does not imply that it may not be worthwhile for its own sake, provided that too much is not expected of it. A few people have tried and are still trying to produce food without the help of chemical fertilizers and sprays, and a few people—perhaps a growing number—prefer to buy food thus produced. Who dares to say that they are wrong? A large majority of people are not interested and much prefer to swim with the stream, and to dismiss the objectors to food grown by modern methods as being mere faddists.

New techniques are adopted by farmers because they know that if they do not keep up to date they will be squeezed out of business. Modern farming has become much more a business than a way of life. The pressure towards an ever more complete industrialization of agriculture is still growing. Farmers are officially encouraged to expect nothing less, in Britain, where certain minimum prices are fixed by the Government, farmers are told that these prices will be based on an expected increase of so much per cent per annum in their "efficiency", and the measure of that efficiency is exclusively financial. That is why most of the few farms trying in one way or another to fight against contemporary trends have already been squeezed out. They have found out that what was economically possible yesterday is not so today, and will be less so tomorrow.[9]

One thing is abundantly clear. It is unlikely that the growing population of the world can be fed at all in the future otherwise than by the employment of modern scientific agricultural techniques. For it to be fed without using those techniques, a condition would be the abolition of all the quantitative and sentimental ideals of modern civilization and the desires they engender, and the recovery of a sympathy with

Hunza people of N.W. India, and *Farmers of Forty Centuries* by F.H. King (Emmaus, PA: Rodale Press, 1973), a study on Chinese peasantries.

[9] If anyone wants to protect himself from contemporary trends and influences which he believes to be pernicious by growing his own food on his own land in his own way, as he has a perfect right to do, he will get no help and little sympathy. He must be in a position to face an economic isolation which is in practice extremely difficult to realize. It is even more difficult to realize an isolation from the influence of modern civilization in other domains, yet, unless this can be done, the purpose of an economic isolation will be only very partially fulfilled.

and an understanding of Nature now in abeyance. It is undeniable that very dense populations have fed themselves for long periods without modern techniques,[10] but their approach to life and its problems and their sense of values were so different from ours that we cannot as a society even understand them, let alone live as they did.

Wherever the line that divides the artificial from the natural may be drawn, their separation has now reached a point at which one can say that the agricultural revolution which has followed on the heels of the industrial revolution has brought about something like a divorce between man and Nature. Formerly, man lived more or less in harmony with Nature, and played his part in maintaining what we call a "balance of Nature". That natural balance, if we could but see it so, represents a fulfillment of the divine ordinances whereby all living things are related one to another through their common origin in God, and those ordinances have both a gentle and a rigorous aspect, a fact which modern sentimentality refuses to recognize.[11] From the modern point of view, ancient man was "superstitious", meaning that his motives appear often to have been other than purely rational. No account is taken of the fact that those motives may have been in origin super-rational; that agriculture—in common with all other human activities, social, artistic, military, and so forth—can ever have been sacred. We often describe it as having been traditional. The words "sacred" and "traditional" are, or ought to be, very close together in meaning; today both have come to be more or less assimilated in meaning to the word "superstitious", which properly speaking is

---

[10] See note 8. The works referred to are equally informative in connection with the feeding of large populations from small areas of workable land.

[11] When we speak disparagingly of the "law of the jungle" we are looking only at the rigorous aspect of the divine ordinances. It is undeniable that wild animals are liable to misfortunes which sometimes appear to us to be cruel and even unnecessarily so, but it is doubtful whether they are any worse than those to which humanity is liable, more particularly because human troubles are so much more varied, subtle, and persistent. It is evident to the most casual observations that wild animals seem almost always to be vigorous and well nourished, or else dead. Nature's method of eliminating disease and injury, and with them the suffering they cause, may seem harsh in our eyes, but they are undeniably effective, and where the conscious apprehension of death is, as far as we can see, absent or only momentary, they could scarcely be more merciful, given that pain in one form or another is inevitable in a world which is necessarily imperfect. The wild animals certainly look happier than we do.

applicable to things that have lost their virtue through the loss of their attachment to their divine origin. The ancient practices cannot be understood in purely economic terms; and when no other terms are regarded as seriously significant, they cannot be understood at all. [12]

Our ancestors no doubt realized, consciously or unconsciously or semi-consciously, that there is no end to the complexities and the subtleties of the relationships between living things, so that they are beyond the power of the human brain alone to resolve. Our ancestors were not overweeningly inquisitive about their environment, having been taught by their religions and traditions to accept their human situation. The justification of all such teaching is that the direct and unelaborated human experience provides as much as, and more than, most people can comprehend. Too wide a range of enquiry can distract attention from experiences which, though outwardly simple and even commonplace, are symbolically adequate to provide a support for spiritual needs. [13]

The surface of an expanding sphere moves away from the center which is the principle of its sphericity, and at the same time, as the surface expands, its constituent parts move away from one another. Such is the image of all outward-looking and peripheral knowledge; in becoming more extensive its constituent parts move away from each other and away from their common principle. [14] In this analogy the surface of the sphere represents the visible universe, the world of appearances with which alone modern science is concerned, while the

[12] Many of the ancient practices have in fact become superstitions in the proper sense of the word, and that perhaps is why they no longer seem to be effective (an instance would be the regulation of sowing and planting by the phases of the moon). The attitude of ancient man towards Nature was probably one of a more or less non-analytical acceptance, accompanied by a sense of reverence for the wonderful works of God, a reverence too often caricatured nowadays as "nature-worship".

[13] An excessive inquisitiveness concentrates attention on matters the outward complexity of which creates an illusion of comprehensiveness, although in reality they are concerned only with appearances, and are therefore superficial.

[14] What, one wonders, is the reality underlying modern astronomical theories of an expanding universe? To what extent do they reflect the purely outward-looking tendencies of the modern mentality? It is perfectly possible that the physical universe should appear to be expanding when looked at from a particular point of view, necessarily limited but not necessarily illegitimate; whereas from a different point of view, no less legitimate put perhaps less limited, it would appear otherwise.

whole sphere, surface included, represents reality as a whole, centered on unity. The surface is indefinite in extent; it has no boundaries, and no part of it is principial with respect to any other. A search for truth confined to the surface can have no finality. If finality is sought in the surface, the search for it inevitably becomes more and more extensive and fragmented. The resulting multiplicity and diversity are represented as an enrichment, but it is a false and ultimately harmful enrichment because it is more and more quantitative and out of touch with the purely qualitative center.

⤞➔❋⬅◉⤝

The apparent need for experimental research grows rapidly as the field covered by observation grows. Each single experiment can cover only an ever smaller fraction of that field. The approach of science, being experimental, is the approach of trial and error, that is to say, it is purely empirical. If it be true that sound practice, in agriculture or in anything else, can be established on no other foundation, it follows that inquisitiveness and inventiveness are the true measure of intelligence. If that be so, the intelligence of our ancestors was indeed inferior to our own. One must then envisage the recent occurrence of a change in the power of the human brain so great, so rapid, and so world-wide that no theory of evolution conceived as a gradual process of adaptation could possibly account for it.[15] What has really happened is that a change of outlook, which can take place without the acquisition of any new powers, has brought about so many changes in our lives that it has been mistaken for an acquisition of new powers.

We have chosen the direction in which we want to go, and we have arrived at a point at which the only hope for the future seems to lie in the extension and acceleration of research, so that changes in the chosen direction may take place more and more quickly. This acceleration is extremely bad for agriculture, and if it is bad for agriculture it is bad for humanity.

---

[15] It could only be accounted for as being something like what biologists call a mutation; but it would be a mutation of a magnitude and a universality to which our present knowledge can suggest no parallel.

The soil, animals, and plants have a limited range of adaptability, and adaptation is slow within that range. When the process of forcing up output has reached a certain point, it will have gone too far. By then it will be too late. Nobody can say what that point is, because before any innovation has had a chance of a fair trial, and before the creatures involved—men included—have had a chance to adapt themselves to it, it has already been superseded by another. There is no chance at all of assessing or anticipating long-term effects, simply because they can only be assessed at the end of a long term; there is simply not time to take more than the most obvious and immediate effects into account.

The one thing we know about these long-term changes is how complex and unpredictable they are, and that they are often irreversible, as for instance in the case of soil erosion. Any attempt to predict their nature is mere guesswork. So far the dangers seem to be, in the soil, loss of texture and trace element deficiencies, in animals and plants liability to diseases and to genetic troubles, and in agriculture as a whole, invasions of weeds and pests. So far, and up to a point, science has been more or less able to keep pace with tendencies in these directions as the need has arisen, but new problems arise ever more quickly. All this emphasizes the growing dependence of agriculture on a complicated and vulnerable scientific and industrial organization over which it has little control.

Perhaps this is the place to mention the recent development of the relatively new science of genetics, which offers possibilities of the artificial production of what would be in effect new species of plants and animals. So far most of its work has been confined to inducing variations in existing species or hybrids by the selection and combination of existing genes, but the production of artificial genes has been seriously propounded. Whether something of that kind is possible or not, future developments are sure to be much more far-reaching than present achievements. We have good reason to know how potentially dangerous to living creatures experiments on the structure of atoms can be. What then, of experiments on the genetic constitutions of creatures themselves? The unintentional production of uncontrollable monstrosities, though they might be no larger than viruses, cannot be ruled out. A discovery that would be described journalistically as a "major breakthrough" is greatly to be feared, if only because it would encourage the attribution to humanity of a new "creative" power. A greater and more insidious danger may be a qualitative deterioration in the animals and plants with which we are so closely associated.[16] And will such experiments always be confined to plants and animals? Experiments on the human constitution itself are not likely to be long deferred.

⫸✦❊❈❭✦⫷

In looking at the picture of modern agriculture as a whole, and more particularly at the factor of acceleration that dominates it, it is difficult to see how a severe crisis can be avoided, or even postponed for very long. It is impossible to predict the form it might take, chiefly because its proximate cause might not be internal to agriculture. It might for example be connected with its loss of independence and self-sufficiency. It might also be connected directly or indirectly with the growth of world population. It is not at all difficult to envisage a situation in which the demand for cheap food had been replaced by a demand for food at any price. There would then still be pressure, perhaps fiercer even than it is now, and it would certainly be even more quantitative and even less qualitative. The nature of any future crisis is impossible to foresee; but insofar as it affects agriculture as a whole, it will affect every man on earth. Meanwhile, in Britain an average of 50,000 acres of agricultural land are being permanently alienated for other purposes every year.

---

[16] Our association with plants and animals is one of mutual dependence. Our dependence for survival on the plants is total, our dependence on the animals is less so, though in practice it is real enough; in both cases the quantitative aspect is more evident than the qualitative, although we ignore the latter at our peril. The plants and animals on the other hand, expect for cultivated species and varieties, are not physically dependent on us in the same way; they could survive if we were to disappear. Scientifically speaking, to say that the dependence of the plants and animals on man is of a spiritual order means nothing, because science is not equipped to take account of that order; nevertheless it is the truth, and therefore must be stated. The function of humanity is essentially spiritual and mediatorial and it is exercised on behalf of the whole creation. When it is neglected the whole creation suffers. Therefore the plants and animals will bear witness against this generation of men in the day of judgment, despite all our societies for the conversation of Nature and for the prevention of cruelty.

One of the forms such a crisis might take is that of what used to be called an "act of God"; for instance, it might be precipitated by a readjustment of the earth's crust. It is worthwhile to remember that, in the days when unpreventable disasters were attributed specifically to God, it was at the same time customary to thank Him for benefits received. The two attitudes combined represent an acknowledgment of dependence on God, good for the soul. It is good for the soul because it keeps it in touch with reality. Nothing is worse for the soul because nothing is more false, than any assumption of its independence of God in matters great or small. If in the past disasters were "acts of God", they are so still; if they were then "judgments" they are so still. This we admit involuntarily when we use the word "crisis", the literal meaning of which is "judgment".[17]

Both the soul of man and the crust of the earth are subject to God's over-riding dispositions and to His judgments. The world including its inhabitants is multiple, but by virtue of its origin in the divine Unity it constitutes a unity. Whatever may affect one part affects the whole, and whatever affects the whole affects every part. That being so, it would be strange if changes in the crust of the earth and in human mentality were mutually independent. It is not so much a case of a change in one causing a change in the other, as of their proceeding from a common cause. All things move together, towards the fulfillment of the plan of the Great Architect of the Universe, and are interrelated at all stages and not only in their critical or explosive or conspicuous phases. Preparatory phases may not be recognized as such. They may be imperceptible in the case of changes in the earth's crust, while at the same time evident in human affairs, wherein they can be "signs of the times" to anyone who can read them.

The accomplishment of any phase may be a disaster from the human point of view, not least when it is accompanied by a terrestrial upheaval. We forget that a terrestrial upheaval, though it is a death from the point of view of what precedes it, is a birth from the point of view of what follows it. The world, or a world, is reborn, and it is reborn on a new soil more fertile than that of the ancient worn-out

---

[17] That the course of events in these days should be made up of a succession of "crises" following one another ever more closely, is probably more significant than most people seem to think.

lands. And if the cataclysm is a divine judgment so far as the preceding humanity is concerned, it can also be the divine inauguration of a new humanity, restored to its Edenic state because no longer remote from a direct divine intervention and forgetful of it. And so a new cycle begins, and somewhere in its course an agriculture of some kind will become necessary, as it did with Adam.

Science agrees with religion concerning the periodical occurrence of terrestrial cataclysms, but the two differ profoundly concerning their implications.[18] Science can only see a way out for man through a hypothetical enlargement of his inventiveness, whereby the even more hypothetical opportunities for a human life on the terrestrial pattern afforded by the stellar universe might be opened up to exploration and exploitation.

Religion offers a release of an entirely different kind. It is a release from all entanglements, physical or otherwise, and man can only find it in the unchanging Center of his own being, and of all being, wherein the Spirit dwells eternally and by its radiation confers on all that is peripheral whatever qualitative excellence it may possess.

If we seem to have wandered at times rather far from agriculture, it is because agriculture cannot be considered in isolation and at the same time realistically. It is the principal expression of our relation to Nature, far more so, for instance, than any aesthetic or sentimental relationship; it is woven into the texture of our whole existence and touches us at every point.

---

[18] The Hindu cosmology takes full account of the succession of cycles through which every "world" and every humanity passes on the way to its final reintegration in the Absolute. The first chapter of the Book of Genesis and the New Testament (in particular the twenty-fourth chapter of St. Matthew's Gospel and the Book of Revelation) appear to be concerned only with the cycle in which the present humanity is involved; nevertheless, since every cycle, whether great or small, is a manifestation of universal laws, all cycles are basically analogues; the Biblical statement is therefore of more general application than it may at first sight appear to be. In other religions the point of view may be different, but in every case there is an adaptation of a comprehensive truth to the particular mentality of the people to whom the message is addressed. The message is always essentially the same.

From our creatural point of view, there is God and there is Nature and there is also man, whose body and mind are one with Nature, but who is made in the image and likeness of God. Man is thus by appointment mediator between God and Nature. Man cannot exercise his mediatory function effectively if he allows his gaze to wander from the God who appointed him to it and who is always present to guide him if he will look for guidance. If he uses his God-given dominion over Nature, not in view of God, but of his own aggrandizement, he soon finds himself lonely and insignificant, vainly struggling against the forces of Nature. In the end even his own powers are turned against himself.

Nature manifests in change the changeless dispositions of the Almighty God. Nature has no choice. We have a choice, and we have exercised it in a manner and up to a point at which there seems to be no escape from the involvements it has brought upon us. The industrialization of agriculture is one of those involvements, and it may well prove to be not the least of them.

6. Compassion in World Farming[1]

I have been closely connected with agriculture (in the broad sense, including horticulture both commercial and private) for over fifty years, mostly actively engaged in it. So I can claim to see at least that period in perspective. Tractors and chemical fertilizers came into their own after the first war, but the changes that have taken place since the second war are much greater, and constantly accelerating; and now the computer will accelerate them still further. Increasingly all natural rhythms are violated, and it is only a question of time before we find out in what currency the penalty will be paid.

The sole objective of industry is to cheapen production. Agriculture is now an industry and is treated as such both officially and by a vast majority of the general public. The government allow for so much per cent annual increase in "efficiency" in the February price reviews. The public buys its food by eye and demands standardization and ease of preparation and little more. Under four per cent of our working population is on the land, and the annual reduction is regarded as an achievement. Factory farming in one form or another is an absolutely inevitable consequence.

As to what an individual can do in his own garden, or in feeding himself and his family, all one can say is that it appears to be largely a matter of taste—and taste has of course its proper place in the scheme of things. But it is difficult to see how the pressure of economic "progress" is to be escaped in any enterprise on a commercial scale, at least for more than a very short time. I will give two examples to illustrate what I mean:

One. About eight years ago we (my farming company) found ourselves with a set of old dairy buildings on our hands. We decided to use them for housing a poultry unit, with two thousand five hundred laying hens, a few on deep litter, but mostly in covered yards

---

[1] This article is previously unpublished in book form. Written c. 1975, it could be said to function as a postscript to Lord Northbourne's early writings on the subject of agriculture. The facts related in the article's second paragraph pertain to the time they were written. —Editors

with a run-out into open yards. They are fairly crowded, in units of about two hundred and fifty, but are free to run about, and they get grain thrown into the litter, which they spend hours scratching for. Food and water ad lib. The staff is one man, who also does the chick rearing. They have laid well by modern standards. The price of eggs has fallen continuously in relation to all costs throughout this period. Three years ago we made some minor alterations which have enabled us to keep three thousand birds with the same accommodation and staff. Even so, the position is becoming more and more precarious, and the question of closing down will have to be considered. Although our initial capital costs were low, eggs can be produced more cheaply by people who run ten thousand birds with one person and fully automated equipment. This production is more "economic", and we are probably going to be squeezed out, as thousands of smaller producers have been before us. When we started, our show was quite modern: now it is out of date.

Two. Our farms are nearly all arable, and we practice ley farming because we do not believe in growing more than three grain crops in a row.[2] The leys are grazed by sheep, well suited to this dry chalky land. Till three years ago we had two ewes and progeny per acre. (The story is more complex than this, but I reduce it to essentials.) The return per acre was insufficient. So we doubled the number of ewes to four per acre; we treat them and the lambs and the pastures intensively, and sell all progeny as fat lambs as quickly as possible. This can only be done by systematic dosing of animals against parasitic infections, and stimulation of the grass with artificial fertilizers. It has however become possible, at least theoretically, to produce lambs still more cheaply by hormone treatment of ewes to make them lamb twice a year with a higher proportion of twins, the lambs being taken away at birth and reared artificially for sale at an early age. Shall we be squeezed out of business here as well?

That is what we are up against.

The question of factory farming, however, is in a sense a side issue; in attacking it one is attacking a symptom of the tendencies of the

---

[2] In ley farming crops are rotated with three-year legume and grass pastures for livestock. It is an alternative to crop-fallow practices or to rotation with other crops such as sugar beet. Literally, "ley" means "meadow". —Editors

modern world without touching the cause. Neither laws nor protests directed against any of its features will affect in the slightest degree the sources of the overriding pressures that bring it about. Nor will laws and protests produce "compassion" in the only sense in which it could be effective in the present context. In that sense it means a "sense of oneness with", and this implies understanding as well as sentiment.[3]

What we have lost is our sense of oneness—or sympathy or "compassion"—with Nature as a whole. Pity for any particular case of suffering is not the same thing; it is of course to be encouraged, and it always accompanies true compassion, but it does not carry the same implication of oneness or understanding, and therefore cannot attain by itself to more than a limited objective.

Our primordial and wholly unsentimental oneness with Nature has been destroyed by the outlook of which industrialism is a consequence. It cannot be restored while that outlook retains its dominance. The industrial-scientific-humanistic outlook is the converse of the traditional outlook. They are incompatible, and we have chosen between them; now we cannot escape the consequences of our choice. Obviously it is necessary and right to try to mitigate some of the consequences, but it is a mistake to suppose that one is doing anything to check the movement that gave rise to them.

For instance: the production of proteins by industrial processes may well be the most practicable expedient for feeding over-populated countries; nevertheless it represents a further step in the industrialization of agriculture, and that step, like most of the others, is likely to prove to be in practice irreversible, and to become the foundation for further "advances" in the same direction, and therewith to lead to further, and worse, problems.

The whole subject is of course a vast one. I have only touched on one or two points. To end on a personal note: I don't like pumping sheep full of drugs (though they appear to thrive on it); nor killing weeds with hormone sprays (they show every evidence of torture in the etymological sense of the word);[4] nor forcing crop yields to the

[3] We should perhaps more often use the word "sympathy" in that sense, which is the exact etymological equivalent of "compassion", derived from the Greek instead of from the Latin.

[4] From the Latin, *tortura*, "twisting, torment". —Editors

limit with chemicals, etc. What are the alternatives? To try to put the clock back, when I can see so many reasons why it is not possible to do so? To conduct some wild experiment which could not possibly have any sound foundation and would therefore be useless even if—as is most unlikely—it were to achieve apparent success? To adopt some half-measures connected with either or both of the above, having to some extent done so in the past and learnt better? Or to stop farming? This last is the only practical one: but there is still enough left in farming and especially in gardening to make it preferable to anything else. It is not all drugs and chemicals, nor ever will be.

II

ON THE VALUE OF
TRADITION

The ideology of progress envisages the perfectibility of man in terms of his terrestrial development, and relegates it to a hypothetical future, whereas tradition envisages the perfectibility of man in terms of salvation or sanctification, and proclaims that it is realizable here and now.

From "Looking Back on Progress"

7. Religion and Tradition[1]

The word "religion" is often used today simply to mean whatever an individual or a group regards as being true, or that whereby conduct is regulated. Even Communism is sometimes loosely called a religion, regardless of its origin and its tendencies, and regardless of the fact that it is no more than a construction of the human mind. Such things as Communism may be substitutes for religion, but to call them religions is an abuse of the word which can give rise to a very pernicious kind of confusion.

In its original and only valid sense the word "religion" applies only to something which is, above all, not a construction of the human mind, but is, on the contrary, of divine origin, so that it can be said to be supernatural, revealed, or mysterious. Its purpose is to provide an effective link between the world and God. The word "Religion" is used hereafter in this strict sense, and to emphasize this it is spelt with a capital R.[2]

All that follows is applicable to the Christian Religion. In the main it is also applicable to what are sometimes called the great Religions of the world. It is assumed here that each has its validity for a particular group of peoples, despite outward differences and even apparent contradictions. What matters for each person is adherence to one Religion, normally that of the country of one's birth, rather than attempts to reconcile it with others, or purely academic excursions into the field of comparative religion.

The completeness and uniqueness of a Religion implies that from the point of view of its followers it is preferable to any other. It really is so for them, but not necessarily for other people. There may often be good reason for defending it against other Religions in order to preserve its purity and the coherence of its symbolism. That does not alter the fact that all "orthodox" Religions—that is to say those that are linked by an unbroken chain of tradition to an authentic Revelation—are paths that lead to the same summit. If that were

---

[1] From *Religion in the Modern World* (1963). —Editors

[2] In this anthology, such usage is confined to this article. —Editors

not so, God would have denied the possibility of salvation to a vast majority of the earth's inhabitants, past and present. It is surprising how cheerfully many of the followers of a Religion based on love and charity accept this conclusion.

Paths that lead to a summit are widely separated near the base of the mountain, but they get nearer together as they rise. The wise climber takes the path on which he finds himself and does not worry too much about people on other paths. He can see his path but cannot see theirs properly. He will waste an enormous amount of his own time if he keeps on trying to find another and better path. He will waste other people's time if he tries to persuade them to abandon theirs, however sure he is that his is the best.

Religion is founded on the belief—or rather on the certainty—that God has shown His love, as well as His justice and His wisdom, to the world in the first place and most directly in His Revelation of Himself through the founder (or founders) of the Religion in question. This implies that the founder did not invent that Religion, his part being entirely receptive, insofar as a distinction can be made between his divine and human nature.

Revelation is therefore by definition something greater than anything purely human, including reason. Its validity is beyond rational or observational proof or disproof; nevertheless it would not be what it is if it did not contain internally the evidence of its own truth. That evidence will be acceptable or discernible or self-evident to the eye of faith or of wisdom, although it may not be accessible to analytical investigation.

Revelation enters into the definition of Religion because it is the foundation of everything in the world that has hitherto been called Religion—and not least of the Christian Religion. Revealed Religion does not deny the possibility of individual inspiration—far from it; but it offers itself as the one universal and accessible means of grace available to all both collectively and individually, and as a framework within which individual inspiration can thrive unimpeded and can exercise its influence freely.

In His infinite Mercy, God has given us both freedom and a means of grace. Can we expect to be able to claim the one and refuse the other with impunity? Religion therefore implies not only an abstract belief in God, but also a concrete belief in His Revelation of Himself, His "descent into form". The imitation of that form then becomes the concrete or practical aspect of Religion, the means whereby it is made real and effective in the world rather than being merely notional or theoretical.

From this point of view, man is much more than a mere thinking animal. He is privileged above all other creatures in being given dominion over them as well as by the gifts of reason and of free will. Those privileges are accorded to him in his capacity as responsible guardian of revealed Religion, and for no other reason.

If, like all other creatures, man could not help following the commandments of God, as the plant cannot help turning towards the sun, then his situation would be neutral with respect to good and evil as theirs is. There would then be open to him no possibility better than this world—no heaven; and correlatively no possibility worse than this world—no hell.

The whole duty of man, and his whole advantage, reside in the preservation intact of the chain of tradition that connects him with Revelation. This applies with particular force in these days to the more specifically religious aspect of tradition.[3]

The word "Tradition" will hereafter be spelt with a capital T because it suffers from the same kind of vague usage as the word "Religion".[4] It is often used as if it were equivalent to "custom" or "style". Properly speaking, Tradition comprises all the distinctive characteristics that are derived from the past, and make a civilization what it is, including those that can be more specifically described as religious. Religion could be said to be the way whereby man serves God most directly. The other aspects of Tradition comprise all the less direct, but scarcely less essential ways, such as service to a hierarchical superior, obedience to the appropriate laws, defending Tradition against assaults from without, and so on.

The notion of Tradition is no mere arbitrary or invented one. Its foundations lie at the very root of our being. It can be accounted for in a way that is exceedingly simple and impregnably logical—for anyone who understands it. The Beginning and the End are the same;[5]

---

[3] There are others that have been largely forgotten, or that survive unnoticed.

[4] In this anthology, such usage is confined to this article. —Editors

[5] "I am the Alpha and Omega", Rev. 1:8.

therefore to be effectively linked to the Beginning is already to have found the End.

If these notions of Revelation and Tradition are accepted, it becomes evident that a Revelation must be accepted as a whole and not in part. The doctrinal, ritual, and ethical prescriptions of Religion are inseparable. A belief in God which rejects any of them is not Religion; indeed it is precisely one of those compromises by which people try to salve their consciences without too much trouble. Such a belief in God may perhaps be better than nothing, but it is something purely individual, whereas Religion is supra-individual. This is a very vital point.

The three elements mentioned—*doctrinal, ritual,* and *ethical*— can be discerned in every Religion. There is a correspondence between them and the three main divisions of the human faculties—intellectual, active, and volitive—so that Religion neglects nothing human. These three elements will now be considered in order.

Doctrine is fundamental. It is the intellectual element concerned with the comprehension and formulation of truth and the combating of falsehood. As such it is necessarily the province of a relatively small intellectual elect which stands at the head of a hierarchy through which the truth is interpreted to the multitude in a form which they can accept.

However simple the primary formulation of a truth may appear to be (for example, "God is Love"), its interpretation in terms of common experience is anything but simple. Insofar as the more elevated aspects of truth are concerned it must inevitably be dogmatic. Dogma and dogmatism are almost terms of abuse in these days. It is true enough that dogmatism applied to human affairs which are matters of opinion or of taste cannot be justified, but the case is very different when Religion is concerned. Dogma is a necessary feature of a Religion which is intended for everyone, since a large majority are not capable of grasping the more profound doctrinal truths in any other form. A doctrine fully comprehensible to the average intelligence would not be very profound. It would be intellectually insignificant and so would have no defense against perversion.

For example, every Religion either insists on the reality of heaven and hell, or expresses the same fundamental truth in a different way. This insistence is dogmatic, in the sense that heaven and hell represent something that is by definition beyond the limits of life on earth. They cannot be proved or disproved by means that appertain to that life on earth alone. Nevertheless if there is something greater than man there must also be a life greater than human life. That life is not subject to the same limitations as human life and so not imaginable or ascertainable by the individual as such. Some would accept this insofar as it relates to heaven, but not to hell. This is pure sentimentalism. Either man is not free to choose, a mere machine without responsibility, or he is free to choose and must take the consequences of his choice. No question of arbitrary reward or punishment is involved; it is merely a question of cause and effect.[6]

Ritual is the second essential element in Religion. It is derived directly from the original Revelation, which it recapitulates in a certain sense. This is particularly evident in the case of the Eucharist. God must be worshipped not only in thought and word but also in deed. No act proceeding from the human will alone could adequately meet this need; God has therefore told us what we must do. However simple a ritual based on Revelation may appear to be, we can be sure that its significance is inexhaustible and that its mysterious power extends beyond the confines of this world. It is effective simply by virtue of what it is and independently of the degree to which we may think we understand it. All this of course applies only to ritual that can be said to be strictly "orthodox", in the sense that it is an integral part of a revealed Religion. Without ritual there is no Religion.

---

[6] The perspective of reward and punishment is nevertheless legitimate and useful, otherwise it would not be characteristic of several Religions. Essentially it is simply an application of the law of compensation. As in so many other cases, a symbolical presentation in terms of familiar human situations brings the truth much nearer for most people than could any presentation in less familiar terms. This generation, with its literalism, has lost the habit of thinking in symbols: hence, among other things, its difficulty in understanding the Holy Scriptures. Symbolism, however, is not only every bit as precise as literalism, but also much less limitative. Literalism narrows the truth, symbolism broadens and enlivens it without in any way departing from it. A symbol in this sense is a reflection on the terrestrial plane of a truth subsisting on a higher plane. The symbol, whether it be dogmatic in form or not, is therefore the necessary vehicle of doctrine.

Closely associated with the specific acts appertaining to an orthodox ritual, and not independent of it, is the reading or recitation of the Sacred Scriptures and the recitation of a revealed or canonical form of prayer (e.g., The Lord's Prayer). Such reading and recitation are not effective outside the framework of the Religion to which they belong. Within that framework they are indispensable. This is particularly true in these days when the psychic environment, instead of being traditional and thereby providing an ever-present corrective to error, is so actively hostile and subversive. The effectiveness of this reading and recitation is not conditional on a purely mental comprehension. In the absence of its corrective influence the soul has no point of reference, no anchorage, no refuge, nothing to which it can—and must—return again and again in its inevitable wanderings. There can be no substitute for these indispensable graces.

There is one other grace, closely related to those last mentioned, whose benefit is strictly contingent on a traditional attachment. It takes many different forms in different Traditions: a divine Name or Names, a formula or a visible symbol. It is as it were incorporated in the gift of the original Revelation. It is an essential element in the formulae or prayers used in the methods of spiritual training associated with many Religions. No gift of God is more precious than this.

The third element in Religion is the ethical or moral. Without virtue the soul cannot become fit to be a receptacle of grace. That is what virtue is for; it is by no means mere social convenience.

The two other elements of Religion, doctrine and ritual, are concerned with man's relation to God, and therefore with the first ("and great") of the two New Testament commandments.[7] Virtue is concerned with man's relation to his "neighbor", that is, with everything that is not himself, but most immediately with his human neighbor. The neighbor exists by the will of God, so that to serve him is to serve God, and to offend him is to offend God. That is why the second commandment is "like unto" the first; it also explains why in giving offence the soul harms itself more than its victim.

---

[7] "Jesus said . . . Thou shalt love the Lord thy God with all thy heart, and with all thy soul, and with all thy mind. This is the first and great commandment. And the second is like unto it, Thou shalt love thy neighbor as thyself" (Matt. 22:37-39). —Editors

As to what constitutes offence, the best guidance is that afforded by the code of conduct or legislation that forms part of every Tradition. This may not be the same everywhere because of differences in conditions. Virtue is indispensable, but it is not an end in itself. Its efficacy reaches beyond the confines of the social field in which its operation is usually considered, and indeed beyond the confines of this world.

The first of the two commandments is greater than the second, but neither can be dispensed with. They are not essentially different, but only accidentally so. A single celestial truth is manifested terrestrially in two different modes.

Superimposed on the threefold division outlined above there is another division, much less easily defined. Every Religion has an exoteric, dogmatic, and moral aspect, and an esoteric, metaphysical, and mystical aspect. The two may not be rigidly separated, and the latter may be little more than an intensification of the former. Sometimes they are separated, and may have distinct names: for instance in the Far East they are called respectively Confucianism and Taoism; in Judaism the esoteric aspect is called the Kabbala, and in Islam, Sufism, or Tasawwuf. In Christianity and Buddhism there is no real separation, though in practice the esoteric aspect is usually the province of specialized organizations, often of a monastic type.

Esoterism is necessarily the province, or the calling, of a specially qualified and trained minority. It takes so many forms that no attempt at description could be satisfactory. Esoterism is the "heart" of Religion, and exoterism the "body". Esoterism, broadly speaking, is the repository and guardian of the mystery or secret which is the mainspring of Religion. By its derivation (from the Greek "to keep the mouth shut") the word "mystery" does not mean something that is unknown, but something that cannot be absolutely or adequately expressed in words, but which is not for that reason unknowable. That is always its meaning when it is used in connection with Religion. The ancient Greek mysteries were the esoteric aspect of their Religion and mythology.

The resemblance between the words "secret" and "sacred" is no accident.[8] The modern hatred and suspicion of the secret, of everything that is not laid open to public inspection, is also a hatred of the sacred,

---

[8] Decadence and Idolatry, p. 95, note 6.

and of the "mysterious" in the true sense of the word. The mystery is secret because it is inexpressible, and it is inexpressible because it concerns the Infinite, about which nothing exhaustive can be said, because speech and thought are always in some way limitative.

As we have seen, it is the specific function of humanity, occupying as it does a central position in the world, to keep that world in touch with the Infinite. Within humanity it is the specific function of those who follow an esoteric path to apprehend the mystery of the Infinite as directly as possible. The apprehension of those who follow an exoteric way is less direct, but none the less real. Its foundation is belief rather than vision, but there may not always in fact be a rigid line of demarcation.

From all this it is easy to see that the choice between adherence to Religion and its neglect or rejection has something absolute about it. If Religion is true, then there is nothing else that really counts, and the only practical thing to do is to follow it as best one can. If it is untrue, then the only thing to do is to "eat, drink, and be merry, for tomorrow we die". There can be no compromise. Religion cannot be an optional extra.

The choice between the acceptance or rejection of a particular form of Religion does not always seem to be as simple as the above would imply. The Religion we choose must be orthodox in the sense that in the first place it is derived from an authentic Revelation, and in the second place that it is connected to its origin by an unbroken chain of Tradition. This means that it must be neither heretical nor schismatic. The criterion of orthodoxy is conformity to a traditional law and symbolism, and to an intrinsic truth. However, the boundary between legitimate adaptation and deviation may sometimes be extremely difficult to define.

The preceding pages have been devoted to the presentation of certain positive criteria. Those that follow deal with certain modern tendencies in relation to the decay of Religion—or more accurately of religious faith, for Religion as such remains what it always was.[9] For some they may help to indicate a basis for the exercise of a corresponding negative discrimination.

---

[9] Although written in a different context, this reference to future pages hold true for the present anthology. —Editors

8. Looking Back on Progress[1]

Any intelligible conception of progress must be directional; that is to say, it must imply the conception simultaneously of a goal. When the conception of progress is applied to humanity as a whole, or to any section of it, the way in which that goal is conceived depends on the answers given to certain questions that are as old as mankind: questions such as "What is the universe?" "What is life?" "What is man?"

The search for answers to such questions is nothing less than the unending search of humanity for a stable principle to which all experience can be referred. That search is being pursued in one way or another as intensively today as ever before. As always, the directions in which it is pursued are contingent on the tendencies of the prevailing mentality.

The purpose of this chapter is to draw attention to the contrast between two mentalities. One or the other is almost always predominant. They arrive at different answers to the kind of questions already mentioned, and they can conveniently be distinguished as "traditional" and "progressive". In subsequent chapters that contrast will be amplified from various points of view.[2]

The traditional mentality, in the sense in which the word is used here, is characteristic of societies in which a revealed religion, together with the accompanying tradition, exercises a predominant influence. The progressive mentality is one in which a science founded on observation, together with a humanistic philosophy based on that science, is the mainspring of thought and action. Only within the last few centuries has the latter mentality become predominant.

Almost everyone would agree that a profound change of outlook has taken place during that period, and that it first became predominant in Western Europe, from whence it has spread to the rest of the world.

---

[1] From *Looking Back on Progress* (1970). This article was originally titled "Introductory". —Editors

[2] Although written in a different context, this statement holds true for the present anthology. —Editors

This change is commonly regarded as being of the nature of an awakening to reality, or as an opening up of new horizons, or as a development of powers previously latent, and in any case as representing a progress leading from a state of relative ignorance and subservience to one of relative awareness and freedom.

The present confused and unhappy state of the world proves that the hoped-for results of this change of outlook have not yet been realized. Nevertheless, the world seems to see no hope of their realization except by way of an intensification and acceleration of the intellectual, social, and economic developments consequent on this change. Is it not time to question the validity of the direction of our present aims, rather than thinking only about our efficiency in pursuing them?

The fact that the unending search of humanity is essentially a search for freedom from the constraints that seem to be inseparable from terrestrial life proves that we are conscious that our terrestrial situation is in a real sense a bondage. Less often are we fully conscious of the dual nature of that bondage. For we are bound in the first place by the constraints imposed on us by our environment, that is to say, by everyone and everything that is other than ourselves; this is our outward situation, the "destiny we meet". We are bound also to our own individual physical and mental heritage, which we did not choose for ourselves; this is our ego, our inward situation, the "destiny we are".[3]

The fact that we can be aware of our subjection to this double bondage, and can see it as such, is proof (if proof were needed) that our whole being is more than its terrestrial manifestation. We are strangers here, and we know it, even when we behave as though the place belonged to us and as if we were answerable to nothing and nobody but ourselves.

We are always more or less consciously trying to escape from some aspect of our double bondage. Two main lines of action are possible, related respectively to the two sides of its dual nature. One is to try to free the ego from the constraints imposed on it by its environment, that is to say, to improve its outward situation. That is what most of

---

[3] Frithjof Schuon defines the empirical ego as "the web of our tendencies and experiences; it is the 'I' that aspires to happiness and whose form is modified upon contact with the phenomena it undergoes or produces" (*Prayer Fashions Man* [Bloomington, IN: World Wisdom, 2005], p. 194). —Editors

us are trying to do for most of the time. The other is to try to escape from the limitations of the ego as such. In other words, we can aspire to freedom *for* our terrestrial nature, or we can aspire to freedom *from* our terrestrial nature.

The choice is not between two alternative and more or less equivalent options. If our main objective is to bring our environment into subjection so that it may not restrict the freedom of our ego, we are not even going halfway towards release from our double bondage. So long as we are not inwardly free, we cannot take advantage of whatever our environment may have to offer, even though it should be wholly under our command and at our disposal.

Progress achieved towards the satisfaction of terrestrial needs, desires, and fancies contributes nothing by itself towards inward freedom; on the contrary, when pursued beyond what is necessary, it tends more and more to supplant and to suppress the search for inward freedom, thereby defeating its own ends. Yet it is precisely such a progress that has become almost the sole aim of contemporary humanity. Its goal is to possess or to command everything in its environment. This last sentence describes very simply the way we have chosen. It is the way of those who give first place to the freeing of the ego from outward constraints, and it is the natural choice of the mentality that in this chapter has been called "progressive".

It is less easy to describe the other way. That way is associated with the traditional mentality. Its final goal is not for the inner self or ego to command things external to itself, but rather to surpass itself. The knowledge that it seeks above all is not a knowledge of the outer world but a knowledge that will enable it to command itself, and this implies a knowledge of itself. It does not deny the validity nor the necessity of some command over and some knowledge of the outer world, but this must not supplant or suppress self-knowledge.

Our inmost being is really the only thing we do know for sure, though our knowledge of it is non-distinctive and intuitive. It alone is our one absolute certainty. We can be in doubt and in dispute about outward things and their relationships, but not about our own existence, without which there would be no perception, no knowledge, no doubt, and no dispute. Yet, although our intuitive awareness of it is the very starting-point of all our awareness, we cannot say what constitutes our own reality. As soon as we try to distinguish it by observation, we are mentally trying to situate it outside itself so that it may examine itself, which is absurd, and is made even more so by the fact that it is essentially single and not multiple. Consequently, anything that we succeed in distinguishing is not the object of our search.[4]

Thus we are faced with the apparent paradox of an inward reality and unity which we cannot observe, although we are aware of it more surely than we are of anything. We know moreover that everyone else is in the same position, so we must have a word for it. It can only be a token word, a name and not a description; and no word is more applicable than the word "spirit". That word derives from the Latin *spiritus*, meaning "wind" or "breath". The ubiquitous and vivifying air, invisible in itself, but perceptible through its dynamic functions as wind or breath, is an adequate or natural symbol on the material plane of the unseizable principle of our being that we call "spirit".[5]

Human individuals differ one from another in the degrees of development of their faculties, but the existence of any one individual is not different in kind from the existence of any other; all are animated by the same principle of being. When we want to emphasize the transcendence of that principle with respect to ourselves or to the universe, or to emphasize its intrinsic uniqueness, we usually refer to it as "the Spirit" with a capital S; but we also use the word without a capital, and sometimes in the plural, to express all sorts of different and more limited ideas. Such usages can give rise to confusion; nevertheless they can also serve to remind the discerning of the immanence, the ubiquity, and (if the word be allowable) the "non-specificity" of

[4] Self-knowledge cannot come by observation. Observation implies a duality between observer and observed, knower and known. Nothing that can be observed is identifiable with the observer. Despite its overriding importance it is a fact which a science based wholly on observation can only ignore. If we cannot possibly know distinctively that within us which knows (either in sensorial or in cognitive mode) then our bodies and our souls (to the extent that they can be objects of distinctive knowledge) are external or peripheral with respect to our inmost being, to the "self that knows".

[5] The characteristics of an adequate or natural symbol are analogous on their own plane to those of a prototype on a higher plane, the symbol being necessarily on the plane of the observable and communicable. Our senses are adapted only to two planes of existence, the physical and the psychic. To suggest that these two planes comprise all possibility is to make our senses the measure of all things which, in view of their obvious limitations, is childish.

the Spirit itself.[6] Our passion for exact definition, when it is indulged to excess, hides from us much that is precious, and even that which is most precious of all.

The Spirit is that of which the world and we ourselves are manifestations. Manifestation is an exteriorization or a deployment, implying change and movement in an outward direction; correspondingly, the Spirit, the changeless and motionless Origin, is inward with respect to its manifestations, including ourselves. Although it is not strictly speaking localizable, we must look inward in order to find it.

We are often told that the objective of the "way" we have collectively chosen, the outward-looking way, is to free the human spirit from bondage. If that is true, we are certainly going the wrong way about it. Our main endeavors are directed to the feeding—one might say to the fattening—of the desiring soul; of that aspect of the soul which is indissolubly attached to the body during life, and is the tightest of all the bonds that constrain the spirit, and the most difficult to identify and to loosen.

The way which we have rejected, the inward-looking way, seeks to free the human spirit from all its bonds by freeing it from those that are internal in the sense that they are part of the ego. It is they that confine the spirit most closely. In its purest form, this way is the way of the saint, whose goal is the unseizable Spirit and whose inward state it is beyond the power of words to convey.[7]

The withdrawal of the saint from the world, in his search for that which is within himself, is sometimes criticized as being selfish, on the grounds that he does not appear to be doing what he might do for the good of other people. The truth is the exact opposite. He is seeking a truth that can only be found by inner experience and not by observation, and it is the very truth without which humanity is lost. He is not seeking to obtain anything to satisfy his selfish ego, on the contrary, he is seeking to give himself wholly to God in love, and thereby to learn

---

[6] Apart from this article, Lord Northbourne generally followed a simplified usage, using only "spirit". —Editors

[7] Therefore anyone who tries to convey the nature of that inward state in words necessarily fails. This may not matter when both speaker and hearer are aware of the inadequacy of words in this connection; but when the inevitable failure is hidden in a morass of psychological jargon, which convinces many people by its apparent profundity that it has penetrated to the depths, then it matters very much indeed.

what love really is. The repercussions of his intense activity, which is undertaken on behalf of humanity, are unpredictable, and they are independent of whether he is a public figure or totally unknown to his fellow men. The inward experience of the saint brings a supra-rational certitude, whereas observation brings no more than probability, which is not the same as certitude, even when it is of a very high order. The modern world is conscious of many of its own deficiencies; it does not appear to be at all troubled about its lack of saints, although that is the deficiency that matters most of all and cannot be compensated for by anything else.

But everyone cannot be a saint, so this same way is by extension the collective way of all communities whose traditions, laws, customs, and habitual outlook are predominantly directed towards the pursuit of sanctity, and therefore towards the support of the saint as its vehicle, either directly through religious rites and observances and the selection and training of individuals, or indirectly through the maintenance and defense of a political, economic, and social order so directed that the main aim can be effectively pursued within it.

This kind of indirect support is normally the principal function of a large majority. By its exercise the participation of everyone in the pursuit of sanctity is made possible, whatever his situation or capacity. Such, in principle, is the framework of a traditional civilization, although it is of course never perfectly realized. Such a society is never immune from degeneration and abuse, as we can see all too clearly today.

All civilizations were originally traditional in outlook; each one has attributed its own origin to an initial divine revelation or inspiration, and has regarded itself as the appointed preserver and guardian of the content of that revelation.

This generalization is valid despite great differences in the outward forms of traditional civilizations, despite their many and obvious imperfections, and despite their impermanence. Their differences manifest the fact that the Spirit cannot be confined by any specific form. It can however manifest itself fully in an indefinity of different forms, sometimes mutually incompatible, without betraying itself, and always revealing itself. Their impermanence is a simple consequence of the fact that no civilization has ever been perfect, since it is a human and a temporal phenomenon; it is a manifestation of the Spirit, but it is not the Spirit itself which alone is imperishable.

Everything, save the Spirit itself, carries within itself the seeds of its own dissolution.

-→═◈→✵✦←◈═←-

Anyone who is disposed to emphasize the defects of traditional civilizations would do well to look dispassionately at our modern progressive—and therefore anti-traditional—civilization, and to look at it as it is, and not at what he thinks it is meant to be, or could be if only we could overcome this or that problem, or if only so-and-so would see sense. He should look at what it has in fact produced in the way of contentment, peace, beauty, or freedom, and then at what it has in fact produced in the way of anxiety, war and rivalry, ugliness (in the despoiling of Nature and in the arts), and subjection to its own insatiable desires and to the inexhaustible demands of the machine. Then he should consider, no less dispassionately, what its prospects of sustainability appear to be, bearing in mind that all its present tendencies are bound to be accentuated in the future, their accentuation being in fact its principal objective. More and more and faster and faster is the cry, as if the end of a continuous quantitative expansion could be anything but dispersion and fragmentation, either gradual or explosive.

Some such questionings are at the back of many people's minds in one form or another today. Yet it seldom seems to occur to anyone to question the doctrine of progress in principle rather than merely in some of its consequences, nor yet to wonder seriously whether traditional civilizations may after all have possessed something we have lost, something that made life worth living even under conditions of poverty and hardship. Do we so excel in wisdom and virtue as to have the right to assume that they—our ancestors physically and intellectually—clung to tradition merely from stupidity, from a false sense of where their true interests lay, or from a superstitious blindness to the realities underlying their lives on earth? We are prepared to admit that they often produced sanctity and nobility in man and incomparable beauty in art, but we look down upon them for their submission to a traditional hierarchy, and for their acceptance of their often humble situations in it, and for their relative contentment with service to it. We think that they accepted these things because they knew no better, since they lacked a vision of the possibilities open to humanity. The question is, of course, whether it is the followers of tradition or the devotees of progress who are lacking in a vision of those possibilities.

If, as most people assume today, this life comprises all the possibilities open to humanity individually or collectively, then the satisfaction of the ego, the mitigation of pain, and the postponement of death are indeed the best objectives we can choose, and we rightly accord first place to them. If, however, as the traditional view has it, death is a passage to another state of being in which we shall be confronted with the truth and see ourselves as we really are, and if pain is a reminder of the imperfection of our present state and as such not only inevitable but at least potentially beneficent, and if the salvation of the immortal soul takes precedence over the satisfaction of the ego, then the objectives named appear in a very different light. They do not become invalid, but to give them first place becomes both foolish and wicked. It seems to most people today to be foolish and even wicked to give them any other place. The attitudes and actions of traditional peoples seem to us often to be marked by both incomprehension and callousness. But what is the use of our achievements in mitigating pain and in postponing death if they are accompanied by the loss of the very thing that made life and death and pain both comprehensible and purposeful?

Tradition and hierarchy are inseparable. Together they constitute a chain linking civilization with the Spirit in successional mode and in simultaneous mode respectively; in time to a spiritual origin and in space to a spiritual center. The origin inspires the center, and the center perpetuates the origin.[8] The whole structure is founded on the

---

[8] The use of the word "center" and cognate words in this connection is of course symbolical. The sphere is the type of all spatial forms and the most generalized. The center of a sphere is the point to which all its dimensions are referred; it defines the sphere regardless of its size or qualitative constitution. The center is dimensionless, but its influence pervades and coordinates the entire space; it is thus an adequate symbol of the dimensionless spiritual origin of all things, and that not only in a verbal sense, but also in the concrete form of the sacred locality, be it a temple, a holy city, a holy mountain, or the heart of man. For the spiritual center is in reality everywhere,

conception of the reality of divine revelation. Revelation alone confers on the chain of tradition its directional or centripetal force. Human beings are always to some extent mutually interdependent; they are always linked together by chains of various sorts, physical, economic, or ideological. But such chains are accidental; human desires may give them a direction, which is always centrifugal rather than centripetal. If the chain of tradition is anything at all, it is inherently directional and centripetal. It links mankind to its divine origin, and not to human wants or imaginings.

Revealed religion is therefore the heart of tradition; without it tradition would be an empty shell, a form without significance; it would be no more than mere social convention. Conversely, tradition, with all its many manifestations that are not specifically religious in form, is the indispensable support of religion. Without that support religion cannot be integrated with life, it becomes a thing apart, a supplement rather than the principal directing force; it tends to degenerate into a vague individual belief in God, or into a mere ideology competing with other ideologies on their own plane.

Religion and tradition are inseparable, they are two closely related aspects of the same thing. They are however seldom met with in their pristine purity, since their temporal manifestations necessarily carry within themselves the seeds of their own dissolution, as has already been indicated. Those seeds germinate slowly but, like weeds in a crop, once well established can overwhelm the crop and even virtually replace it altogether. The process is gradual but accelerative. At most times there is a mixture of crop and weed in varying proportions. The assessment of the exact proportion of each present at any given time

---

and it is therefore unseizable. For that reason limited and localized beings who aspire towards it have need of a symbolical location to which they can direct their attention. And who can doubt that the Holy Spirit does indeed dwell in such places?

The fact that mankind feels the need of a symbolical center to which he can direct his aspirations makes possible, in periods of spiritual decadence, the substitution for the sacred center of other centers which are anything but sacred, but are simply rallying points for the delusions and passions of a humanity that has lost touch with a traditional center. They give rise to their own orders or systems which are often misleadingly referred to as hierarchies. The word "hierarchy" comes from the Greek and means "sacred order" and nothing else; it ought therefore to be applied only to a strictly traditional order, wherein all authority, even in its social aspects, derives its legitimacy from the sacred center.

may be difficult; but it is always possible to discern and to describe the intrinsic nature of each.

The point of departure of the traditional approach to reality is everywhere and always the same. This is true despite great differences in the historical development of traditional civilizations. Existence is envisaged as proceeding from an origin or prime cause which is transcendent with respect to all its productions, and is symbolically the center from which all existence radiates without ever becoming detached from it, on pain of ceasing to be. It is the center not only of the universe, the macrocosm, but also of the individual being, the microcosm, since the latter reflects the wholeness of the former.

In any community, its own particular sacred center, and in the individual, the heart, represents or symbolizes the universal center.[9] Therefore the gaze of the intelligent individual in search of the source of existence, or, what amounts to the same thing, the source of truth, is directed inwards, towards the sacred center of his particular world, and at the same time towards the center of his own being. His outlook on all that he sees and knows is conditioned by the direction of his aspiration. In more familiar words, he "seeks the Kingdom of Heaven where it is to be found", namely, "within you". It is worth noting that the word "you" (or *vos* in Latin) can equally well be taken to be addressed to the collectivity with its more or less localized sacred center, or to the individual with his heart. Wherever tradition is the controlling principle of human activity, every man, whether he be intelligent or not, and whatever his function, is (consciously or otherwise) involved in this centripetal tendency.

---

[9] The psycho-physical complex that constitutes a human individual is a coherent unit, a little world on its own, a microcosm. All its organs are mutually interdependent, and each has a distinct function. Most people nowadays would regard the brain as performing the highest function of all, but the function of the brain, and the nervous system that is continuous with it, is mainly one of interpretation and coordination. It is the heart, and not the brain, that vivifies the whole, and is therefore the source of all its potentialities, including the potentiality of intelligence. The correspondence on their respective planes between the heart and the spiritual center is therefore far from being merely fanciful. (See also note 8, pp. 78-79.) When the heart is spiritually inert, the individual is not truly alive, but is a mere machine, however active the mind or the body may be. When the heart is spiritually active, the individual is truly alive, and is at peace whether he be outwardly active or not. "I sleep, but my heart waketh" (Song of Songs 5:2).

The point of departure of the progressive outlook on reality, closely associated as it is with modern science, is observation. It looks exclusively outwards towards its environment, and not inwards towards the principle of its own being, which is at the same time the principle of all being. It does not consider existence as such, but only things that exist, and it regards their forms and qualities as products of their observable structure and their interaction with each other. It seeks to discern and to define the modes of operation of these interactions, hoping to discover some kind of fundamental law governing all relationships, and thus to arrive at something which, if not the absolutely prime cause of all things, represents at least as near an approach thereto as can be made by the human mind. Its point of departure precludes its taking into account anything which is not within the capacity of the human mind. God, therefore, must either be rejected or be rationalized and humanized, and the consequence is that religion is eventually reduced to the status of an unproved hypothesis, "improbable" first in the etymological[10] and then in the contemporary sense of the word. Thence it is but a step to the total rejection of religion, or to its substitution by ideologies or fancies originating exclusively in the brain or the sentiments of men. Tradition dies. Man is in no doubt about his own reality, and thus becomes supreme in his own eyes. At this point it becomes possible to say that man is now god.[11]

Nothing then remains but to glorify as far as possible man's achievements in subordinating his environment to his desires, a difficult task, in view not only of the triviality of those achievements on a terrestrial, and still more on a cosmic, scale, but above all in view of their conspicuous failure to satisfy. However, such talk is eagerly swallowed by a public acutely anxious about its own future, and all too ready to escape from facts into the realm of anticipations and to

---

[10] "Not capable of standing to test". —Editors

[11] These very words constitute as it were the text of the Reith lectures on the B.B.C. for 1967, given by Prof. R. MacLean. But he is not the first to make a public statement to this effect. Some years ago a pronouncement stating that "the people are now god" came from Soviet Russia, certainly without official disapproval. In the Russian case it appeared that man was considered to be qualified for a divine status by his merits rather than by his capacities, whereas in Prof. MacLean's case the main qualification appears to be ingenuity.

delude itself by considering, not what is, but what could be, if only science could have its way.

The outward look is separative. It emphasizes the duality between observer and observed, knower and known, man and Nature. Our environment becomes something to be exploited, albeit "sustainably". We become more conscious of it as an obstacle to the fulfillment of our desires than of our oneness with it. And since our human neighbor is, for each one of us, part of his environment, men become more and more separated one from another. The separativity of the outward look, when it is not balanced by its inward counterpart, divides man from his neighbor as well as from God, so that there is no longer a human family with God as its "Father" and Nature as its "Mother". Reality itself is departmentalized; it tends to disintegrate, and man becomes ever more lonely and puzzled.

By contrast, the inward look is unitive. The seeker who finds the center, the knower who knows himself, sees both himself and the out-side world, Nature and his neighbor, as one through their connection with that center, not through their chance linkages with each other. Unity becomes the reality, separativity and relativity the illusion. Powerful though that illusion be, yet for him it is so to speak trans-parent. Yet he knows that he as an individual does not occupy a situ-ation fundamentally different from that of his neighbor. Unity, which is indivisible, cannot therefore appertain to him alone. If he is sane, he knows that he as an individual is not God; or alternatively, that if he can in any legitimate sense be said to be one with God, the same can be said of his neighbor. He knows that his own separate existence is in the last analysis both illusory and paradoxical; but this knowledge is all a part of his overriding certitude that God is, and alone is wholly real, and that Nature, his neighbor, and himself, distinct though they be and even often in conflict, are one in God, and in God alone.

If the traditional view is the right one, the idea that progress, in the modern sense of the word, could ever fulfill the hopes and plans of its advocates must be deceptive, not primarily because men are weak, stupid, passionate, and sometimes vicious, nor yet because human desires are so often mutually incompatible, but primarily because the advocates of a scientific and progressive humanism are looking away from the luminous source of their being, which is reflected in the divine spark in their own hearts. They are looking towards a universe which, in the absence of a valid principle, appears to be made up of particles and blind forces in ceaseless conflict with the desires and delusions of the human ego. Accordingly, they inflate and even deify the human ego in order to convince it that victory is possible. The voice of a progressive humanism proclaims that man has at last found the means of satisfying his desires, thus opening up the possibility of his becoming the creator of an earthly paradise. He can at last see his way to getting all he wants from his environment, provided that he will work hard and be reasonable.

The voice of tradition on the other hand, when it is not enfeebled or afraid to speak out, proclaims that the worth, the dignity, the whole justification of human life lies in the preservation of the chain that binds man to God, who is his origin, preserver, and end, whose Paradise is the only Paradise; and further, that in order to find that Paradise man must seek it in the sacred center, and not in the periphery.

The measure of our bondage is the strength of our attachment to the world of our experience and the extent of our submission to the desires engendered by that attachment. We deceive ourselves if we seek to escape from our bondage by way of the satisfaction of those desires. The measure of our deception is the extent of our failure to realize that those desires, being fed to excess, will multiply and plague us the more. Instead, we can seek to forestall and counteract too strong an attachment to the world by giving priority to a conscious and active aspiration towards the eternal Principle of our being which, being changeless, is above and beyond all attachment and all desire.

We have the freedom to choose which of these two attitudes or tendencies shall predominate and which shall be subordinate in directing the course of our lives. Collectively we have chosen, and must accept the consequences, but the individual is always free to conform to that collective choice or to reject it. If he rejects it, he can act only within the limits of the possibilities of his individuality and his situation. God does not ask the impossible of anyone. Tradition and all it implies being virtually a dead letter, he will get little help from his environment and much hindrance. He will have to face not only open hostility, but also much more subtle and often tempting subversive influences, which are of many different kinds and have invaded every domain, even the very domain of religion itself.

It may be thought that compromise of some kind must be possible, but the situation is such that compromise can never be anything but superficial and illusory. The opposition between the traditional and the progressive outlooks is strictly analogous to that between East and West, upward and downward, inward and outward, or any other two diametrically opposed directions. Since life is all movement and change, necessitating choice at every turn, an inward choice between the two directions is inescapable, even though it may seem to be involuntary or unconscious. That choice, and it alone, determines the orientation of the soul and therewith its fate. At the same time it determines the ultimate effect of every act.

In these days when circumstances seem to impose compromise, it is no small thing to assert the impossibility of an effective compromise between the two ways of approach to truth here designated as traditional and progressive. Individuals and societies frequently attempt compromises between things that are in reality incompatible, but when that is the case any apparent compromise is illusory and cannot endure. One or the other of the two factors involved is bound to win in the end. This generalization applies fully to the present case, and it is not difficult to see which of the two approaches in question appears now to be winning. The question is whether its final victory is possible. If it is impossible that the approach of modern science should penetrate to the foundations of the reality of existence, simply because that science is looking in the wrong direction, then the fact that tradition is disappearing and religion seems to be in eclipse does not affect in the slightest degree the certainty of the final victory of the approach that leads to truth, although the form that victory will take cannot be predicted.

Before concluding this chapter, three further points must be made. In the first place, it is often suggested that either modern psychology, or a philosophy that has developed in parallel with modern science, is working in the same direction as that pursued by traditional sages and philosophers and by the few who still seek to follow them, and that it is thus making an approach to the same goal. That is not so. The approach of modern psychology and philosophy coincides consciously and deliberately with that of modern science. It is a search for an outward and distinctive knowledge, either in order to gain more control over the environment or ourselves, or with no avowed objective other than that of increasing the sum of human knowledge. In either case, what is involved is the exteriorization and examination of phenomena with as much scientific detachment as possible. The word detachment is very significant, because it implies the most complete separation possible between subject and object, knower and known. Such is the way of science. It has its own validity and produces its own kind of results; its dispassion is exemplary; nevertheless, the direction of its approach is diametrically opposed to that of what has, so far very briefly, been described as the traditional way. It therefore cannot lead to the same goal.[12]

The second point is more fundamental. There is an apparent illogicality in saying that the nature, or the end-point, of what one is talking about cannot be specified in words, and then going on talking about it. Might it not be better to retire within oneself and be silent? Well, it might. To do so would at least avoid the risk of leaving the reader puzzled or angry or, worse, bored. It is a serious risk. The reasons for taking that risk could be stated in many ways, among others as follows.

Words are primarily evocative; their descriptive use is conditional on their evocative power. They convey no meaning at all unless they fall into correspondence with some potentiality present or latent in the hearer. Only then do they evoke a response of any kind. The possibility of their descriptive use depends on their evocative power, but description is restricted to the plane of our terrestrial life. Words are in any case all derived from our common experience on that plane.

---

[12] If this is true in principle, nevertheless its application to particular cases is often difficult. In the case of psychology, the difficulty resides in the fact that, in its investigation of the "sub-conscious", it often fails to distinguish between the "supra-conscious", and the "infra-conscious", that is to say, between what is too exalted to descend into the distinctive consciousness and what is too debased to be raised to that level. It might be thought that such a distinction must be self-evident; but a right discrimination between the two is not within the power of the mind, because the "sub-conscious" is by definition excluded from the conscious mind; it can therefore only be accomplished by way of an interior or spiritual vision. Where that vision is lacking, either accidentally or because an approach that excludes it is adopted on principle, the result is a fatal confusion. The approach of much contemporary philosophy excludes that vision on principle; it is therefore liable to lead to error, however plausible its arguments may seem to be on the purely mental plane.

If that plane alone comprises the whole of reality there is no further argument; but, if there are other planes of reality, they too are accessible to the purely evocative potentiality of words by virtue of the analogical relationship subsisting between all planes, and constituting the basis of all true symbolism.[13] Those who would limit the use and understanding of words to their purely descriptive function are, among other things, reducing to the commonplace all the Sacred Scriptures, and all the great poetry, writings, and sayings that have ever pierced the veil of the terrestrial involvement of mankind. Let us admit once and for all that this world is no better than commonplace unless it is lifted out of itself towards a plane higher than its own. By the Grace of God it can be, provided that we do not insist on limiting our understanding of symbols, verbal symbols included, to that of their most outward or "literal" significance.

Finally: some people say that there is a conflict between religion and science, others say that there is not. Who is right? The two incompatibles, which for the sake of brevity have been labeled "tradition" and "progress", are not identifiable with religion and with science respectively, in the first place because there is and always has been a sacred science. Sacred science is not restricted in its outlook as modern science is. It sees the temporal universe of phenomena as no more than an appearance, and it seeks a supra-phenomenal and intemporal reality, just as religion does, but it follows a path which is parallel to, rather than coincident with, the path of religion, at least until both attain to the summit.

In the second place, a religion founded on revelation remains now as always indissolubly linked with tradition, and now as always it is centered on the supra-phenomenal and intemporal, even when, as a result of human weakness, it is not as evidently so as it might be. Meanwhile, science in its modern form has lost sight of the supra-phenomenal and intemporal, and has taken on the role of prophet, guide, and provider to an ideology of progress having as its goal a temporal and terrestrial utopia.

There is a conflict, but it is not between religion and science as such, for they can be regarded as two normal, necessary, and parallel approaches to truth, provided always that the hierarchical superiority

[13] See note 5, p. 74.

of the religious approach is recognized and acted upon. The conflict is between the two points of view here designated respectively as traditional and progressive. Religion and science come into conflict only insofar as they are associated with the one or with the other.

Attempts at compromise between the traditional and progressive points of view, as applied to the origin and destiny of man and of the universe, can only lead to confusion. Their mutual incompatibility is total and unequivocal. The ideology of progress envisages the perfectibility of man in terms of his terrestrial development, and relegates it to a hypothetical future, whereas tradition envisages the perfectibility of man in terms of salvation or sanctification, and proclaims that it is realizable here and now.

9. Decadence and Idolatry[1]

The word decadence means falling off or falling away. The contemporary decadence of religion, the existence of which few would dispute, is something very much more than a mere reduction in the number of its adherents or in the influence it exercises.

Decadence is not the same thing as either deviation or perversion. Decadence is an enfeeblement, deviation is a going astray, and perversion is a reversal of intent. Or it could be said that decadence is a loss of power, deviation a waste of power, and perversion an abuse of power. Nevertheless decadence, deviation, and perversion overlap and merge one into another. If decadence is here treated separately it is only in order to avoid a descriptive confusion as great as that prevailing in the situation described. That situation is highly unstable and constantly changing. All that can be attempted is a background sketch into which details can be fitted as they arise.

Anyone who understands what tradition is will also understand that a falling away from the primordial purity and perfection of a new revelation is inevitable as time goes on. He will understand too that it is not the spirit of religion that becomes decadent or even dies, it is only its temporary embodiment in a human society. The vital spark is inextinguishable and must be present in the world for so long as the world endures. At certain times the spark is more closely hidden than at others; and just such a time is the present.

Although the spark may be hard to locate it is not at all difficult to specify the nature of some of the clouds that hide it. They do so by distracting attention from it or by distorting the rays it emits.

The profane point of view, as its influence spreads, gradually creates a new domain for itself, composed of elements extracted from the pre-existent traditional domain together with new elements derived from itself. It is this relatively new domain which people usually have in view when they speak of "ordinary life" or "everyday life" or "real life". The domain ruled by tradition becomes correspondingly restricted to its more specifically religious aspect, which gradually

[1] From *Religion in the Modern World* (1963). —Editors

becomes virtually the only effective guardian of the vital spark. It does so only for so long, of course, as it retains its orthodoxy. On this last aspect of the question there will be more to say later on. Meanwhile "ordinary" life continues to claim an ever-growing share of most people's attention.

The progressive restriction of the domain of tradition and religion is brought about in part by annexation and in part by the introduction of new distractions, most of them apparently in themselves harmless, and nearly always presented as new benefits. Industrialism was hailed on its advent as the dawn of a new era of prosperity; it has now annexed almost every productive activity and every traditional craft, including agriculture, thereby subordinating the true good of humanity to the work of its own proliferation. In the process it has annexed, profaned, and commercialized the holy day, together with the sports, dancing, and music normally associated with it. Even the annexation of the intellectual field has been passed off as an advance: this position has been very effectively consolidated by the annexation of virtually the whole field of education.

A further consolidation has been effected through the development of distractions which, especially when made to appear new and exciting, absorb attention which might otherwise be directed to things less ephemeral, while providing a momentary compensation for the destruction of all that really makes life worth living. Not all these distractions are equally crude and obvious. Among those that are less so may be cited the enormous growth of clubs and societies, harmless and well-meaning in themselves, which tend to give their growing number of members a certain sense of unity and of belonging to something. This can act as a substitute for the far deeper sense of unity inherent in attachment to a common tradition, and can cause the latter to be undervalued or forgotten.

More obviously distracting is the flood of reading matter, wherein if anything good appears it is immediately overwhelmed by the next wave. The question of merit scarcely counts in comparison to the effectiveness of sheer weight and insistence.

Still more obviously distracting is the gigantic overgrowth of public entertainment, culminating in television, the most pervasive and seductive of all distractions, not least to the young. It invades the very homes of the people, so that they no longer live in those homes centered on the once sacred hearth (symbol of the spark that animates all things), however simply yet realistically, but in a hallucinatory and hypnotic world divorced from all reality, even the relative reality of ordinary life. There is no need to multiply examples: the broad and evident fact is that nobody nowadays has time for religion. There is too much else that must not be missed.

In all this hurly-burly it would be very surprising if religious faith, doctrine, and practice remained unscathed. The impact of the notion of progress produces the idea that religion needs to be brought up to date. This can mean only one thing, namely that it must be made more worldly, more humanistic, more democratic, and that it must be made to conform to what may be called for the sake of brevity the standards of truth set by modern science and philosophy; and finally that the element of mystery (in the true sense of the word) must be reduced to a minimum or eliminated.

Now the element in religion that can most easily be made to appear to conform to the above conditions is the third, the ethical or moral, though this conformity can never be more than a deceptive appearance. It is very difficult to force either doctrine, whether its expression be exegetic or dogmatic, or orthodox ritual to conform to the requirements of a modern progressive ideology; it is much simpler just to let them slip into the background. Hence the very notion of religion becomes progressively reduced in scope, not only among those who are hostile or indifferent to it, but also among its adherents, by the suppression of doctrine and ritual and the over-emphasis of its ethical aspect. This last in its turn tends to assume a more and more humanistic, almost a sociological form, till all too often it becomes little more than a kind of idealism based on the hope of a triumph of virtue over vice, whereby the world is to become an easier and pleasanter place to live in.

In the end the establishment of the Kingdom of Heaven comes to be identified with the promotion of the physical and psychic welfare of mankind. In current usage, idealism is contrasted with realism, and religion tends to be relegated to the former, and so by implication to a domain of relative unreality. An idealism of this kind is a mere utopianism; and the opponents of religion do not miss the opportunity of making religion out to be a utopianism based on superstition, whereas they claim that their own utopianism is practical or scientific.

Unfortunately we do in fact often see religion (or something that passes for such) and scientific humanism competing in the same field as purveyors of social welfare. But good will is not enough: indeed it is by no means a prerogative of religion, and still less of the Christian religion alone.[2] Morality is not enough, and its insufficiency is one of the reasons why virtue, and the religion with which it is increasingly identified, tends to take on an appearance of dullness. When virtue is put into practice in the name of humanity and not in the name of God it loses its *raison d'être.*[3]

The conception of virtue has itself become sentimentalized and softened, to the detriment of the more forceful and combative virtues, like fortitude, indifference to death, fervor, watchfulness, and nobility, and most of all in the substitution of a vague and feeble tolerance for an active opposition to worldliness. Pathetic attempts are sometimes made to make out that religion is exciting, even as exciting as a television show; but when the notions that animate it have become more or less equated with moralism, and a rather feeble moralism at that, it certainly is nothing of the kind. Hence the common idea that religion is a killjoy, and that to be religious is to be sanctimonious and dull.

That might not matter so much if the idea were not extended to include sanctity. A saint is often thought to be no more than someone who is uncomfortably virtuous. A saint is indeed virtuous, because he is a saint; but he is not a saint because he is virtuous. No amount of virtue is by itself a qualification for sainthood. That qualification is of a different order, and may even, when founded on *gnosis*, lie on a plane where the antithesis of good and bad has already been surpassed. The world depends on its saints, for it is they who keep it in touch with God, independently of whether or not anyone is aware of their presence or of their sainthood. It is not the scientist, not the entrepreneur, nor yet the altruist who is the real benefactor of humanity, but the saint.

The scientific approach to religion necessarily involves treating it as no more than a particular phenomenon among other phenomena. Looked at in this way it appears as one of the aspects of the psychological make-up of humanity. It is seen as something that exists only in

---

[2] It is impossible not to wonder how it has come about that a certain sentence in the original Greek has come to be so often translated "On earth peace, good will to men" (Luke 2:14) when what it means is "Peace on earth to men of right intent".

[3] See chapter 13, "What Am I?" —Editors

order to fulfill a need inherent in human nature—a need comparable in kind to the need for sleep or food or recreation.

This is a subtle misrepresentation because it is a half-truth. It conceals the fact that sleeping and eating and recreation do not constitute the justification of human existence, whereas religion does. To try to explain everything by attributing it to human nature is merely begging the question, and is therefore only pseudo-scientific; but such explanations are often made and widely accepted, though all they do is to eliminate everything that could raise human nature above itself.

Not unrelated to this, and no less destructive, is the notion that there are two domains in human nature, one that of the intelligence and the other that of feeling, and that modern science represents the first, while religion is concerned only with the second. As regards the first half of this proposition, enough has already been said; as regards the second, the more decadent forms of religion undeniably give it a certain plausibility. Religion, however, is either founded on truth, in which case it is also founded on intelligence (insofar as that word has any useful meaning), or it is not, in which case it is nothing.

At this point decadence and perversion become less and less easy to distinguish. The existence of a very real decadence makes it more and more easy for the enemies of religion to misrepresent it, and even for those who are not its enemies to become increasingly blind to its real nature. For instance, there is a very prevalent idea to the effect that some at least of the more obvious oppositions and confusions of the present day can be attributed to the fact that the world has not yet got rid of the differences which exist and always have existed between the various religions and traditions. In this way it is possible to make religion a scapegoat for troubles arising from a very different cause. This leads to the suggestion that it must be, if not abolished as soon as possible, at least reformed, purified, or universalized, which inevitably implies the elimination of most of its essentials; its reduction to some kind of moralism with which, it is assumed, all men could be persuaded to agree. This tendency is closely related to the desire to get rid of the institutional forms of religion.[4]

---

[4] Another instance is the liberal individualism that permeates certain sects or branches of several Religions. It is essentially anti-traditional and, although perversion may be

The Sacred Scriptures have not escaped the scrutiny demanded by contemporary intellectualism. It is not the Scriptures that are harmed by this process, but only the scrutinizers themselves and those who pay heed to them. If the Scriptures are indeed the Word of God and not merely the words of men, they are independent of the limitations of the mind of man, and cannot be harmed by its criticism, whether or not the latter be called "higher". The purpose of the Scriptures will not be discernible to anyone who approaches them in that spirit, and his findings can only be misleading.

The purpose of the Scriptures is not to convey information, nor yet to exercise verbal persuasion, nor yet even to be understood in any restricted or purely mental sense. Their purpose is to reveal, or to support the revelation of, the incommunicable secrets of Infinity to those whose whole being (and not mind alone) is so constituted as to vibrate in unison with them. The orthodox commentaries and traditional interpretations are providential aids to this end.

When orthodox commentaries and traditional interpretations are thrust aside in favor of critical assessments, most people, even if not led astray by the critics, are left with no alternative but to make what they can of the most obvious and literal meaning of the words of the Scriptures. That meaning is always valid, but it constitutes but a fragment of the whole, and one that is all too easily misinterpreted or distorted when it is isolated and exposed to the play of individual opinion, or to the subtle attacks of more diabolical forces.

The Sacred Scriptures are integral parts of the traditions to which they belong, and are only fully comprehensible in the light of their respective traditions. Every tradition provides safeguards against their misinterpretation. In Christianity in the past only the clergy had the right to expound the Scriptures; indeed for a long time it was only the clergy who knew the language in which they were written. The situation is—or was—similar in Judaism; it is effectively similar wherever literacy is not the only measure of intelligence. In Hinduism only a brahmin may study the Vedas.

This generation, hating all that is superior to itself, wants to drag down to its own level everything that could help it if only it would

too strong a word for it, yet it paves the way to perversion, and may merge with it in the end.

humble itself and recognize its own desperate need of help. It prefers to pick out from the Sacred Scriptures such parts as can be made to appear to support its own dreary sentimental moralism and utopianism, and to ignore the rest.[5]

The softening of the significance of the Sacred Scriptures affects both their outward meaning, accessible to all, and their interpretation through contemporary representatives of the traditional hierarchies. One of its most important aspects is that which concerns the punishment of the wicked, and particularly those who set up idols in place of God. Yet there is no Sacred Scripture that is not emphatic and decisive on this point, whatever may be the symbolism in which it is clothed. In Christianity this aspect seems to have become particularly associated with the Old Testament, which is perhaps one reason why the Old Testament is now so largely set aside, as if it were no more than a sketchy history of a primitive people who worshipped a rather violent tribal god. If it were not in reality something very different indeed it would not stand at the heart of one of the world's great civilizations, nor would it be among the canonical books of Christianity.

The scriptural condemnations of those who worship idols are related to a much more comprehensive and widespread set of circumstances than many people suppose. Anything that is worshipped in place of God is an idol, whether it is given some material representation such as a statue or picture, or whether it exists only in the form of an ideal.[6]

Whatever a man regards as the ultimate end and justification of his life, and as embodying the fulfillment of his desires, is the thing he worships, whether or not he renders lip service to anything else. If this view of the real nature of idolatry is correct, it becomes evident that

---

[5] This is no empty accusation, particularly so far as Christians are concerned, for there is no Scripture that is outwardly more severe or more demanding than the Gospels: "Ye generation of vipers, how can ye escape the damnation of hell?" (addressed to highly respectable and respected citizens); "If thy right hand offend thee, cut it off"; "Sell that thou hast, and give to the poor"; "Blessed are ye, when men shall revile you and persecute you"; and so on. These four quotations are respectively from Matt. 23:33; 5:30; 19:21; and 5:11. The following are no less relevant: Matt. 5:20, 39, and 48; 8:12; 10:34-7; 12:36; 19:24; 22:14; 24:2; Luke 14:26-33.

[6] According to the Hindu science called *Nirukta*, resemblances between words are significant and not accidental; the science in question consists in the interpretation of such resemblances.

the profane point of view is not only in principle agnostic, but also in principle idolatrous, and that in the highest possible degree.

Man, alone among all creatures, embodies the possibility of a conscious and voluntary affirmation of God (to his own infinite advantage). This inevitably implies that he also embodies the complementary possibility—that of a denial of God (to his own infinite detriment). From a human point of view there is no possibility of merit in the absence of a possibility of demerit. From a metaphysical point of view both possibilities have their appropriate degree of reality. Thus it is impossible, not only that there should be no idolatry in the world, but also that it should not be developed up to the limit of its potentialities. It is equally impossible that idolaters should not reap the reward of their idolatry, and they must do so, unless they repent in time, that is to say, in this life while they are still free to do so.

If this generation could see the hand of God in all things—in the earthquake no less than in the evening calm, in death no less than in life—it would not be what it is; but it only sees blind forces on the one hand, and its own temporal desires on the other. This is a delusion. When nothing else is seen, a delusion can become the mainspring of action, and so for us it is today. Action so motivated is not likely to come to anything, for it is not founded on truth.

God is Truth; the fact that this implies His perfect justice is repugnant to modern sentimental idealism, which, even when it recognizes that on the terrestrial plane there can be no true mercy without justice, still fails to see that God's perfect justice is implicit in His infinite mercy. He will therefore not withhold His hand for ever from those who put idols of their own construction in His place and who attribute their own commonplace ideals to Him.[7]

---

[7] For an explanation of the non-arbitrary nature of God's perfect justice, see p. 67 and note 6 on the same page. —Editors

10. Intellectual Freedom[1]

The meaning currently attached to the words "intellectual freedom" is very clearly exemplified in the demand that state schools and state aided schools should be neutral in their approach to religion, that religious education should be restricted to the giving of factual information about religion, and that no regular school assembly should be religious in character or content. It is argued that no "prejudice" in favor of religion as such, or of any particular religion, should be instilled into children, who must be free to decide for themselves as individuals whether to accept the truth and the authority of religion or not, or, more generally, free to decide what source of truth and what authority, if any, they should accept. This represents the extension to children of an individualistic "freedom of thought" which has long been widely commended as a sign of intellectual maturity in their elders, and scarcely less widely accepted by them and put into practice in the form of "permissiveness" in behavior.

It is not uncommon today to argue for "intellectual honesty". People who adopt any particular point of view may not like being told that they are enslaved by prejudice, but they resent even more deeply an accusation of dishonesty. Dishonesty is deliberate; it implies deceit practiced for one's own advantage, even though that deceit be only self-deceit. A factor of morality as well as of intelligence is thereby introduced; animosity is aroused and any discussion drops to a lower level.

It is of course a fact that any two people can be as honest to God and to themselves as it is possible for fallible humanity to be, and can still fail to arrive at the same conclusions. That is what people who use the phrase "intellectual honesty" do not seem to accept. If one were to adopt their attitude one would say "do not choose to accept", thereby labeling them as hypocrites, as they so often label people who do not see eye to eye with themselves.

The idea of "intellectual honesty" is the same however it may be expressed. It is derived from the principles of scientific research, with

---

[1] This article is previously unpublished in book form. —Editors

their insistence that no conclusion is fully valid until it has been shown to be in conformity with everything that observation can disclose. That, precisely, is what constitutes and characterizes the scientific approach.

The great changes resulting from the applications of science to industry have led to the growth of the idea that no approach to truth other than the scientific is valid, and therefore that no conception can be said to represent the truth until it has been checked by observation and deduction from observation. This in turn has led to the calling in question of every assumption, every system, every tradition, and every belief that has ever constituted the background of a civilization, and their submission to an investigation which claims to be scientific (whether it be really so or not).

When the arrival of that better world which the progress of science was to have made possible is disappointingly delayed, the relative stability of the ancient traditions leads to their being regarded as obstacles to progress, and being blamed for the delay. Their elimination or supersession can then be claimed as a liberation of the human spirit.

The assumptions, systems, and traditions of the past were based on religion. It constituted their background even when they were not specifically religious in character. Religion, when it is true to itself, postulates that there are truths—and those the most important truths of all—which are neither discoverable nor provable by the faculties of observation and deduction alone, but are accessible only to something that can be called vision or intuition or faith.

To judge the content of religious faith, which is by definition unquestioning, by purely secular preconceptions and prejudices on the grounds that it is unscientific is therefore to deny the very foundations of religion. The opponents of religion lose no opportunity to do just this, and to class religious faith as servile and unworthy of the newly won independence of mankind. They apply similar derogatory epithets to the more or less unquestioning personal loyalties which have until recently been the basis of the unity of all social groupings, from the family upwards, in every civilization. Those loyalties are derived from the hierarchical aspects of religion and its accompanying traditions; any picture of the situation that takes no account of them is therefore incomplete.

Thus the idea has grown up that the scientific approach can alone properly be said to be intellectual, whereas the approach of religion cannot, and that therefore the tendency of religion is to impede intellectuality. This is not to be wondered at in people for whom the word "intellectuality" implies no more than conformity to the scientific approach. The goal of intellectuality is a better understanding of the origin, nature, and end of man and of the universe. It is just such an understanding that religion claims to offer. Insofar as that claim is justified, religion, very far from impeding intellectuality, is an essential part of it. That is the crux of the whole question, yet how seldom do those who seek to defend religion put the question in that form! One can hardly expect its opponents to do so.

Nevertheless, despite all the propaganda for so-called intellectual freedom, the collectivity, the mass of the people, will always have faith in something, and will always follow someone. What philosopher, they ask, what scientist, what President, what demagogue, what quack, what mushroom Messiah will bring them the comfort and the freedom they seek? This is no new phenomenon. The Psalmist says, "There be many that say: who will show us any good?" (Ps. 4:6). Now, in the virtual absence of an established source of authority, the phenomenon has entered into a new dimension, and the cry "who will show us any good?" has become almost universal.

The average mentality, in its search for an authority it need not question, seems instinctively to know itself better than many who seek to guide it seem to know it. The average mentality is by definition mediocre. That is not to its discredit. Mental capacity is, and always will be variable, and while that is so the average mentality will be in the middle range of capacity. It is also a mathematical certainty that it will always be represented by a large majority. It is not reasonable to expect it to be able to formulate the great critical decisions on which everything depends, least of all when those decisions involve a discernment between truth and error, as, for instance, when the issue is between religion and anti-religion in all its many forms and disguises.

Most really critical decisions are of that order; they demand a wisdom that is profound and not commonplace and is therefore rare. Most people are in fact more or less conscious of their limitations and of their dependence on guidance "from above", whatever the sense in which the word "above" may be understood, so that, although they have been told that authority is now in their hands and that they can and must exercise it through the medium of their votes, they will still look for an authority which they can accept without having to think everything out for themselves.

That such an authority existed when it was vested in religion is undeniable. People then looked for guidance, at least in matters of principle, to the religious hierarchy which was guardian and expositor of the spirit and of the teaching of the founder of their religion. Even kings did so, kings whose temporal power was exercised by divine right; but that right conferred on them their temporal functions only which, in principle if not always in practice, did not impinge on the functions of the spiritual authority; it was indeed the main duty of kings to support and defend that authority. This system did not always work perfectly; no system, however admirable, is proof against the imperfections inherent in human individuals and societies. These imperfections are variable in kind and are seldom seen for what they are by those who manifest them at any particular time. Every age seems to have its own characteristic failings and to be much less aware of them than of the failings of its predecessors. The obvious imperfections which marred the operation of the hierarchical system make it easy to attribute them to the people's acceptance of the authority of religion, and to make insufficient allowances for the variety and extent of human perversity and weakness. This is especially true if one is encouraged to do so by an unquestioning faith in the conception of progressive evolution of the human race, with its corollary of the superiority of the present age in every domain, spiritual as well as material.

However that may be, it is apparent that current problems are too complex, too remote, too specialized, too subtle, or too profound to be within the competence of the average mentality, with its enormous numerical preponderance. The best opinions can only be those of an intellectual elite composed of people who can see the human situation most penetratingly, most synthetically, most realistically, and most dispassionately, and such people are necessarily few. Whoever they may be, they alone can put things in their proper place and can escape from being confused or overwhelmed by the weight of the indefinite multiplicity of facts, and of the opinions derived from them, under which our scientific civilization is laboring. It is obvious that such people's opinions ought to prevail; and perhaps they would, if other people's opinions as to who they are did not differ so widely and change so frequently as they do.

These things are seen, clearly or dimly, by most people; but today the necessity of rule by majority vote is an article of faith. The only solution seems to be that the constituent members of society should be educated up to their responsibilities, so that they may vote intelligently. It would seem however that people must on no account be taught what to think; that would be to deny them intellectual freedom and would open the way to a tendentious advocacy in the field of religion; they must therefore presumably only be made familiar with as many facts as possible, and then if possible be taught how to think; how to assess the relevance of facts, how to relate one to another, and then how to discriminate between the indefinity of ideas and opinions that can be based on them. The practicality of this conception is, to say the least, questionable. All that need be said here is that it ignores two facts: one is that though the average of intelligence be raised, it is still an average and not an optimum; the other is that the opinions of the most highly educated people differ at least as widely as do the opinions of those less favored. One suspects that what the advocates of education as a panacea are really thinking in most cases, though they may not realize it, is that other people, if they were properly educated, would then think as they themselves do, and then all would be well. This is very natural, we probably all do it to some extent, but it is too simple to be true.

To expect the impossible of the average adult mentality is foolish; it merely leads to the replacement of intelligence by prejudices that are often largely emotional in origin, and thence to the passing of authority into the hands of any individual or group that is able to seize it. To expect the impossible of children is even more foolish, and it is at the same time cruel. Children are not yet equipped to decide what is best for them even in the simple affairs of daily life; how much less so when fundamental assumptions are in question! Let them be encouraged to think by all means, but only on the simplest issues; they can only be happy when the really adult issues do not arise at all for them, but are covered by an established and unquestioned code of behavior. Moreover it is nothing less than the truth that most adults are in a comparable position. Everyone, child or man, needs a framework, an "establishment", to limit the range of his responsibilities to matters that are within his competence. Children need it even more than do their elders, and it is the first duty of their elders to provide it for them—first their parents, then their teachers. The rigidity of such a framework can be, and perhaps often has been, carried to excess; but that error is probably less damaging in the end than its opposite. Rigidity or otherwise is a question of degree; much more crucial is the question of the foundation on which the framework is built up. For there will always be a framework, there will always be authority, there will always be an "establishment", good or bad, simply because people cannot get on without it and are always seeking it, whatever the theoretical anarchists may say.

In the past the foundation of the social framework was religion. The authority of religion, firstly in matters of fundamental truth concerning the origin and destiny of man and the direction in which the ultimate good is to be sought, and secondly and consequentially in the field of morality and ethics, used to be regarded as final because it was regarded as of divine origin.

If indeed an eternal and all-wise God has revealed Himself to man, it is anything but intelligent to accept as final any authority other than that of this revelation, embodied, as it necessarily is if it is to be handed down from generation to generation, in forms doctrinal, ritual, and moral; and the guardianship of these forms is no less necessarily the function of a specially trained and qualified hierarchy. It certainly seems that this conception must either be substantially true or not true at all. If it is true, the fear of the Lord is in truth "the beginning of wisdom" (Ps. 111:10); it is a first condition without which there can be no real wisdom, and so no well-founded authority, no stable framework within which the inherently limited abilities of humanity can each find its proper place.

Science offers no alternative framework. The best it can offer is material wealth in a wide sense of the term, that is to say, the satisfaction of a wide variety of desires. It does not conceive of any means of achieving that escape from desires we call "contentment" otherwise than through the satisfaction of those desires. It has not yet learnt that there is no limit to the multiplication of desires, nor that, since different people's desires are often mutually incompatible, an indefinite multiplication of desires increases conflict as well as discontent.

The scientific outlook on the origin, nature, and destiny of man, varied though it be within certain limits, leads only to two alternative attitudes. The first, which is the more scientific, is one of an ultimate despair arising from the inevitability of terrestrial, solar, and cosmic cataclysms. The second appears to take no account of the first, and is less scientific both for that reason and because it is based on nothing more than a rather vague hypothesis; it is a utopianism based on the notion of progressive evolution of the human race. The latter has so strong an emotional appeal that it has in practice attained the status of a dogma, unexamined and unquestioned. The first attitude is an ultimate hopelessness, the second is a consolation eagerly grasped at in the prevailing intellectual and social confusion.

The point at issue here is one of truth and not of consolation. The consolations of religion are often spoken of, as if its purpose were to make this life easy. The only real consolation religion offers, and it is no small one, is that of making sense of the world, even when the world seems to be unbearable. Promises of celestial bliss are always conditional, and they are balanced by promises of hell (to reduce a situation covering a very wide range of possibilities to very simple but nevertheless adequate terms). The notion of a life of pleasure ending in total annihilation can be more "consolatory" than the truth, the rigorous aspects of which are so commonly glossed over.

How then, it will be asked, has it come about that the authority of religion has become so weakened? There are two possible answers. The first is that it is because the principles of religion, which are founded on the conception of divinity and revelation, and on the precedence of the eternal over the temporal, are in themselves false or inadequate. If this answer is right, the matter ends there.

The second possible answer is that it is because human failings have allowed the principles of religion to become overlaid and obscured by conceptions or preoccupations which are confined to the universe of phenomena and thereby tend to exclude the divine and the eternal. If the second answer is right, the decline of the authority of religion must be attributed to a substitution of mutable opinion for immutable principles, or of hypothesis for faith, as the foundation of authority. The substitution has been gradual, but by it the conception and the content of revealed religion has by imperceptible degrees been changed, so that eventually religion has ceased to be a foundation and becomes more and more an optional extra, more and more subjected to the uncertainties of opinion, less and less the accepted background and collective of opinion. At the heart of this change lies an enfeeblement of the conception of Divinity, whereby Divinity loses the quality of absoluteness from which the uniqueness of the authority of religion is derived, and becomes relativized.

The form of the questions that often arise concerning the nature of Divinity is revealing in this connection. It is usually something like "is there a God?" or "does God exist?" or "is God a reality?" or "what is God like?". In any such form they are really "leading questions", since they imply that God can properly be considered as one factor in our situation among others; that God "as He is in Himself"—to use an admittedly but inevitably equivocal phrase—can be objectivized distinctively, like the objects of our perceptions and imaginations; that He is not even as real as those objects unless He can be brought into comparison with them; in short, that God is a relativity like everything else we can perceive or know.

It is true that God as Creator can be considered as "relativizing Himself" in His creation, insofar as His creation is a manifestation of His qualities and attributes; but that manifestation is not God "as He is in Himself". To suppose that it is so is the error of pantheism.

It is no less true that every relativity is a Divine manifestation; the conception of God as "Creator" of all things implies nothing less than that. But God is not *a* reality; He does not "exist" distinctively as do His manifestations; as Creator He is the origin of all existence and of all distinctive realities. As such He alone is absolute reality, He is Reality Itself. The reality of all things, from the universe in its entirety to the most evanescent of dreams, is relative and more or less fugitive and illusory; God is the one and only absolute reality and absolute certitude; He alone is That which "cannot not be". By Him alone the universe is sustained; from Him all things come and to Him all things must return. Woe betide those beings who have any choice in the matter if they fail to prepare themselves for that return. Allowing for the inadequacy of words in this connection, such is the foundation of religion, and nothing less will serve. It is not compatible with compromise of any kind.

Of this order, though not necessarily in this form, is the vision that has inspired and guided mankind since the dawn of time. It is a vision and not a deduction; like physical vision it is direct, immediate, "concrete" and convincing; it is "supra-rational" in the sense that, as with physical vision, it is not preceded but followed by reasoning.

In comparison, how dismally trivial are the basic conceptions of humanism, scientism, and secularism, and how unworthy are they of a humanity to which, alone of all creatures, the possibility of a celestial vision has been granted! Uncountable millions have seen things in the light of this celestial vision, always more or less imperfectly because the full blaze of the truth is too strong for the creature, always from within the framework of their religion, guided by the symbol, the spoken word, and the radiance of the saints, and in endless different ways, each according to the light that is in him, whether it be bright or dim, white or colored. It is written: "and if that light be darkness, how great is that darkness!" (Matt. 6:23).

If every relativity is a Divine manifestation, anything can in principle be seen as a "symbol" of Divinity, since it is as it were a reflection on the terrestrial plane of some aspect of the Divine nature. Not least among those symbols is man, "made in God's image and likeness". It is this that justifies, and even necessitates, the use of anthropomorphic symbolisms, whether in the form of sculptures or pictures or fables or parables, for the communication of religious truths that are in their essence ineffable. The spiritual potentiality of the symbol may however always become obscured or lost when the outward or literal or "human" significance of the symbol is taken to be its principal or its only significance. The symbol then becomes an "idol". Thus, in the case of anthropomorphic symbols, the conception of Divinity can come to be increasingly assimilated to the outward form of the symbol. In other words, man may tend increasingly to make God in his own image, to "measure" God by his own capacities and characteristics, so that God becomes, not God, but a more or less magnified and particularized image of man. This is an "idolization", not of a graven image, but of the image that man himself is; and it is the ultimate idolatry.

Since however this idolatry is not recognized as such by its perpetrators, they will tend to attribute an idolatrous intention to anyone who uses symbols, anthropomorphic or otherwise, with a right intention, especially if the symbols in question are those of a religious nature which they have been taught to hold in contempt or to dismiss as "primitive". The conception of Divinity—or the celestial vision—would not however be what it is if only one particular symbolical formulation could be used to suggest it. When the Absolute is in question, the creature tied to relativity must be content with whatever point of view is his by nature or by upbringing; what is important is, firstly, that this point of view should be compatible with the truth, and secondly, that it should not be taken to be more that it is.

At the heart of the decadence of religion lies this kind of relativization of the conception of Divinity, inevitably accompanied by a loss of the celestial vision. The repercussions of this vision, where it exists and whatever form it may assume, are limitless, they cannot but reach into every department of life; its consequences may take a lot of working out, and much may be gained or lost in the process, but the vision itself is of a total simplicity and directness. That is why it is often more accessible to those whose minds are simple and direct than to those whose minds are complex and analytical, and that is why it is accessible to children, and to those who are able to receive it "as a child". It is precisely the opportunity of a glimpse of this vision that so many people are seeking to deny to our children by limiting their contact with religion to mere information concerning the forms it assumes. The final decision however does not rest with man, it rests with God, since vision is a grace, and is therefore neither procurable nor disposable at will. Those who would seek to impede its operation do themselves more harm even than they do to the children.

From the point of view of the militant atheist or agnostic it is good policy to deny participation in religion to children, since, as they know well, religion can only be communicated by participation (always excepting the possibility of a special grace). Information alone, especially if treated as purely historical and conveyed by an agnostic, can be a very good medium for anti-religious propaganda; for no teacher—or parent—can help communicating his own point of view to those he is teaching, whatever the subject of the lesson.

Humanism, through at least some of its avowed representatives, has adopted other tactics, and is now claiming equality of status with revealed religion, and has been admitted in that guise by representatives of the ancient religions to some of their discussions. Apparently those representatives cannot see that the ideals of humanism are fundamentally the same as those of atheism, secularism, and agnosticism in all their forms, insofar as they idolize man by putting him in the place of God as the first object of all service and all devotion. Alas! how many people who profess to be religious do just that, although to do so is to deny—or to distort beyond recognition—the very vision on which their religion is founded. Religion is infinitely more than a mere system of ideas, philosophical, ethical, or otherwise, and its primary function is not one of making this life more agreeable, but of the salvation of souls; its concern with the intemporal takes precedence of, and alone justifies, any concern it may show for the temporal.[2]

What we are in fact witnessing is a dissolution of the sacred traditions. They can properly be called "sacred" because they are derived from revealed religion and are its normal support. It is they that hold a civilization together and give it its distinctive quality. There has never been a stable and coherent civilization constituted on any other foundation—remembering that coherence and stability are necessarily always relative—and there never will be, for the simple reason that humanity is not independent of God, to whom it is linked by revelation and tradition. Without them there is no framework within which freedom, intellectual or otherwise (and itself also necessarily always relative) can be realized without its turning into license and leading to chaos. Tradition however is by no means merely a negative or protective force. In its more important positive and constructive aspect it canalizes thought and activity into ways that are truly profitable, because they lead away from attachment to the world and the ego and towards attachment to a spiritual center.

The sacred traditions in all their diversity manifest the unity of the Absolute; they do so most evidently in what may be called their common celestial orientation; the message is always essentially the same though the symbolical "language" that conveys it be diverse. It is the diversity of that language that strikes most forcibly the modern literalistic mentality, thereby clouding or even discrediting the universal message. If however there is that which transcends and comprehends all human experience, that message can evidently not be reduced to any single formulation, although paradoxically the diverse traditional formulations can each suggest it adequately, provided only that those who live within their influence are so attuned to them that they can recognize them as reflecting on the terrestrial plane realities subsisting on a higher plane. Any such recognition is truly intellectual, since it implies a grasp of fundamental truths at least in some degree; and that is precisely what the human intellect is for.

Everything that had a beginning must have an end, and the sacred traditions are no exception. This applies, however, exclusively to their

---

[2] Elsewhere the author has reminded readers of the order of Christ's two commandments, which places love of God before love of the neighbor; see pp. 68-69. —Editors

outward forms, their content being universal and imperishable; it is therefore only from a temporal point of view that they must seem to die. As they split up and dissolve there is less and less to hold society together; in the end nothing remains but secular ideologies, pseudo-traditions of purely human invention, looking earthwards and not heavenwards, having no principle of unity more stable than collective opinion, and therefore always in opposition one to another as well as to sacred tradition itself.

Is all this mere prejudice? If it is true, no; if it is untrue, yes. Prejudice implies the assertion of an opinion based on an unsure foundation, and the only sure foundation for opinion is truth—the whole truth, and not a partial truth. Supporters of the doctrine of intellectual freedom would limit the conception of truth to truth that can be supported by evidence, and it is an article of faith with them that the only valid evidence in the last analysis is the evidence of the senses. The evidence of the senses, however highly developed it may be, reveals the characteristics of the visible universe and nothing more, and so, unless the visible universe contains its own cause within itself—that is to say, unless it "created itself"—scientific investigation can never elucidate the ultimate reason for anything whatever, and least of all for existence as such.

Is it not prejudice or presumption or both to deny that any man can see, or ever has seen, more than the human eye can see, or heard more than the human ear can hear, or known more than can be categorically stated in words; in short, that no man's understanding can be more penetrating or profound than one's own? Or to claim that the scientific approach is the only valid approach to truth, despite the fact that the conclusions of science may be true while still representing no more than a partial truth? Admittedly no dialectical proof of the validity of the religious approach is possible; it seems to be forgotten however that this is equally true of the scientific approach. The only "proof" in either case resides in the quality of the vision on which the approach is founded, that is to say, on the "light that is in you", whether that light be bright or dim or even darkness itself.

Even apart from all this, is it practical or realistic or scientific or even common-sensical to suppose that, provided that the average mentality is "intellectually free" in the sense of having no preconceptions—and thus operating as it were *in vacuo*—it will absorb from its environment whatever is good for it and reject whatever is bad, or even that a sufficient majority will do so? This indeed would postulate a faith in human nature that is not supported by the available evidence. The advocates of intellectual freedom are too intelligent to have any such faith; what they really want is that the average intelligence should be "free" to absorb what may be called the "scientific prejudice" that now predominates in their environment.

Must we then admit something that most of our contemporaries are reluctant or unable to admit, namely, that in the past, and insofar as religion was the final authority, a vision more penetrating than ours provided the foundation for authority? If so, it will be said, the people of those times ought to have behaved more wisely than we do, and ought therefore to have been more harmonious and more contented. The common assumption is, not only that they knew less than we do, but also that they endured so much discomfort and hardship that they cannot possibly have been more contented than we are. Contentment is a difficult thing to prove or disprove at a distance; but one who has passed the Psalmist's three-score years and ten can at least assert that people, even poor people, were in general more contented before the 1914-18 war than they are now, although not nearly so well provided with comforts and luxuries. Incidentally they were also more often people of strong individuality, "characters" or "personalities" as we might say; not of course always either virtuous or agreeable, but qualitatively distinctive, not mere drops in an ocean of mediocrity. And they were more content with their lot than we are. What then is the true criterion of contentment? Can it be anything but the acceptance of one's lot, whatever it may be? Or in other words, knowing one's place and fulfilling faithfully whatever function may be associated with it, with a pride in the quality of the product as the principal incentive rather than any tangible reward; knowing, perhaps, that not to want is better than to have; and above all being intelligent enough not to place one's best hopes in nothing but the satisfactions which a short sojourn in this world can bring. All these things are criteria of contentment, and at the same time they are universal ethical constituents of every religion and tradition.

There are those who think that such criteria of contentment represent something despicable, that they imply a servile submission, a sterile social and intellectual slavery, unworthy of the representatives of an advanced civilization. Let them then propose something better able to bring contentment to a world that is necessarily imperfect because it is other than God, who alone is Perfection; and let it be something more practical than an intellectual vacuum masquerading as freedom.

The more remote from God the world becomes, the more imperfect it becomes. If the confusion, fear, and discontent of our times seem to be reaching towards an extreme, despite a technological development bringing a wealth and a luxury unparalleled in history, why is an exactly coincident decay of religion scarcely ever suggested as a causal factor? To attribute any part of this increase of discontent to an allegedly servile and unintelligent clinging to religion by a diminishing sector of society is a *non sequitur* of which any normal schoolchild would be rightly ashamed.

No: anyone who clings to religion is clinging, not to an arbitrary framework of man's devising, but to the only framework that can serve as a starting-point for the realization of an inward freedom that is independent of terrestrial contingencies. Moreover this inward freedom is a truly intellectual freedom insofar as it is founded on an integral vision of truth, on a vision which is unified at its source because it comes from within and is not derived exclusively from the observation of the dispersed and fugitive relativities of this world. An outlook which limits itself in principle or in practice to the things of this world is nothing less than an intellectual bondage, since it denies to men the possibility of an inward freedom which is not only the only real freedom, but is also, whether they know it or not, the very freedom they are always seeking.

Let the Psalmist have the last word. He says, "The Lord is King, be the people never so impatient: He sitteth between the Cherubim, be the earth never so unquiet"[3] (Ps. 99:1).

---

[3] From the Book of Common Prayer translation. —Editors

11. Change in the Churches[1]

The Christian religion is represented in the world by several Churches and many sects, each of which claims a certain exclusiveness. In two important respects however the situations of all are identical. In the first place, they all claim to be devoted to the person of Christ and to be followers and interpreters of His teachings. In the second place, they are all subjected to pressures and influences that are peculiar to modern times and have not been felt to anything like the same extent in the past. The observations which follow are concerned with nothing but the relationship between those claims and those pressures. It would therefore be both unnecessary and confusing to attempt to introduce questions arising only from the existence of divisions between Churches and sects. That is why "the Churches" are here spoken of collectively, without reference to distinctions or subdivisions.

An urge to make changes is strong in the Christian Churches today. Doctrines, liturgies, scriptural language and interpretation, the approach to moral questions, organization and administration; all are involved. The whole field cannot be surveyed here, but the changes which will be mentioned will suffice to exemplify a very general tendency. Most of these changes, including those that have a reunion of Churches or sects in view, originate in a consciousness of weakness in the face of anti-religion and indifference to religion: a consciousness often manifested in the form of questions such as "why have the Churches lost so much support and influence"? The natural reaction is to try to win back that support and influence by accommodating the teaching and the forms of religion to the prevailing tendencies of the present age. The aspects of those tendencies most relevant to the present discussion can be summarized as follows:

One: Confidence in the approach to truth characteristic of modern science, with its insistence on the observational or dialectical proof of all postulates, and the equation of intelligence with conformity to that approach. Two: A belief in progressive evolution so firmly held that

---

[1] This article is previously unpublished in book form. —Editors

111

disappointment with the results of technology does little to weaken the dogma of the superiority of the present age in all domains. Three: An egalitarian hatred of authority combined with a failure to distinguish between the validity of one source of authority and another, and an eventual attribution of authority to public opinion alone. Hence a desire to bring everything within the mental range of the average intelligence. Four: An activism demanding ceaseless movement and distraction, and despising contemplation. Five: The placing of man on a pedestal, as if his corporeal existence were its own justification, and as if he had nothing better to do than to seek his own survival and his own gratification, like the animals.

These tendencies are each and all inimical to religion. At the same time they are characteristic of an attitude of mind for which the best single word available is "humanism". There is a philosophical humanism which is in principle either atheistic or agnostic, and either denies religion or seeks to eliminate all mystery from it; and there is a popular or sentimental humanism, accompanying and supporting its philosophical counterpart, which has no clearly definable principles but, even when it does not deny religion, puts the service of man above the service of God. The order of the two New Testament Commandments, which express perfectly the very essence of religion, is thereby inverted; it is as if man had been created, not for the disinterested service of God, but to serve God, if at all, in order that he himself may attain to peace and prosperity on earth; it is as if religion were made for man and not man for religion.

The popular manifestation of the humanist spirit is the more dangerous; it is in effect the enemy within the gates, for it is often not openly or even consciously opposed to religion. A whole-hearted opponent is always liable to conversion and will remain whole-hearted thereafter—the classic example being of course St. Paul—whereas there is little hope for the half-hearted (see Rev. 3:14-16).

In all their manifestations these two kinds of humanism lean heavily on modern science, the discoveries of which are confined, not only in practice but also in principle, to the domain of the "things which are seen and are temporal" (2 Cor. 4:18); science therefore gives these things priority over the "things which are not seen and are eternal"; naturally so, and even rightly so from its own exclusive point of view. The fault of those who accord intellectual priority to the scientific point of view is precisely that of failing to recognize its exclusiveness, and therewith the limits within which it is applicable.

The question is: to what extent are the changes now taking place within certain churches biased in the direction of making concessions,[2] either for the sake of popular appeal, or in the hope of arriving at a formal reunion with some other Church? The least one can say is that this bias is precisely what the humanist element, inside the Churches as well as outside, is working for, apparently with conspicuous success. "The Church must adapt itself to the modern world"—that is one of the formulae; despite the fact that the attitude of the modern world is predominately one of opposition and indifference to religion, or, more particularly on the philosophical side, one of trying so to speak to take religion over.

As concerns the liturgy and the scriptures, the emphasis in contemporary changes is centered mainly on facilitating the mental or verbal comprehension of their content, and on a more outwardly active participation by congregations in religious services. Whatever may be the intrinsic merit of any such objectives, they must tend to depreciate both a humble acceptance of things that surpass the comprehension of the mind alone, and also a submissive and often silent participation in an ineffable mystery, a participation that by its very passivity acknowledges the supremacy of the Divine activity. People thus tend to be misled into supposing, on the one hand, that nothing is true or valid unless it can be put to the proof and reduced to an exclusive verbal formulation, and on the other hand that the effective element in religious observance is their own activity rather than the activity of the Divine Grace. At the same time, the changes in the forms of ritual and in the language of the Scriptures support these tendencies insofar as they lead to a loss of familiarity. An ingrained and habitual familiarity with scriptural and ritual forms can provide a permanent foundation for the deployment of their hidden power, by way of an unsought penetration into daily life and thought, leading to a gradual awakening of their innermost meaning, but by Grace and not by calculation.

The new translations of the Bible have of course certain merits. They can claim to convey the meaning of the original languages in

---

[2] Concessions may be disguised in many ways.

a number of critical passages more accurately than the King James Authorized or Revised versions. They can also claim to make the Bible seem less remote or alien to contemporary readers. Nevertheless, no translator can avoid being himself affected by the outlook of his own times, and so unconsciously weighting the alternatives that present themselves to him so as to conform to that outlook; and in modernizing the language he is expressing himself in a manner characteristic of his times. If those times are characterized above all by anti-religious tendencies, something of those tendencies will creep into the new translation despite the best of intentions to the contrary. This infiltration may be difficult to detect, but there is direct evidence of it in a loss of beauty or of "poetic" quality which is fairly generally admitted; that at least is entirely characteristic of modern times. So is the making of change for its own sake where the original language is neither obscure not archaic, which is conspicuous in the New English Bible, and can only serve to accelerate the loss of familiarity already mentioned. The same may be held to apply with force to many liturgical changes, especially in the Mass or Eucharist, made apparently for the sake of change. What precisely, it may reasonably be asked, is wrong with the older forms? Finally, there is another aspect of the matter which may be the most important of all, however unacceptable it may be to the modern mentality. It is this: the sacred scriptures are "mysterious" in the sense that they contain much more—even infinitely more—than is comprised in any strictly literal translation. That is why the Church as such used at one time to be the only legitimate interpreter of the Bible to the people; the dangers of profane, analytical, or "vulgar" interpretations were recognized. Nowadays such interpretations seem increasingly to be facilitated and even to be sought and welcomed. Who can say what the result may be?

The introduction of changes into the liturgy of other forms of worship is often justified or excused on the grounds that it is experimental. Any human invention may legitimately be put to the test. If however the forms of worship are something more than mere human inventions, their eligibility for any such treatment becomes questionable. If they are not something more than that, how can they be spiritually effective? Insofar as they are in some way or in some degree divinely inspired, guided, or appointed it is very foolish to put them to the test, and no good can come of it, since the degree or quality of their inspiration cannot be measured. In practice the only thing that can be used as a criterion in any experiment is their apparent effect on the worshipper, or in other words, what the worshipper appears to get out of his worship, and not what he gives to it. What he gives to it is what affects the state of his soul, but since it is known to God alone, it cannot be used as a criterion, although it alone really matters. The experimental approach guarantees that attention will be directed to the production of quick satisfactions in the worshipper rather than to the state of his soul although the latter is the proper and only real concern of any Church. A false criterion cannot but produce deceptive results; the only criterion that could lead to a useful result will not become apparent until the Day of Judgment; the experimental approach to the forms of worship is therefore unworkable in practice as well as being objectionable in principle.

The ultimate effect of these changes taken together seems likely to be an ever-increasing emphasis on the rationalization and democratization of religion: that is to say, on the limitation of its content to whatever seems to be susceptible of dialectical proof, and at the same time to whatever may be acceptable on emotive rather than on doctrinal grounds. Increasingly the supra-rational—which is the beginning and the end of religion—will be suppressed, and truth will give way to sentiment; for truth is often harsh.

Admittedly the liturgies and the versions of the scriptures now being supplanted are the result of changes made in the past, some of them with the same sort of end in view as that of the present changes. Some may have been desirable and some not. In any case, they and their effects are with us, and the question now at issue is not whether change as such is desirable, but the direction in which further change, if any, should take place. The object of the changes now taking place and projected is ostensibly to bring religion nearer to the people. Does this necessarily mean that they will bring the people nearer to God? No, for they cannot do so if the essentials of religion are sacrificed to popular acceptability. These essentials are enshrined above all in the original and fundamental doctrines of Christianity.

The aspects of the Christian doctrine most difficult to reconcile with the humanist outlook in all its forms are those that are related to the Biblical emphasis on a rejection of the world and the search for a kingdom that is not of this world, on the need for salvation of the immortal soul and on the inescapability of a Divine Judgment of great severity.[3] Hence these aspects tend nowadays to be glossed over—or one might say be "taken as read"—in favor of an emphasis on aspects of doctrine which are—or which appear to be—concerned more with contemporary human relationships and their hoped-for immediate effects than with the ultimate fate of souls; in short on those aspects that can most easily be made to appear to coincide with the humanist outlook, with its ideal of an ultimate realization of a world-wide prosperity and absence of outward conflict. Any such utopian ideal, though it is represented as a realization of God's Kingdom on earth, or rather especially when it is so represented, distracts attention from the true goal of religion, and from the true function of the Churches, which is the salvation *here and now*, before it is too late, of the souls in their charge.

For this life is insignificant except as a way to the salvation of its immortal part. Man is insignificant—a mere thinking animal—except insofar as he is effectively God's representative on earth, the "mediator" through whom the whole creation is brought back to God. The professedly religious humanist justifies his utopian planning by saying that God gave us our faculties to be used; nevertheless religion teaches us that they ought not to be used for our own—or even our successors'—temporal satisfaction, but rather in order that they may return to God refined and purified.

Observe how the dominance of the scientific outlook reduces man to a factual insignificance, from which he vainly tries to escape by seeking to bend the creation to his puny will! But our hearts are hardened: the symbolical center of our being is no longer melted by the Divine fire that transforms the base metal; our minds are agitated, dispersed, and fragmented: their potentially contemplative function is dissipated in movement without issue. To melt the heart and calm the mind so that they may become receptive to the Divine Grace and Truth: that is what religion is for, and that is what religion alone can accomplish. It alone can do so in the face of all adversity, and even—though less easily—in the face of worldly success, because it is, through its founders, the interpreter and vehicle of the single immutable truth and underlies and conditions all contingent truths.

---

[3] For an explanation of the non-arbitrary nature of God's perfect justice, see p. 67 and note 6 on the same page. —Editors

Nothing that could properly be called a renewal or revival of religion can take place otherwise than on a foundation of truth, that is to say, of sound doctrine, presented fearlessly and with its priorities right. We know from the Bible that there will be a great renewal, and that it will come suddenly and in an unexpected form, and there will be "a new heaven and a new earth" (Rev. 21:1) and not the old ones refurbished. Any lesser renewals that may precede it will be of the same Divine origin or they will not be renewals at all. Like the great renewal they cannot be expected to come by way of dialectical compromises, not indeed by any human contrivance; they must come by way of a "judgment" or "crisis" of some kind, wherein falsity will in some degree be swept away, just as it will be wholly swept away in preparation for the great renewal.

It is often suggested that the promised earthly paradise will in some way be evolved out of the modern world; that it will take the form of a continuation or a fulfillment of what we call progress, with a full realization of all the potential benefits of that progress to be achieved by the application of scientific knowledge wholly for constructive and no longer for destructive purposes; in short that what the modern world has gained will not be lost. Such notions are seldom contradicted by representatives of the Churches; they are "consoling" and are therefore allowed to persist even by many who must know in their hearts that they are nonsense, and that the conception of the great renewal implies a fresh start, right from the beginning.

The primary function of the Churches is therefore to be ready, and to help their adherents to be ready, for that great judgment and renewal; not forgetting that on that day all those who have died previously will be judged according to their works, and that therefore (since we cannot know when that day will be) those now living must be offered *here and now*, while change is still possible for them, not comfort and prosperity, but a means towards the salvation of their immortal souls. This surely, and nothing else, represents the essential function and the central doctrine of Christianity.

Suppose that the Churches were boldly to proclaim their central doctrine, and to insist on all its consequences, without a thought for the probable effects of their doing so, and especially not for their own success nor even for their survival, leaving the results in the hands of God, thus at last truly obedient to Christ's command to them to "take no thought for the morrow"; if they would tell the world that they neither seek nor offer what everyone else is seeking and offering; that what they seek and offer is not an unhampered enjoyment of progress; that it is something infinitely more than a way of making people behave better one to another;[4] if the Churches did this, what would be the result? Nobody can tell: it might be derision or persecution or merely an even greater numerical decline; but it might in the end bring about the release of a power and influence now in eclipse. All we know is that truth must prevail in the end; what that end may be and when it will come we cannot know. That the result would be a change is beyond dispute, and it would be a change involving a real reversal of most contemporary tendencies.

A precautionary observation seems to be called for at this point in order to avoid a possible confusion between things that are on different planes. If the Churches were to accept the kind of changes suggested and act accordingly, their action would not by itself constitute a spiritual renewal in the sense in which these words have been used above, for such a renewal can only come from Divine Grace, and only at a time and in a manner willed by God. What the Churches would be doing is to help their members to be ready to meet the inevitable fate of all creatures, while preparing themselves as Churches for a renewal they know must come sooner or later. A renewal can be prepared for, and it can—and must—be prayed for; that is as far as the will of man can go. At the same time the Churches would then be doing all that they have been commanded to do.

In order to be ready, they must hold on at all costs to what they have got, and what they have got is what has been handed down to them by tradition. Now, if ever, the integrity of tradition should be maintained as nearly as possible, and that implies a minimum of outward change, for never in history has there been a time when innovation was more likely to do harm than good. But the Churches seem to be obsessed by the supposed newly acquired powers of humanity to control its own destiny and to construct by its own ingenuity, without reference to God, or with reference to God as scarcely more than a formality, a paradise situated in time and not in eternity.

---

[4] For there is nothing in the least religious in the commonplace and self-evident idea that if people could be persuaded to be kinder one to another the world would be a pleasanter place to live in.

What could be more contrary to the teaching of the Gospels, severe and uncompromising as it is, and to what could the more ancient parable of the Tower of Babel be more appositely applied? The Churches are in danger of finding out too late that, in glossing over their essential function and the truth on which it is based in favor of compromises with humanism, they are risking the loss of their real and only source of strength, and therewith the very justification of their existence.

III

METAPHYSICAL PRINCIPLES

The plane of existence is the plane of contrasts, and on it error, evil, and ugliness remain what they are. It is natural to us to try to avoid them in this world, and it is far from useless to do so; not however primarily because success in doing so makes life more agreeable, but because truth, goodness, and beauty, as they are manifested in this world are nearer to reality than their contraries. In their existential manifestations they do but prefigure their own intrinsic and principial nature. . . .

From "On Truth, Goodness, and Beauty"

12. "With God All Things Are Possible"[1]

The very existence of our universe, in its fullest extension in space and in time, and with all that it contains both quantitative and qualitative, proves that it is among the things that are possible with God. It is gratuitous to assume that nothing else is possible with God simply because nothing else is at present accessible to us.

Our universe is governed by certain conditions, the chief of which are form, number, time, space, and mass or energy, and our faculties are adapted to these conditions and not to any others. If we choose to assume that no other conditions exist or are possible, we are simply assuming that there is nothing beyond what is, in fact or in principle, within the grasp of human perception or the powers of deduction of the human mind. That, if you come to think of it, is a curiously presumptuous thing to do. It makes human limitations the measure of the power of God. It is also curiously naive to behave as if the mind of man, without the help of anything to raise it above its inherent and obvious limitations, could be supposed to be capable of comprehending (in the double sense of enclosing and understanding) not only all that is, not excepting its own self, but also all that is possible. The power of God, as our text states so clearly, comprehends all-possibility. All-possibility is infinitely more than all actuality, and we can never perceive more than a small fraction even of actuality, let alone of possibility.

The word "infinitely" has just been used, but not carelessly or conventionally. Once one has abandoned the idea that possibility is limited by the conditions of our terrestrial experience, there is no conceivable reason to assign any limit to it whatsoever. This is exactly what our text says in apparently very simple words. Here, as always, the simplest wording is the least restrictive and the best adapted to convey a highly comprehensive and far-reaching conception. By reason of its very simplicity it contains in potentiality more than any prolonged explanatory statement could convey.

---

[1] From *Looking Back on Progress* (1970). —Editors

A true statement made in theological terms, as this one is, necessarily corresponds to a truth that can be stated in metaphysical terms. In this case that truth could be called the illimitation of all-possibility. The choice of terms is a matter of opportunity alone.

The metaphysical conception of all-possibility and its illimitation is fundamental. Once it is grasped it does not matter so much what it is called, since all terms are limitative, and here it is a question of an absence of limits. The conception of all-possibility is in fact logically inescapable, for if possibility were limited it would have to be limited by something, and that something would itself be a possibility, for if it were not a possibility, it would be pure nothingness, and so could not be the cause of a limitation (or of anything else).

The conception of all-possibility cannot be grasped at all unless the mind can be freed, at least to some extent, from habits of thought arising from its confinement within the body, which tend to limit its range to the phenomena of terrestrial experience. Language in particular, the means whereby we communicate our thoughts, is derived almost entirely from our terrestrial experience, and for that reason no verbal statement of the metaphysical theory of all-possibility can convey its full content, or can be intrinsically complete and unequivocal. That fact by no means invalidates the theory, it is only a consequence of its comprehensiveness.[2] Nevertheless, a little further explanation must be attempted.

Every identifiable or definable possibility, whether it be simple or complex, that is to say, every object, every event, and every combination of the two, is limited by the fact that there are other possibilities distinct from it and external to it. If that were not the case, it would not be in any way distinguishable in itself, for by definition no possibility is external to all-possibility, which is therefore not limited by any possibility.

It might however be thought that impossibility, being as it were the opposite of possibility, must be distinct from all-possibility and external to it, or in other words that possibility ends where impossibility begins. But impossibility does not begin anywhere, it is another

---

[2] For an exposition of the theory of all-possibility, the reader must be referred to two works by René Guénon: *The Symbolism of the Cross* and *The Multiple States of Being* (Ghent, NY: Sophia Perennis, 2004).

word for "nothing", a mere conception, purely negative, denying everything that has been or is or could be. Entities have beginnings and ends, total non-entity has neither. If impossibility has no beginning, possibility has no end.

Definable entities, insofar as they are considered as existing in their own right, by virtue of what they seem to be rather than by virtue of what they obviously are not, can be regarded as so many limitations of all-possibility. From that point of view their existence represents a sort of departure from all possibility, as it were a step in a "descent" towards impossibility, which however can never be reached, as the word itself implies. Such a point of view is admissible, and can be useful provided that it is recognized as partial and provisional. It is no more than that because nothing exists in its own right, but only by virtue of its participation in all-possibility. In the last analysis, all-possibility, being limited neither by possibility nor by impossibility, is limitless. As such it is neither definable nor imaginable, since there is nothing outside it to supply either the likeness or the contrast on which identification depends.

For these or similar reasons many people, especially those who pride themselves on being practical or up-to-date, would say that the conception of all-possibility is unnecessary, or at least that it is a purely mental conception embodied in a play of words having no relevance to the solution of current problems, and that therefore the question of its inescapability or otherwise is purely academic. Yet if the conception corresponds to a truth that is fundamental to an understanding of the nature of existence it cannot be negligible. On the contrary, it is vital that it should be grasped by all who are capable of doing so, at least to some extent and in one form or another, whether metaphysical or religious. One of its religious forms is that enshrined in our text. Moreover, since the conception cannot be fully grasped by the mind alone, but involves the whole man, heart as well as mind, the simplicity and directness of that text is very significant.

The physical universe that affects our senses can be regarded as a single complex possibility, that is to say, as a system that can be identified and in principle described. We spend a lot of time trying to formulate its laws, which amounts to defining its limits as precisely as we can. Independently of how far we succeed, the simple fact that the universe is subject to laws, and that its possibilities are limited by those laws, proves that it does not coincide with all-possibility, that is to say that it is not infinite and not alone, and that there is something external to it. That being so, what can be conceived as being external to it other than the indefinity of possibilities postulated by the theory of all-possibility? Any other assumption is arbitrary—this one has an impregnable logical foundation. It is true that it cannot be verified by observation; but neither can any other more limited assumption, since nothing outside our universe can be accessible to observation by us, who, for so long as we rely exclusively on our powers of observation and deduction, are looking at the universe from within and can by no means survey it from without.

Man, and man alone, can recognize the fact that the universe he knows is subject to laws. He fails to make the right deductions from this fact, and so tends to identify the universe with all-possibility. He is tempted to do so more and more as the extent of his knowledge of its observable features increases.

Surely it is evident that more ancient views of the nature of the universe, such as would usually be called "religious" or "traditional", although on the physical side less extensive and often less accurate, were really much more comprehensive. At least they took into account possibilities far more extensive than those comprised in our terrestrial state. Furthermore it must not be forgotten that all our means of communication are derived from our common terrestrial experience, so that the nature of wider possibilities can only be conveyed symbolically and never descriptively. The various images made use of to represent them cannot therefore be expected to coincide formally.

Modern scientific knowledge reveals much that was previously unknown, yet it conceals or supplants much more. In aiming at completeness in one aspect of the picture it suppresses the picture as a whole.

Man's awareness of the limitations of his universe implies that there is something in him that can penetrate beyond its bounds, that is to say, beyond the world of phenomena, although his powers of observation can never do so, however well developed they may be.[3] It is just

---

[3] It may be mentioned in parentheses that phenomena such as are sometimes called "paranormal" are still phenomena, and as such they are of this world, and, as with normal phenomena, their outward form is one thing and the interpretation of its significance is another.

this possibility of seeing the limitations of this world that marks the uniqueness of man and enables him to rise above his terrestrial limitations. When he fails to take advantage of that possibility by neglecting or rejecting the divine revelations which alone can shed light on the mystery of existence—a mystery which is beyond the reach of his natural or unaided mind and senses—he becomes no more than a thinking animal, subject to the same laws as the animals, and having no superior rights save those arising from his superior ingenuity. Hence the universal concern of religious doctrines with a certain detachment from the world as a necessary condition for the realization of man's true destiny.

Our universe, being subject to definable laws, excludes anything that is incompatible with those laws. It can be regarded as a system of mutually compatible possibilities, or "compossibles" as they can conveniently be called. The compossibles constituting a system such as our universe are not assembled by chance nor by any arbitrary choice, they simply constitute a system because they are what they are. The number of possible systems is indefinite, not only because the number of possibilities that can be assembled into systems is indefinite, but also because any given possibility can form part of a plurality of different systems, each of which is defined by a unique set of conditions, and has its own relative internal unity, and its own relative reality. The reality of each is however derived entirely from its participation in all-possibility, which alone is absolutely real and wholly itself. Whatever else may be or may not be, all-possibility "cannot not be". The one thing that is inconceivable is its limitation.

All the rest follows. It is vain to seek to formulate the ultimate reason why things are what they are; they are what they are because it is possible that they should be so, and therefore impossible that they should not be so; and they are in a particular system—our own universe for instance, because they are compatible with the conditions that define that system. In theological terms one could say that they are what they are and where they are because God made them so and gave them their place. If that sounds a bit old-fashioned, it is nonetheless much better sense than a good deal that is said today about the origin and nature of our universe.

⟶◉→✳︎←◉⟵

All the above is scarcely as much as a sketch of the theory of all-possibility. It may however be just enough to convey by contrast some idea of the complete inadequacy of the modern scientific outlook, which equates what man can see and know with the whole of reality. In attributing a sort of absolute validity to this outlook, scientific man is taking a fraction of a fraction to be unity. At the same time he is making himself insignificant, a mere trivial accident in the evolutionary process of an apparently arbitrary and purposeless mechanism. For so long as he continues to try to squeeze reality into the miserably inadequate vessel of his own brain he will continue himself to become more and more insignificant.

A living terrestrial being, a human being for example, can, like the universe itself, be regarded as a coherent system of compossibles, an assemblage of inter-related potentialities, manifested in a mode which accords with the conditions that characterize this universe. Those potentialities constitute an individual being distinct from all others because they are what they are and for no other reason; as in the case of the universe, their assembly is in no sense fortuitous or arbitrary; and they remain for ever what they are, whether manifested or not. They can be manifested under a variety of conditions without losing their cohesion, their individuality, because its source is in their intrinsic nature and is not external to it. Their manifestation under particularized conditions, for instance those peculiar to our universe, realizes only such potentialities as are concordant with those conditions, but not others, so that it appears both as a realization and as a limitation. The total being in all its potentiality is not realized, but only as it were one possible aspect of it. A different aspect, perhaps less limited, perhaps more so, must characterize its manifestation under other conditions, but the total being must remain what it was and is.

Only in a total release from all the limitations inherent in manifestation can the being realize its full potentiality. In more familiar words, man has an immortal soul capable of perfection, and its sojourn on this earth is but a partial and passing phase. On this earth we have a body, but it is not ourselves, it belongs to this universe, wherein it reflects potentialities inherent in our being. At death we leave this universe and are therefore parted from our bodies, but this does not affect our real being and its potentialities, which can and must be then reflected in some other "universe" in a new mode, according to whatever conditions may prevail. These may include some kind of duration and extension, corresponding to, but not identifiable with, our time and space, as well as something corresponding to the "materiality" that conditions our bodies, but such possibilities are far beyond the range of our imagination. St. Paul says of our bodies, "It is sown a natural body, it is raised a spiritual body. There is a spiritual body and a natural body."[4] The doctrine of the resurrection of the body gives rise to many doubts and difficulties, even in the minds of believers. It need not do so, since the possibilities manifested in the body cannot be annihilated.

In our present state we are involved in time and space, wherein possibilities are manifested in succession and in extension; but they can equally well be considered as co-existing in a non-temporal and non-spatial state (although this does not come naturally to us because of our present involvement in time and space). Our present viewpoint is not for that reason false or distorted, but it is particularized in a special way. The fact that a more generalized conception can be reached, at least by some people, is direct evidence of our situation on the central and "vertical" axis connecting the whole hierarchy of possible states, each of which can be envisaged as a "horizontal" expansion of a point on this axis. Such a picture of our situation is evidently symbolical; as such, its content is virtually inexhaustible.[5]

Sometimes it may be helpful to think of the present as permanent and as alone wholly real. In it alone can we act or be acted upon; it summarizes the past and conditions the future; it alone is always with us, it is stationary while events move past it; it will still be when everything else has gone; it is the container, events are its ever-changing content.

Comparably, space is spherical, and a sphere is defined by the relation of its parts to its center; it may revolve or expand or contract, but always by reference to its center, which contains and regulates all its potentiality. In the terrestrial state the symbol (the likeness) of eternity is the present, and the symbol of infinity is the dimensionless center, the point. The present is eternal, the center is ubiquitous.

---

[4] 1 Cor. 15:44.

[5] *The Symbolism of the Cross* (see note 2) is mainly concerned with the development of this symbolism.

Eternity is not a very long time, nor is infinity a very capacious space. And in the last analysis eternity and infinity are not two, but one, and all-possibility is one of the names of that indivisible Unity.

⊷═◉→☀←◉═⊷

Let us return again to theology and consider what religion teaches. Being concerned with humanity alone, for the good reason that humanity represents the central and only fully conscious element in the universe, religion is only indirectly concerned with the multiple states of being as they affect non-human entities, animate or inanimate.

All living beings "have the same religion as ours" as Black Elk says of the birds,[6] that is to say, they express their dependence on God each in its own way, in their forms and their behavior (see also for example Ps. 19:1–3, and 104:21). Having little or no consciousness of their individuality they are not tempted to the sort of presumption of independence that beguiles us. They have therefore not only no capacity for, but also no need for, anything corresponding to the external forms of religion as we know them.

The doctrines of the great religions are formulated in many different ways and expressed through a very varied imagery, but integral to them is always the idea that the human being has an essential and immortal part which passes through a plurality of states, of which this present life is one. The "monotheistic" religions teach, for instance, that man has an immortal soul, given to him by God, and destined after its earthly death, in which it is separated from the body, to pass on to Paradise, purgatory, or hell, the choice depending on what it has done during its sojourn on earth. This no doubt is a great simplification of the situation in its entirety; nevertheless, it expresses the metaphysical truth adequately, and in a manner adapted to the needs and capacities of the people who are called upon to accept it, for whom it is unnecessary to know more than this. It is however vital for the state of their souls that they should not know less than this, and that they

---

[6] *Black Elk Speaks*, by John G. Neihardt (Lincoln: Univ. of Nebraska Press, 1961), p. 199.

should order their lives accordingly, that is to say, as a preparation for an inevitable change of state.

At death we drop all our terrestrial characteristics, all bodily and mental forms, for they are but the temporary manifestation of the possibilities inherent in and characteristic of the immortal center which is our real being, and that real being takes on another form, reflecting its proper nature in its new surroundings.

While subject to terrestrial conditions (or to any others), the individual being does not become something other than it is in principle or in potentiality, but it is passing through a phase of limitation, as it has done before and will do again. It will be a different phase every time; it has been said that "we pass this way but once", and this is necessarily true; the timeless co-existence of all things in all-possibility excludes any repetition, simply because two identical possibilities are not two but one. That is why religion treats the judgment that faces all beings after death as final, for so it is from the point of view of terrestrial existence, which is what a terrestrial religion is primarily concerned with. Religion could not, however, present the truth without taking account of non-terrestrial states: in the monotheistic religions they are referred to as paradises, purgatories, and hell, and are situated symbolically "above" or "beneath" this world.

It will have become clear that within a given set of conditions or compossibles (in other words, in a particular universe), every possibility compatible with those conditions must be manifested, the universe in question being a manifestation of all-possibility in a particular mode. Therefore possibilities of distinction, of contrast, of definition, also of opposition, contradiction, and negation, and even of a sort of apparent negation of itself, cannot be excluded. Manifestation consists precisely in this kind of throwing into relief of one possibility by its separation from another, or by the possibility of its apparent negation, without which everything would remain in the permanent indistinction and non-manifestation of all-possibility itself. But if things were to remain in that state, all-possibility would not be all-possibility, since the possibilities of distinction and opposition, that is to say, of manifestation, would be excluded, and that is impossible. In the non-manifestation

of all-possibility there is no separateness and no negation (for negation implies a separation), there is only the unimaginable perfection
of totality—but we have here already passed far beyond what words
alone can convey.

This is the only complete answer to people who say, "If all things
are possible with God, why does not He eliminate evil and ugliness
and pain?" There are other answers of course, some good and some
bad, but they are all vulnerable in one way or another. If God were
to eliminate these things, there would be no manifestation, no world,
and no salvation; but more than that, there would be no completion,
no perfection, no fulfillment.

St Paul says that "all things work together for good to them that
love God".[7] This is a comprehensive statement of the metaphysical
truth in theological terms. We read too in the Book of Genesis[8] that,
from the third day of the creation, when the distinctively manifested
features of this universe begin to appear, God saw that each of them
was good. Finally, He "saw everything that He had made, and, behold,
it was very good". As in the case of our text, the simplicity and directness of these words confers on them a power and a range that would
be diminished by any dialectical expansion or elaboration. As it is with
fundamental statements of truth such as these, so it is with faith. A
simple and direct faith is stronger and more far-reaching than a faith
justified or sustained mainly by philosophical or quasi-philosophical
considerations. Insofar as the latter is of the brain alone it is peripheral
and mobile. Simple faith is of the heart, it subsists at the center and
illumines the whole being, brain and all. With it, philosophy can live,
without it, philosophy is a dead thing.

As limited beings, we cannot know all-possibility, still less imagine
or visualize it in any way, since it cannot be compared or contrasted
with anything, nothing being outside it or separable from it. Yet at
the same time the universe we can know is nothing but a reflection
or refraction of all-possibility, and derives all its qualities and all its
reality therefrom.

---

[7] Rom. 8:28.

[8] Gen. 1:9-31.

St Paul said, "Now we see through a glass, darkly".[9] Only if we look upon the universe as a partial refraction of all-possibility, and not as if it were itself identifiable with all-possibility, can we "see God in all things". It is just in this sense that He is "in all things", and that all things subsist only "in God" and not in themselves. At the same time all things, to the extent that their appearance is taken for the reality, play the part of so many veils, hiding the Presence of Him with whom all things are possible.

[9] 1 Cor. 13:12.

13. What Am I?[1]

That which perceives is what each of us knows as "I".

There is no perception unaccompanied by a change in the perceiver. A visible external object, for instance, initiates a complex series of changes in the eye, its nerves, and the brain; but none of these organs considered together or separately can be said to see, nor do the changes they undergo constitute vision. There is something else, something that interprets the changes and deduces the qualities of the object seen not only separately as form, color, texture, size, etc., but also synthetically, so that it is instantly recognized as a man or an apple or a star.

If the mechanism (eye-nerve-brain) is faulty, and equally if the faculty of interpretation is limited or lacking (as it so evidently is in varying degrees in all animals), the object is not perceived for what it is, or is not perceived at all. Similarly with the other senses. Similarly also with all deduction originating in sense-perception.

Thus there can be no awareness which is not already potentially present in the individual who is aware. What we perceive or know is what we are capable of perceiving and knowing, rather than what there is to be perceived and known. "My" perception and "my" knowledge comprise far more of "me" than of the indefinite range of possibilities that constitute my environment, and *a fortiori* of the limitless possibilities of the Infinite. My knowledge is objective only to the extent that there is a real correspondence between my own nature and the nature of the universe. Hence the answer to all questions connected directly or indirectly with the nature or the reality or the objectivity of the universe or of anything within it is contingent on, or can be reduced to, the single crucial question: "What am I?"

That question can never be fully answered by observation. I am more than anything that I can observe or feel or think about. Observation, sensation, and mentation imply a duality between myself and some object that is not myself. We commonly speak of "my" body or "my" soul in the same way as we speak of "my" feelings or "my"

[1] From *Religion in the Modern World* (1963). —Editors

hand or "my" dog. I am however certainly nothing that I can be said to possess. We also commonly use phrases like "I said to myself" or "I am ashamed of myself". Who then or what is the "I" that says these things? It is not my body; it is not my soul. It cannot be the "myself" of which "I" am ashamed, nor can it be said to be anything in particular other than these.

If I argue that I am a man and I know what a man is, I delude myself; for I do not know what a man is unless I know what I am. If I practice introspection in the psychological sense, I am merely trying to isolate parts or qualities of my total being and to observe them objectively. The ultimate "I", the "pure subject", eludes all research.

Traditionally the ultimate "I" is the Self or Personality (with initial capitals) considered as being transcendent with respect to everything distinctive—including the lesser self or personality which is the individual ego, perceptible and distinctively knowable. The transcendent Self can never be specified or objectivized, proved or disproved: yet it is the one ultimate certitude lying at the heart of the being of every one of us. To realize what that transpersonal self is to realize "what I am", and thereby to have at my disposal the indispensable key to all knowledge.

How, then, to find the answer to the question "what am I?" Evidently modern science and philosophy are likely to take us farther from it rather than nearer to it, for before they could make any approach to the answer they would have to cease to be what they are. It is in the nature of the case that the answer can never be categorical; insofar as it can be expressed at all it must be expressed symbolically. Perhaps enough hints have already been given as to where the appropriate symbols may be sought.

There will be no harm in devoting a little attention to its obvious corollary: "What is my neighbor?" From his point of view (to which I must accord an authority equal to my own) it is he who is "I" and I whom am his neighbor. Are we then simply two creatures of the same species who naturally look at things in the same way? Or alternatively, is it that the same transcendent Self is manifested in us both, so that an essential unity is reflected in an apparent duality?

The modern scientific approach cannot get beyond the first answer. It sometimes tries to, and then it is inevitably led into an attempt to define the Self, which, being not other than the ultimate "I", is indefinable. The result is therefore a distortion of the truth.

The second answer is the answer of tradition, and therefore of religion. Since religion must cater for the needs of all men, it has to interpret that answer in such a way that all men may understand it, not so much mentally as existentially; not so much in their brains as in their hearts, so that, whether or not they may be able to express the truth in words, they may be enabled to live according to it.

That is the essence and origin of the religious virtues, of which charity may be taken as an example. Charity is an essential component of all religions (the Christian religion is far from having any sort of monopoly) because, in the last analysis and in its only pure form, charity is the recognition of the fundamental identity of myself and my neighbor.

If my only certitude, the one thing it does not occur to me to question, is that I am "I", I cannot, unless I am a solipsist, refuse to recognize that my neighbor is no less "I" than I am. If that is the case why should I behave as if my "I" were other or better than his? Should I not "do unto him as I would that he should do unto me", "love him as myself"?

Instead, the tendency is always to pay attention to our apparent distinction and to the details of the relatively small differences between us. We each embody but a tiny fragment of the indefinitely extensive possibilities of our common "being"; it is "being" and its indefinite possibilities that are real: all the rest is but a fragmented manifestation of those possibilities in a temporal and distinctive mode.

All but the underlying and non-distinctive reality of being is therefore in a very real sense illusory, a reflection that vanishes when the conditions that produced it change, and with precisely the degree of reality that attaches to a reflection. Insofar as our actions are not in conformity with reality, we blur its reflected image in the world. If we do not act charitably to our neighbor, our actions are not in conformity with the reality of our essential identity; we blur the truth so that it becomes not only less and less visible but also less and less the foundation of our living.

True charity is therefore by no means synonymous with altruism, for altruism as such tends to be more separative than unitive. It starts from the assumption, as its very name indicates, that my neighbor is other than I. Sentiment should not be the prime mover of charity, though sentiment has a part to play. Still less is the word "charity" properly applicable to the mere act of giving something to somebody.

On the contrary, its closest associations are with reality and truth, and with the finding of the answer to the question: "What am I?"

Thus the charity that is common to all religions is above all realistic, being founded on a true view of the nature of things. It does not always coincide with a charity motivated largely by sentiment.

A realistic charity is regulated by two overriding considerations. The first is that, since everything came from God and finds its fulfillment in a return to Him, the service of God comes before the service of man, with the corollary that the latter is useful only insofar as it is an expression of service to God.[2] In terms of Christianity the two New Testament commandments mean what they say. The normal practical expression of service to God being adherence to tradition, that is what comes first, and the charitable act must not interfere with or contradict traditional laws, including those that preserve the equilibrium of society, either because they serve to maintain the social hierarchy, or because they provide for the punishment of the wicked.

The second consideration is that charity is not realistic if it offers a lesser good, or a false good, in place of the true good. This may happen simply because a man does not do to his neighbor as he would like his neighbor to do to him. For example, it may be that he himself would hate to be interfered with and told that he does not know what is good for him, and would be furious if someone ran a subscription to educate or to improve him; but such considerations may not prevent him from doing exactly those things to his neighbor. Owing to his ignorance of what he is and what his neighbor is, he may really not know what is good for either. A man may in all good faith offer to his neighbor something that will distract the latter from what he really needs most—thus offering him a stone in place of bread, or a serpent in place of a fish.[3] No man can give what he does not possess; and that is why to "covet earnestly the best gifts"[4] is the beginning of charity. The passing on of those gifts, once possessed, will look after itself.

Charity is chosen as an example because it is the virtue most evidently related to the question: "What am I?" besides being the cardinal virtue of Christianity. All the other traditional virtues are

[2] See Deut. 6:4-7.

[3] Matt. 7:9-10.

[4] 1 Cor. 12:31.

similarly expressions of a conformity to reality and to truth. They are by no means merely useful conventions or expedients devised to minimize conflict, external or internal, or to make life more agreeable. Therefore, when truth flies out of the window, true virtue soon follows.

It is not their outward forms that make the virtues effective, either for the salvation of the soul or for anything else. What makes them effective in any particular case is their animation by an inward consciousness of, or conformity to, the real nature of the cosmos. It is he who gives "a cup of water" (the most insignificant of charitable acts) "in my name" who will "not lose his reward".[5] The same act performed in any other name, for example in the name of humanity, retains all its natural insignificance and may not even escape from perversion to diabolical ends.

Consciousness of reality can take the form of a metaphysical realization of what I am, implying a simultaneous realization of what my neighbor is. Conformity to reality can find its expression in religious faith, with all that this implies by way of participation in the doctrinal, ritual, and ethical elements of religion. There is no rigid line of demarcation between consciousness and conformity, but the attainment of the former otherwise than by way of the latter is so rare that it can be left out of account as a practical possibility.

The one thing that can be stated categorically is that a true consciousness of reality can never be attained by observation.

[5] Mark 9:41.

14. On Truth, Goodness, and Beauty[1]

There is no end to what could be said about truth, goodness, and beauty in all their various aspects and relationships. The observations that follow are therefore limited to making only one point concerning them, namely, that truth, goodness, and beauty are positive and eternal, whereas their contraries, error, evil, and ugliness are negative and perishable.

This point seems to be worth making because of the prevalence in the modern world of a tendency to attribute an equal status to the positive qualities and to their contraries, simply because they co-exist in this world; because all are facts of observation, all are regarded as being equally real and of equal standing. Such a view is implicit in many modern movements that base their philosophy on a so-called "realism"; most conspicuously perhaps in the arts and in psychology, in which the hideous and the degrading are often accorded a "significance" equal to that of the lovely and the elevating. Deeds count for more than words, and, whatever motives we may profess, truth is sought in these days mainly in its modern scientific form as a foundation for a technology devoted to the promotion of economic progress. Goodness is expected to follow automatically on an increase of material possessions, and beauty is relegated to the status of a luxury which must be ruthlessly sacrificed to economic advantage whenever the two seem to be mutually incompatible. Contrary tendencies are of course discernible, but it is undeniable that those just outlined are in practice predominant at the present time.

Truth, goodness, and beauty are traditionally associated as together representing an ideal of perfection.

Truth must come first because its absence invalidates anything and everything. The word "truth" and the word "reality" are sometimes used as if they were more or less synonymous, but there is a distinction between them which it is helpful to preserve. Truth can be defined as the coincidence of a mental image with reality, while of reality itself all that can be said is that it is what it is, whatever anyone

[1] This article is previously unpublished in book form. —Editors

may think it is. That is to say: reality plays the part of absolute with respect to a truth that is, humanly speaking, almost always in some degree relative.

Reality as such is ubiquitous and is therefore not definable distinctively—for to say that "it is what it is" is not a definition—nevertheless it is the rock on which are founded all truth, all experience, and all possibility of logical thought. If we had found reality in its entirety there would be nothing left to look for; there would be no need to seek for truth, no room for differences of point of view or of opinion, no approximation, no doubt, no denial, no falsehood; there would no longer be any mystery in existence but only pure certitude.

There is nevertheless one thing, one reality, that for everyone of us represents pure certitude, and that is the reality of our own existence; it is the only thing of which we are directly aware, while our awareness of everything else, even of our own distinguishable characteristics, is indirect and arises by way of the perception of the senses and the activity of the mind. Perception may be acute and mental activity may be penetrating, or they may not, but they are always relative; the underlying nature, the reality, of their objects is in no way affected by either; the object remains what it is, only the impression it makes on us is variable.

Reality as such has no contrary, since total unreality is absolute nothingness. Total unreality cannot even be imagined, for a mental image is always concerned with something that manifests reality in some degree, however slightly and however temporarily. Therefore truth, which is conformity to reality, is positive in relation to its contrary, error, which, being nothing but a failure to conform to reality, is purely negative.

The reflection of reality in our minds which we call "truth" is always relative because of the limitations of its human receptacle, which cannot perceive nor contain more than a fragment of all that is. Our corporeal limitations we take for granted; not so, apparently, our mental limitations. Truth being, humanly speaking, liable to imperfection—to say the least of it—has a contrary which we call "error". Error consists simply in the failure of a mental conception to coincide with reality, and, like truth, it exists only in our minds. The mind is like a mirror which reflects reality well or badly according to its own characteristics and condition. If a mirror is not a true plane it will reflect nothing without distortion; if it is tarnished it will reflect nothing clearly. It can, in principle, reflect anything whatever, save only one thing, and that is itself. That of course is why we cannot come to know what we are by observation or by any mental operation, however intense or refined.

We are liable to error, that is to say, to the formation of images that are imperfect reflections of reality. At the limit, those images and the ideas they give rise to can founder in an almost total negation of reality, which however can never become quite total because it would then have no relation to reality and so no existence whatever; nevertheless it can get as near to nothingness as anything can possibly be. In other words the more erroneous error becomes the nearer it is to extinction in nullity. Truth and error are therefore not equal and opposite; on the contrary, the relation between them corresponds to that between reality and illusion. Truth corresponds to that which is and "cannot not be", error tends towards that which has never been and can never be and can therefore never be wholly attained. Truth is essential and eternal, error is accidental and ephemeral.

That being so, error can only be associated in principle with destruction and chaos which, whatever form they may take, cannot be called good or beautiful, if those words have any useful meaning. Goodness and beauty therefore cannot but be on the side of truth, and so of reality, and their contraries, evil and ugliness, on the side of error, and so of illusion.

Truth is associated with the intellect, but the intellect is not all, there is also existence; goodness and beauty are existential rather than intellectual qualities, they are related to doing and being respectively rather than to thinking. They are two and not one because existence is manifested in the two modes just referred to as "doing" and "being": the former is energetic, vital, or dynamic, the latter is stable, substantial, or static. Goodness is the perfection of the dynamic mode and beauty of the static. They are manifested either positively or negatively and in varying degrees and proportions in everything that exists, from the stars in their courses to man in his earthly pilgrimage, but never in absolute perfection, since nothing that exists is perfect in all respects. It has been said that beauty is the splendor of the true; it could also be said to be the peacefulness or the purity of the true. Similarly goodness could be said to be the power of the true, or its nobility or its virtue. These qualities are positive in relation to existence, just as truth is positive in relation to the intellect. Hence their traditional association.

All three are on the side of reality, whereas their contraries, error, evil, and ugliness, are negative and on the side of illusion. Man is intellect, action, and contemplation; he must recognize and seek reality in its three principal manifested aspects; first in the intelligible, then in the existential in its two modes, the dynamic and the static; the true, the good, and the beautiful.

It is not difficult to see that, unless truth is founded on a reality that is independent of the observer, the word itself means nothing, and that therefore truth is positive and error negative. The relation of goodness and beauty to reality is less self-evident because the subjective element in their constitution seems to be more prominent, so that individual opinions concerning what the two words really represent differ even more widely than they do in the case of truth.

That no doubt is why it is sometimes suggested that they are purely subjective and are little more than names given to particular human activities and sensations that are for one reason or another beneficial or pleasurable. Such ideas arise because the mind, stimulated by the senses, reflects the multiplicity and mutability of terrestrial objects rather than the enduring reality of the qualities which, by their presence or their absence, make those objects what they are. We tend to think mainly by comparing and contrasting one object with another, and to regard qualities as if they originated in the objects that manifest them in time and space, forgetting that the object is perishable while the qualities are timeless.

For us the object is the reality and the qualities are the accidents. When this point of view becomes more or less exclusive it obscures the timeless reality of the qualities which, by their presence or absence, make objects what they are and also us what we are. This treatment of the object as the reality and the quality as the accident constitutes precisely the materialistic point of view; its predominance is therefore of fairly recent origin. From that point of view the underlying reality of all things—not only their truth but also their goodness and their beauty—resides in their ponderable substance and not in the imponderable but changeless qualities they manifest; it is to be sought in the images reflected in the mirror of a mind which is not only limited in its capacity, but also in its quality; in the indirect experiences that arise out of observation and deduction, and not in the one direct experience, namely, the being's inward and indivisible consciousness of its own reality, which is its point of contact with the reality of other beings, and the one thing common to all. When reality, and therewith all positive qualities, is situated in relativity, everything becomes conditional, even what passes for truth; goodness becomes self-conscious and uncertain of itself, rather than being radiant and impregnable; beauty becomes equivocal and seductive, rather than being peaceable and purifying.

The traditional point of view which has been largely supplanted by the materialistic, is based not primarily on an outwardly directed observation, but on an inward certainty—call it a conviction or a belief if you like—that reality, and therewith all positive qualities subsist in a timeless absolute of which all things temporal are but reflections. All the great religions and traditions, in their doctrines, in their rituals, through their saints and sages and in the faith of their followers testify to the overriding reality of a plane of perfection of which the plane of terrestrial existence is but a fugitive reflection or refraction in time and in space. This implies that reality, and therefore possibility, is not limited by the conditions that govern our terrestrial existence. If a conception of the limitlessness of reality were impossible to us, we would not perceive the limitative nature of terrestrial conditions; but as things are, our ability to conceive of our own limitation proves that there is something in us that can reach out beyond our present state towards what is greater than ourselves, even though it be not directly accessible to our senses alone which are attuned exclusively to the conditions of terrestrial existence. Once that is admitted, there is no longer any solid reason for questioning the realism of a vision of a plane of perfection on which truth, goodness, and beauty are seen in all their purity, and are no longer known mainly by contrast with their contraries.

The vision of perfection, experienced in the form of the beatific vision of a saint or less directly in the faith of a believer, either reflects reality or it does not. If it does not, it is the most pathetic of delusions; and it is moreover a delusion in which a vast majority of men have stagnated until now, when at last release has come through the rise of the materialistic point of view.

The plane of existence is the plane of contrasts, and on it error, evil, and ugliness remain what they are. It is natural to us to try to avoid them in this world, and it is far from useless to do so; not however primarily because success in doing so makes life more agreeable, but because truth, goodness, and beauty, as they are manifested in this world are nearer to reality than their contraries. In their existential manifestations they do but prefigure their own intrinsic and principial nature; they are but shadows, reflections, signs, symbols, or heralds of what they are really and eternally. It is not enough to seek them in their temporal manifestations alone, not only because to do so may cement our own attachment to a lower plane and thereby hinder assimilation to a higher, but also because it is not by itself an exercise of the function that alone makes man truly human. That function is to aspire here and now towards a celestial perfection that is more real than anything that can be found on the plane of contrasts on which terrestrial life is situated.

Thus, although it has always been generally admitted by right-minded people that truth, goodness, and beauty are, to say the least of it, on the side of righteousness, it is not so generally admitted that truth is infinitely more than conformity to ascertained fact, nor that goodness is infinitely more than a mere abstention from evil or a neighborliness that can make life in this world easier, nor yet that beauty is infinitely more than a subjective impression or a pleasurable accident or a luxury; still less is it admitted that all three are on the side of reality and that their contraries are on the side of illusion.

This generation seeks truth in the infinitely variable permutations and combinations of an inexhaustible multitude of facts; it sees goodness mainly in terms of terrestrial welfare and of outwardly harmonious human relationships; small wonder therefore that so many of its works seem to tend towards the destruction of beauty, and even that this tendency should be specially apparent in the domain of a self-conscious art, dissociated from other activities and pursued for its own sake as a sort of luxury. But beauty is not a luxury. Like truth and goodness it is an essential aspect of reality itself.

Plato says of beauty:

> He [the delivered soul] will see a Beauty eternal, not growing or decaying, not waxing or waning; nor will it be fair here and foul there, nor depending on time and circumstance or place, as if fair to some and foul to others; nor shall Beauty appear to him in the likeness of a face or hand, nor embodied in any form whatever . . . whether of heaven or of earth; but Beauty absolute, separate, simple, and everlasting; which lending of its virtue to all beautiful

things that we see born to decay, itself suffers neither diminution or any other change. (*The Symposium*)

The reality which is the ultimate objective of all search, and in which truth, goodness, and beauty are one, is too all-embracing to be identified with any object of the senses or with any system built up in the mind. It can only be sought by way of something that overrides and synthesizes the brute fact and its mental derivatives, without however necessarily invalidating them on their own plane. That "something" has been called a "thirst for the absolute" or, more familiarly to most of us, a "love of God". Only insofar as we may endeavor to satisfy that thirst or to perfect that love may we be enabled to see, directly and as it were with our own eyes, that truth, goodness, and beauty are essentially real and eternal, positive and Divine, whereas error, evil, and ugliness are correspondingly illusory and fugitive, negative and human, and that it is they, and they alone, that perish.

IV

ART AND SYMBOLISM

Existence is joined to eternity not only through the qualities manifested in it, but also through its rhythms, which, as it were, compensate the irreversible and devouring character of time. We can sense this directly when the repeated and identical vibrations of a string produce a single musical note. Through flowers as through music we can perhaps learn to hear something of the "music of the spheres", wherein the rhythms of the whole creation are unified in one great song of praise.

From "The Beauty of Flowers"

15. Art Ancient and Modern[1]

It has been truly said that "art is the mirror of its times". This implies that the peculiarities characteristic of a given period are reflected in the art of that period. But this is only half the truth, because art not only reflects its times: it also exercises a powerful influence over them.

A work of art is distinguished from other products of human skill by the fact that it is, to a greater or less extent, inspired. This inspiration confers upon it a value or a significance which it would otherwise lack.

Inspiration can be of different kinds and can come from various sources. The difference between a work of art that is ancient in spirit and one that is modern in spirit resides fundamentally in a difference in the nature of its inspiration, and in the source from which that inspiration comes. Neither category can be established by date alone, but art that is ancient in spirit predominates in ancient times, and *vice versa*.

Broadly speaking, the distinction can be expressed in the following way. The artist whose work is ancient in spirit, whatever he may take as his model, derives his inspiration from tradition. This is perhaps most evident when the art in question is specifically religious in character, and when the artist prepares himself for work by prayer, fasting, and meditation, as would be normal for the painting of an icon or a Tibetan *tan'ka*, or in preparation for a religious drama. In such cases the artist can be said to seek his inspiration directly from God, though in addition he is always guided, usually very closely, by traditional rules governing his method, style, and choice of model. If his art is not specifically religious in character, as is the case if he is a craftsman producing articles of daily use, he is similarly guided by tradition in his method, style, and choice of model. Although his inspiration is then in a sense less direct than in the first case, nevertheless it comes from the same source and is no less real. In both cases

---

[1] From *Religion in the Modern World* (1963). —Editors

151

the artist is indeed constrained by tradition. He must not allow free play to his imagination and he must not experiment beyond a certain clearly defined point. This constraint protects him from error, from his own individual weakness in the face of subversive influences and from isolation. The last thing he would wish, if the possibility ever occurred to him, would be to be released from it.

Judging by the admiration that is so justly and universally accorded to them, it certainly cannot be said that works of art that are ancient in spirit bear the marks of a constraint that has impaired their quality or their beauty. If that constraint is, artistically speaking, otherwise than beneficial, how is it that so many common traditional objects—a cottage, a corn stack, a wagon, a scythe, a basket, for example—are so evidently works of art, and at the same time show great variety of form, even within a single country, whereas the corresponding modern objects—a concrete dwelling, a grain silo, a tractor trailer, a mowing machine, a plastic container—are not only often ugly but also increasingly alike all over the world?

The artist whose work is modern in spirit derives his inspiration from his environment rather than from tradition. His environment includes not only the whole of the external world in its endless variety, but also the content of his own imagination. His mind is incapable of forming images that are not derived from his environment, however convinced he may be that they originate in himself.

The environment has always provided art with its models, but not always with its inspiration. Herein resides the fundamental distinction. In Europe the Renaissance marks the period at which the change from one source of inspiration to the other became, rather suddenly, almost complete.

The artist inspired by tradition looks upon his model primarily as a symbol manifesting particular Divine qualities or attributes, and he seeks to embody them in his work, even though very often he would not or could not define his aim in precisely that way. Insofar as he succeeds the work will reflect, more or less directly and positively, some aspect of Ultimate Reality. It will manifest, to a greater or less degree, a supra-individual quality, a celestial as well as a terrestrial beauty. The intrinsic characteristics of the model, that is to say the peculiarities which distinguish it when it is regarded as an independent object, are a secondary consideration, and are often conventionalized, in the sense of being modified so as to conform to a traditional style.

The non-traditional artist who looks to his environment, or to some part of it, for example to his model itself, for inspiration sees his model only as an independent object having particular intrinsic characteristics which he seeks to reproduce in his work. Since he can only reproduce characteristics that are perceptible to him as an individual, his work will itself be individual, that is to say, confined to the plane on which his individuality is manifested; it will not manifest the quality of universality characteristic of traditional art. This is true even though the artist is completely successful in realizing his aim, and even though the qualities reproduced in his work are all desirable and good—such as beauty, strength, tenderness, and so on. The work will not reflect directly and positively some aspect of Ultimate Reality. Yet since there is nothing that does not reflect that Reality, however indirectly, either positively or negatively, it will not be protected by the constraint of tradition from a tendency towards inversion or negation. The modern artist is indeed free: free from the constraint of tradition, and so cut off from its protection. His own judgment is the final arbiter of everything he does. In his isolation and loneliness he has no sure means of discrimination between one kind of influence and another, or between one kind of inspiration and another.

Every worker, and not the artist alone, finds himself in a comparable situation when there has been a departure from the traditional laws and constraints that alone can confer on a civilization as a whole an effective unity, so that all its constituent parts—religion, art, politics, trade, sport—are as one. When the principle of unity has been lost to sight everything becomes individualized. Chaos can only be avoided by some kind of collectivization of human society, in an attempt to reconstruct the missing unity. But any such collectivization is but superficial and lacks a sure foundation. It inevitably takes the form of a grouping together of like with like, rather than a hierarchical organization of like with unlike, such as exists in a traditional civilization. Without a hierarchical organization, a civilization is broken up in the course of its history into a growing number of separate domains, each one representing a particular set of objectives and points of view, for example, religion, politics, economics, science, art, industry, trade, sport, and so on. They are more or less loosely interconnected by such interests as they have in common, but each claims a certain independence and often a certain supremacy, while at the same time each tends to split up into a number of subsidiary domains.

Thus it is that the artistic or "cultural" domain, with which we are here concerned, comes into being as a more or less distinct entity. Its separate existence is a relatively recent phenomenon. For a long time past the arts have played a less and less real and effective part in the life of the community, on which they are now to a large extent superimposed as a luxury or a compensation. In our society the supremacy of modern science and its related domains of industry and economics are in practice unquestioned. Beauty being the quality most particularly sought after in the arts—at least hitherto—a consequence of this separation of domains has been a divorce of beauty from utility. The useful often becomes ugly and the beautiful useless.[2] Beauty ceases to be a quality occurring naturally in the products of human skill; instead, it has to be added artificially or artistically. This tends to happen only when it does not interfere unduly with the economics of production, or when it can be turned into an economic asset and used to promote consumer acceptance.

Thus, while applied art has a connection, purely exterior and economic, with some of the other factors that make up the life of the community, fine art forms a domain of its own within which it becomes increasingly isolated. In this abnormal situation art can only seek its justification within itself; and since the attention of the artist, no less than that of his public, is henceforth directed to his experience of his environment, that is to say, to the experience of the senses, that justification can only be aesthetic, that is to say, concerned with the gratification of the senses.

In the earlier stages of this movement a sufficient aesthetic satisfaction, and with it a certain justification of art, is obtained through the simple representation of the beauties of nature. The recording and aesthetic interpretation of natural beauty becomes the main aim and function of art. It demands a high degree of perceptiveness, discrimination, and skill, and when it is successful its products can be very beautiful. Nothing that is in any way beautiful is wholly despicable or worthless. Nevertheless, such work is no longer traditional in the

---

[2] Beauty becomes a superfluity, a luxury to be cultivated for its own sake, or to be grafted in the form of applied art (the notion of which would have been incomprehensible in an earlier age) on to the ugliness that is characteristic of a profane civilization.

rightful sense of the word. The source of its inspiration is not tradition but the environment. However true to life it may be, it is no longer true to the real nature and destiny of man. However much satisfaction it may give, it takes no account of, and contributes nothing to, the fulfillment of that destiny.

Someone will say: "But surely, even if that be true of profane art, it cannot be true of religious art." Unfortunately it can indeed be true of religious art, particularly if, as is usually the case, the words "religious art" signify no more than an art that takes a religious subject as its model. The criterion of the traditional character of a work is not one of date nor of model: it is one of inspiration and style.

The essential reason why the representation of natural beauty cannot by itself be fully satisfying is that it does not satisfy the fundamental need, unconscious though it often be, for something greater and more enduring than terrestrial experience. It caters in general for a need that is occasional and contingent, and subject to the fluctuations of individual taste and opinion, and even of fashion. Hence the quest for something that will be more fully satisfying, or, in default of satisfaction, that will at least attract attention, puzzle, or horrify. The quest is for novelty and originality at all costs. This is the exact equivalent of the sensationalism so evident in some other domains. The artist, if he is to survive, is virtually compelled to explore his environment (which, be it remembered, includes the content of his imagination) to its uttermost limits in a search for fresh models and fresh sources of inspiration. Having as it were exhausted the resources of those parts of his environment that affect his senses from without, he must probe into that part that affects his sensibilities from within. The regions he explores contain a vast and amorphous array of psychic entities and influences, some derived from his own subconscious mind, others from some kind of collective psychic influence, and others from the psychic world as such. Modern psychology tries to describe and to classify the few elements of this array that are accessible to analysis, and gives them high-sounding scientific names.

In the old days they were called good or bad fairies or spirits, or demons or ghosts or bogeys, and by many other names. It was certainly then recognized that tradition alone, whether religious in form or otherwise, could be relied on to keep them in order, to favor the good influences and suppress the bad.[3]

In the absence of the control which tradition alone can exercise, it is extremely dangerous to venture into the territory of these powerful, ill-defined, and deceptive psychic forces. It is, however, characteristic of the later phases of an historical cycle that all its most subversive and dissolving elements, hitherto kept in the darkness where they normally belong, should be brought into the light of day. Modern psychology has no idea how to set about the destruction of these elements (our ancestors would have said: "how to exorcise them"), nor does it recognize the fact that such things cannot be brought into the light of day otherwise than by their taking possession of some of the elements that make up a human society, which then acts as their vehicle; or in other words, without the occurrence of changes in a human society favorable to the development of their influence, so that a point is eventually reached where their destruction cannot be accomplished without the destruction of the society itself.

A similar failure to recognize the nature of the forces in question accompanies the activities of those artists who deliberately lay themselves open to the influence of psychic forces in an attempt to widen the field from which they draw their inspiration. Small wonder that the result so often seems "satanic" to anyone who has eyes to see or ears to hear, and who is not misled by current mumbo-jumbo about "creative art", "significant form", and so on. The incomprehensibility of much modern art has produced a whole new jargon of apologetics, miscalled criticism, without which that art could not survive the ponderous and unanalytical conservatism of the masses. This conservatism, on the whole negative in character, is not for that reason anti-traditional in tendency. It is in this sense that *vox populi* can also be *vox Dei*.

---

[3] Such was the purpose of many of the traditional sciences that are now virtually obsolete and usually dismissed as mere magic or superstition, as if our ancestors were so idiotic as to be incapable of distinguishing illusory results from real ones, or good from bad. On the contrary, it is the supposed ineffectuality of those sciences that is a delusion, and a dangerous one. Their subsisting residues have become superstitions in the proper sense of the word, namely, ancient forms detached from their origin and no longer comprehended. They are not for that reason deprived of their power, which however is no longer under control.

Let it be clearly understood that no man ever created anything whatsoever; not a speck of dust, not even an idea, for all ideas are derived from pre-existing material. The most that man can do, and that only to a very limited extent, is to select and arrange what is already there.

Significance as such in no way justifies anything, the crux of the matter being what it is that is signified. Forms, and not least the forms of art, can have a significance that is sacred and unitive, or one that is diabolical and disruptive. The latter are often deceptive, for the sacred is profound with the profundity and mystery of the star-spangled heavens, while the diabolical is also profound, but in the opposite sense, with the hot and heavy obscurity of the nether regions. An unguided soul can all too easily mistake the one profundity for the other. The sacred is interior in the sense that it is associated with the spiritual Center that is everywhere; the diabolical is interior in the sense that it is associated with the center of gravity towards which all material things tend.

We are contrasting an inspiration arising from tradition with an inspiration (which ought really to be called a pseudo-inspiration) sought in appearances. This last leads inevitably to a search for a missing inwardness. The artist feels compelled to seek it; very often he finds nothing, but if he finds anything it is almost certainly not a spiritual inwardness, but rather physical or psychic.

Today the validity of a work of art is often assessed on the grounds of the sincerity of the artist. The implication presumably is that he is not trying to deceive or to defraud anyone, but is on the contrary convinced that his approach to his work is valid, and that therefore, provided that he does his work well, its results must be good. This notion is closely related to another, not at all uncommon nowadays, to the effect that whatever one believes to be right is for that reason right. Both notions are equally vicious and equally absurd. They are not so much a contradiction of truth as a denial that there is any such thing as truth.

Curiously enough, the same principle does not seem to be applied to most other domains, such as those of politics or economics or modern science, where it would be generally admitted that a man can be disastrously wrong, however convinced he may be that he is right. This is probably because the things included in the other domains named are regarded as being more or less measurable, whereas those included in the aesthetic domain are too subtle and difficult to define or measure. They are therefore relegated to a region wherein individual opinion and taste are supreme. If that be so, it becomes understandable that the same criteria should be applied to the ultimate or metaphysical truth—or to religion, its most direct expression—since its domain (if this word be still applicable) is so comprehensive as to include all domains, and is accordingly immeasurable.

The change of approach described and its consequential developments can be discerned in all the arts, but perhaps most easily in the visual arts, painting, and sculpture, where the forms chosen by the artist as his models are visible and relatively stable. The forms chosen as models in the literary arts are usually events rather than objects; but events, and thoughts as well, possess form just as do visible objects. They can similarly be taken either as symbols or as mere incidents. Anyone who questions this has only to reflect on the forms of the Sacred Scriptures, and on the substitution of a mere literal rendering for their symbolical interpretation. Architecture, with its predominantly utilitarian bias and non-representational character, reflects the changes in question perhaps most clearly when it is employed in the service of religion: it is sufficient to compare the forms of medieval churches with those of many modernistic churches.

There remains music, the most abstract and non-representational of all the arts, and its associated art, the dance. Each would be worthy of a separate study, but only a few points can be mentioned here.

Certain kinds of modern dancing manifest the spirit of decadence at least as obviously as does any other modern art. Indeed it is open to question whether they still fall into the category of art. Apart from any question of symbolical content, their total lack of the grace and dignity of traditional dancing needs no emphasis.

As for music itself, its abstract character has generally speaking afforded it some protection against those influences to which the more representational arts are more vulnerable. Nevertheless, as in other arts, a growing preoccupation with a purely sensual beauty has led to an urge continually to try to break new ground in the hope of finding new material and new inspiration. This has led, among other things, to the borrowing of elements from the sacred music of other traditions. For instance, the sacred rhythms of African music, which are essentially ritual in origin, acquire, when they are alienated from the tradition to which they belong, all the subversive and deceptive characteristics of superstitions in the proper sense of the word. They lose their sacred character, but not their power, and there is nothing to hold that power in check or to direct it aright. The fact that such considerations are largely rejected by the modern outlook in no way detracts from their reality; indeed incomprehension of such matters is entirely characteristic of the modern outlook.

Although music has to a certain extent been protected by its non-representational character from some of the influences that have affected other arts, yet there is one peculiarity in its history which exemplifies with particular clarity the real nature of the changes that have taken place. In most ancient music a single note of unchanging pitch is sounded continuously throughout the composition; the melody departs from it and returns to it, often frequently, and is as it were no more than a development of possibilities inherent in the continuous note, the "tonic", the origin, the support, and the end of all the rest. Some music of this kind has survived to the present day, for example that of the bagpipes.[4] At a later stage the continuous sounding of the tonic is abandoned, but the melody is still developed in such a way that the tonic, even when unheard, is effectively present; the French *sous-entendu* conveys this exactly; the melody never changes its key or tonality.

Next comes the discovery (really the release of a possibility formerly held in check) of the sensational effect of modulation, a change of key. At first such changes were restricted to a narrow range of keys closely related to the original key, a final return to which was obligatory. Later modulation becomes a dominant element in music, now spread by mechanical reproduction all over the world. It is no longer restricted to nearly related keys, all keys being regarded as equivalent and interchangeable.[5] This involves a loss of both the stability and the

---

[4] The rules governing the development of the melody, and those governing any polyphonic or harmonic additions to it, differ according to the traditional style of the music concerned, and do not affect the immediate point.

[5] This new freedom necessitated the invention of the "well-tempered" scale, in which all keys are effectively interchangeable, because they differ only in pitch, so that there is a complete and exciting freedom of movement between any one and any other; but that freedom cannot be achieved without the sacrifice of the exceedingly fine differences of pitch which distinguish the natural scale from the well-tempered scale, the latter being indeed a more or less artificial compromise.

subtlety of a music in which each key, usually called a mode, is qualitatively different from every other. Thus the tonic, the unchanging
principial note in which traditional melody begins, develops, and
ends, is gradually allowed to slip into the background, and to be overwhelmed by the development of possibilities which, attractive though
they be, and indeed necessary for the full manifestation of all the possibilities inherent in music as an art (and therefore also inherent in the
tonic itself), are none the less negative insofar as they are incompatible
with the maintenance of the audibility of the tonic; or, one might say,
incompatible with its "real presence". A final and totally dissolving
step is taken in the invention of atonal music, wherein any impression of tonality is studiously avoided, as a matter, one might say, of
pseudo-principle.

These developments reflect accurately in the domain of music
the successive stages of the abrogation and final abandonment in all
domains of the traditional laws governing the activities taking place
within those domains. The main purpose and effect of those laws was
to ensure a constant reference back in each domain to the underlying
principle of its existence. That principle cannot be other than the
Principle of all existence; its origin, its support, and its end.

The successive abrogations in all fields of art succeed one another
ever more rapidly; they are, broadly speaking, all undertaken in the
name of freedom. In the arts, as in other domains, each new freedom
is more illusory than its predecessor, since it always consists in a substitution of other constraints for the constraints of tradition. The new
constraints, though often unrecognized as such, confine the artist ever
more closely to terrestrial things, and so cut off his access to heavenly
things, thus depriving him of the only freedom worth having, indeed
of the only real freedom there is.

As time goes on it is inevitable that the qualities normally associated with a work of art should be sacrificed one by one on the altar
of this imaginary freedom, often spoken of as "originality". But only a
work of art that is traditional in spirit can properly be called "original",
because it alone is effectively attached to its real origin. The newer
kind of originality assumes that man, not God, is the origin and the
creator, and that inspiration is individual and not universal.

At last even the ideal of a purely sensual beauty is often sacrificed.
It will perhaps be argued that this is not really so, but that a new kind
of beauty always takes the place of one that has been abandoned, and

that this new beauty is inevitably unrecognized at first and condemned as ugliness, until the public have been educated to it. There is an element of truth in this, but it is contingent on a recognition of the fact that each successive new expression of beauty derives less and less of its inspiration from heavenly things and more and more from earthly things, and from them in descending order. The public is therefore not "educated up" but "educated down". It is a question of getting accustomed to things that are qualitatively inferior; it is as such that they are instinctively resisted at first, however novel and sensational they may be. Their inferiority is directly reflected in their lack of an enduring influence and in the confused quality of that influence, as well as in the perishability of their forms.

An acceptance of the inferior takes place only when there is a failure to distinguish on the one hand between a relative good, dusty and tarnished though it be, which is still not error, and on the other a polished and glittering relative error. Beauty as such is on the side of good; that it should become tarnished is a misfortune. That it should be lost is a disaster.

The saying that "beauty is in the eye of the beholder" is scarcely as much as a half-truth. It belittles beauty by suggesting that it is less than the beholder and dependent on him, or that it is purely subjective in the psychological sense. The saying is true only in the sense that different people see different kinds of beauty, or none at all, as the case may be. It ignores the truth that beauty as a divine attribute is greater than the beholder who is but an individual. Beauty exists on all planes of manifestation: we see only its reflection on a lower plane, whereon it is a manifestation of the Infinite in the finite, a gift of God, a grace, a sign, a symbol, though its vehicle be limited and ephemeral. Fortunate indeed is a person who sees both the vehicle and the beauty it carries for what each really is.

16. The Beauty of Flowers[1]

*The important thing is to understand why it is worth-
while to make a garden—why a garden is (or can be)
much more than just a pleasure for the senses. The
reason is this. God allows us to do our best to imitate
His Paradise, however incompletely, provided that we
never forget that all beauty comes from Him alone and
remains always in Him, without any loss and for ever.*
(From the author's letter to a friend)

Flowers which are attractive by reason of their forms, colors, or scents
have been admired and loved and cultivated for thousands of years;
perhaps never more so than in Europe at the present day. Everyone
knows, or thinks he knows, what a flower is.

About a hundred years ago the modern scientific point of view
began to be applied to flowers. It is necessary to take that point of
view into account, because today so many people think that it is the
only point of view from which we can learn what a flower really is, or
assign to it its proper place in the scheme of things.

From a scientific point of view a flower is characteristic of all
the class of Angiosperms. Whether it be conspicuous and attractive
or not, it is primarily a mechanism for securing the transfer of pollen
from the anther of one flower to the stigma of another of the same
species. In the case of conspicuous flowers, this usually takes place
on the body of an insect. The form, color, and fragrance of flowers is
thought to have been evolved in nature for the purpose of attracting
insects, the intervention of which compensates for the immobility of
plants and makes the impregnation of the ovule by the pollen of a distant individual possible. Alternatively, as everyone knows, pollen may
be transported by wind; in such cases the flower is usually small and
inconspicuous, though the inflorescence may be beautiful in our eyes.

---

[1] From *Looking Back on Progress* (1970). —Editors

From the scientific point of view, flowers have evolved into what they are solely as a result of the interaction of factors connected with the relationship of plants to insects or to wind.

Insofar as flowers are the indispensable precursors of useful seeds and fruits, with honey as a by-product in some cases, there is an obvious economic relationship between flowers and mankind. Man has also taken advantage of the fact that flowers seem to us beautiful, and has tried to accentuate the pleasurable aspects of his relationship to flowers in his development of floriculture. Scientifically speaking, all other kinds of relationship, aesthetic or otherwise, can only be regarded as accidental.

The modern scientific point of view takes account of nothing but the immediate and tangible advantage, "economic" in the broad sense of the word, to the individual or to the race. It could therefore be described as purely utilitarian. It assumes that the qualities and way of life of every living being, including man, can in principle be regarded primarily as expedients for securing the continuity of the existence of the being or its race or species in the face of environmental pressures and competition from other beings or races. If any other influences are admitted they are regarded as secondary.

There are some scientists and philosophers of science who would say that even the above statement is tendentious, in that it makes use of such words as "advantage", "expedients", and "competition", and thereby suggests some kind of underlying purpose in the process of evolution and in existence generally. To them, there is no such purpose, terrestrial life having arisen purely through a fortuitous combination of circumstances, probably unique, and certainly destined eventually to be swallowed up in some equally fortuitous cataclysm. According to this view there exist only blind forces acting upon elementary particles, the resulting associations and dissociations of which constitute the universe and all that it contains. Thus all our experience, all our aspirations, every conception of beauty or goodness or greatness or of any kind of purpose, and of course any kind of theistic conception, can have no ultimate significance whatever.

This is the philosophy of despair, of which Bertrand Russell is one of the chief exponents. It claims to expound the only intellectually acceptable basis for the development of a philosophy of life, and to represent the only possible logical and intelligent deduction from the discoveries of modern science.

Independently of whether they are prepared to accept any particular religious or quasi-religious eschatology, there are probably very few people who can accept in their hearts the view that existence is ultimately meaningless. But the conception of terrestrial life as a struggle for existence, in which every creature or race is fighting for its own advantage, has been thoroughly instilled into our minds by the protagonists of evolutionary ideas.

It is of interest in passing to compare this point of view with another that was very prevalent in the nineteenth century, according to which everything on earth was created, not for its own advantage, nor for the advantage of its race, but for the benefit of mankind. It differed from the evolutionist point of view in being "creationist", and ostensibly founded on a religious rather than a scientific outlook. It perished partly because creationism was superseded by evolutionism, and partly because it met with insuperable difficulties in application. It was necessary to argue that not only many things apparently useless to man, but also his worst enemies, were in fact created for his special and exclusive benefit. It was however very close to the evolutionist point of view in being essentially utilitarian. Both are examples of the tendency to try to account for everything in terms of immediate and tangible advantage and disadvantage. This is none other than the materialist tendency.

Considerations of immediate advantage and disadvantage can be important in terrestrial life, but any theory founded on them alone is totally insufficient to account for the forms and the behavior of living beings, vegetable, animal, and especially human, and no less insufficient to account for their existence, their variety, and their qualities, and not least for their beauty. Beauty is the quality that particularly appeals to us in flowers.

The conception of a universal struggle for existence is highly anthropomorphic. It seems probable that our view of the world of nature as a conflict rather than a harmony is little more than evidence of our own state of mind. It is colored far more strongly than we suppose by that state of mind, whether it be internally harmonious or internally distraught. The picture of flowers manifests a joyous superfluity that accords ill with any conception so grim as that of a universal struggle for existence taken as the influence which has made that picture what it is and has conferred on us the inexplicable and gratuitous benediction of flowers.

Struggle there is, obviously; but it is a result of the temporal limitations that obscure the underlying harmony, the harmony that shines forth from within in the inexplicable beauty of flowers. The struggle is as it were superficial; it does not constitute the basic force that molds the world of nature, still less did it produce the beauty of flowers. The "struggle for existence" theory is that the more brilliant the flower the better its chances of attracting insects and thereby ensuring pollination and the perpetuation of its race. It sounds plausible, but it does not fit the facts. The attractiveness of flowers to insects bears little relation to their brilliance or size. Lubbock pulled the petals off geraniums and found that insects visited them as before. The flowers of vines, of ivy, of box, of gooseberries, of sycamores, are small and green, yet they are objects of hot competition in the insect world, more so perhaps than most conspicuous flowers. *Cotoneaster horizontalis* has the least conspicuous flowers of any of its race, and is much the most attractive to insects. Neither lilies nor magnolias seem to be particularly attractive, whereas roses and poppies and peonies are. There are also contrasts like that between the fig and the yucca, each dependent for pollination on one species of insect, small and specialized: the flowers of the fig are entirely hidden; the large white flowers of the yucca are flaunted in great plumes on stems many feet high. An abundant source of sugar, like the waste from a sugar factory, unadvertised though it be, is far more attractive to bees than the brightest of flowers. In short, the colors and forms of uncultivated flowers cannot be accounted for solely by any theory that confines its attention to their purely functional or utilitarian aspect.

Let us then assume without more ado that the beauty and fragrance of flowers is not an accident nor yet is it manifested for the exclusive and tangible benefit either of the plants themselves or of man. It can of course be maintained, with no possibility of proof either way, that man alone sees beauty as such; it is anyhow a commonplace that all men do not see it in the same way and that some appear to be totally indifferent to it. Hence the saying that beauty is in the eye of the beholder, and so in one sense it is, but this saying can be interpreted in two different ways. On the one hand, it can mean that beauty is purely subjective and therefore has no intrinsic reality independently of its observer, or, on the other hand, that it has an intrinsic reality but that reality is accessible to an individual only to the extent that he is attuned to it.

According to the first interpretation beauty is less than man and is a product of his nature; according to the second it is greater, or at least more universal, than the human individuality as such. The first interpretation is concordant with the scientific and evolutionary outlook. The second is not, because it takes account of something that is outside the purview of science. It implies that beauty is objective and universal, that its reality is independent of its manifestation in nature, and that therefore it is inherently mysterious, intangible, and non-measurable.

If that is so, beauty is by no means a fortuitous attribute of matter; it is something of the universal manifested in the relative. It is a manifestation of the infinite in the finite, and in that case, the real importance of beauty to us does not reside in its pleasurable or aesthetic aspect, but in its symbolism, or in its didactic potentiality.

The traditional association of beauty with truth is then neither sentimental nor fanciful, for the positive qualities, among which is beauty, are immutable realities. Only the material and perishable forms, through which the ever-present potentialities of the qualities may be more or less imperfectly manifested, are ephemeral.

Materialism consists precisely in restricting attention to the perishable form. Whether in its scientific or in its popular guise, it is therefore opposed to all that a religion not tainted with materialism teaches, namely, that the material world can only be accounted for in terms of the non-material, the visible in terms of the invisible, the measurable in terms of the non-measurable; and further that the ultimate truth is enshrined in the latter and not in the former.

This is no way implies that material and measurable things should be ignored or despised, but simply that they should be seen for what they are, namely, signs or symbols of a reality immeasurably greater, more comprehensive, and more enduring than they are, even in their totality. Here, as always, it is a case of preserving a right balance. This can only be done by keeping the essential principles always in view and interpreting the facts of observation accordingly.

The main principle here in view is the metaphysical superiority or transcendence of the intangible and non-measurable over the tangible and measurable, that is to say, of quality over quantity.

Without quantity the universe as we know it could have no existence. Qualities would remain as unmanifested potentialities. Without quality, if anything could then be said to exist, it would have no intelligibility; it would have the completely abstract character of pure number, to which, as René Guénon has shown, the conception of quantity is in the last analysis reducible. Such a situation is not, strictly speaking, conceivable, since one cannot form a conception of unrelieved indistinction, pure chaos. For similar reasons it is not realizable. Nevertheless it is the situation towards which the world is moving, though it can never attain to it fully.

It is not really surprising that an inversion of priorities has culminated, quite logically, in a sort of nihilism, in the philosophy of "unyielding despair" which Bertrand Russell announced specifically, and others of the same persuasion by implication, as the only rational basis for the ordering of human life. If the priorities are kept in the right order, the beauty of flowers, seen as the expression of a principle and not as an accident, can teach us directly, intellectually, and without recourse to sentiment of any kind, that this philosophy of despair is rubbish.

Can one thus metaphorically consign to the waste-paper basket the life's work of so many able and erudite men, highly trained in logic and in exposition, and deeply convinced that they are struggling to save mankind from self-destruction? What have they done to deserve such treatment? Well, what they have done is to consign to the waste-paper basket, metaphorically or otherwise, the whole of the "perennial philosophy" that is enshrined in the sacred Scriptures of the world, all the exposition and exemplification of that philosophy given by the saints and sages whom the world has revered from time immemorial, all religion, all tradition, in short, all that has hitherto given meaning to human life. And, one must add, all that can still give it meaning; not a spurious meaning, as they would have it, but the only true meaning it has.

If they are right, they themselves must be the *avatars* and the prophets of a new age of realism, destined to replace millennia of delusion; but if they are wrong, the word "rubbish" applied to their work is too gentle. It is not their erudition that is in question, nor their logical consistency, nor yet their sincerity (for "sincerity" in its current sense makes no distinction between error and truth); it is the fundamental assumptions on which the logical structure of their philosophy is built.

In the case of the two philosophies here contrasted, their respective starting-points are diametrically opposed, so that, even when there is a superficial resemblance in method or in development, there is still in reality no common measure between them. The one seeks to derive principles from phenomena, the other seeks to see phenomena in the light of their metaphysical principles. The first attempts an impossible task and consequently ends up in a sort of chaos or nihilism; the second attempts a task of supreme difficulty and one that can never be fully accomplished, least of all by the unaided efforts of man, but it is the task that justifies all other tasks.

⤙⥤➤✳❮⥢⤚

Somebody may say: "Are you not doing exactly what you criticize, and trying to arrive at a principle by studying a phenomenon, for surely beauty is a phenomenon, since it is observable."

Any such question misses the point that beauty as such is not a phenomenon and is not observable; what is observable is the material or psychic entity through which beauty is manifested in some degree and in some mode. The endless variety of its modes, in each of which it can achieve a sort of perfection that reflects its universality, bears witness to that very universality, to the fact that beauty is in its essence a principle and not an accident, whether it be manifested in a flower or in a star or in a human soul.

To say that beauty is a principle or an archetypal possibility of the highest metaphysical importance, adds nothing to the direct and incalculable impact of our experience of it. That experience can to a greater or less extent carry us "out of ourselves" by giving us a glimpse of something greater than ourselves, though its vehicle may be only a humble flower. To the extent that it does so, it is an experience of the "supernatural", whether we recognize it as such or not.

Beauty is necessarily something like that, or else it is but a perishable illusion devoid of ultimate significance. If it is devoid of ultimate significance, then so is everything else, ourselves included. A rejection of the supernatural logically and inevitably leads to something like a philosophy of despair.[2] The certitudes or basic assumptions that

---

[2] One could wish that those whose religion implies an acceptance of the supernatural would apply the same kind of logic to the development of their certitude as its rejecters apply to theirs, instead of always trying to justify it in terms of morality

169

provide the starting-points of logic are necessarily themselves supra-logical, in the sense that, like existence itself or the beauty of a flower, they cannot themselves be objects of discursive proof.

There are a few people to whom flowers make no appeal. People's likes and dislikes in relation to flowers are different. The same is of course true of the perception of beauty in its many other forms. These commonplace facts may seem to support the idea that the whole issue turns on the vagaries of individual taste. But if beauty is what it has been said to be in the preceding paragraphs, its universality and tran-scendence imply that there must be some real or quasi-absolute cri-terion whereby it can in principle be judged. The distinction between good and bad taste cannot be wholly arbitrary, nor a matter of fashion or period alone, nor even of the application of any purely human standards of judgment. Distinctions of taste which arise entirely from individual or collective peculiarities are indeed of a very limited and fugitive importance. Other distinctions can however reveal differences of approach that are more profound, because they are connected with the didactic or symbolical aspects of their objects. Distinctions of taste in the floral domain are by no means always of the first kind alone; they may indeed be more revealing than distinctions applied to human artifacts, because they are uncomplicated by local or national differ-ences of style and technique.

In certain circumstances the symbolical aspect of a particular flower predominates, but that occurs only when it is used as part of some formal and established religious or traditional symbolism. One could instance the rose in the center of the cross, where the five-pet-aled flower symbolizes the "quintessence", the unmanifested *quinta essentia* which is central to the four elements and is their principle; the lotus as the throne of the Buddha, horizontal but with upturned petals, and lying on the face of the waters; or the *fleur-de-lys*, which we now know as iris, and the association of its triple form with the Trinity. In such cases the symbolism associated with each flower could be called a specialized symbolism, to which the beauty of the flower is incidental.

or of contingent advantage, which, in the nature of the case, it is impossible to do conclusively.

Here however, we are chiefly concerned with the general symbolism of flowers in its less specialized manifestations, and with the relationship of that symbolism to what would usually be regarded purely as questions of individual or collective taste.

One aspect of the general symbolism of flowers which is often overlooked is the following. As everybody knows, the function of flowers is exclusively concerned with the sexual reproduction of plants. In general those parts of a flower which we most admire, such as the petals, are secondary sexual characters, closely associated with the minute primary characters. The whole assembly is paraded and flaunted with joyful unconcern above the more mundane structural and nutritive organs, and it constitutes what is usually for us the most attractive feature of the plant. In this way flowers exemplify more completely and perfectly than any other living organisms the primordial innocence, beauty, and unselfconsciousness of the sexual function. As a symbol and as something like a perpetual renewal of the primordial Act of creation, that function is essentially sacred; but it can be profaned and prostituted by fallen man, who has lost his innocence and unselfconsciousness and can by no means recover them. The traditional restrictions and taboos which surround the sexual function in all human societies take account of these facts. To many people, especially in these days, those restrictions seem harsh and futile, or even psychologically unsound, but they are adapted to the present needs of fallen man, and above all to the safeguarding of the fate of his soul. The latter consideration plays almost no part in contemporary discussions of what has become a burning question, but it is by far the most important, outweighing all considerations of present ease.

A conscious conformity to God's laws is required of us, in exchange for our gift of free will. The beauty of a perfect but unconscious conformity is demonstrated in flowers, here and now, as a perishable symbol of that which awaits in eternity those whose conformity in this life is fully conscious.

⊷⊶⊷✹⊷⊶⊷

Each manifestation of floral beauty is in some degree unique and incomparable. A wild rose, a Madonna lily, the Pasque flower, the common primrose, most crocus species, fritillaries, lily-of-the-valley, a wild cherry or apple (the latter in its true wild form is rare), Grass of Parnassus. . . . But why continue? for the list might never end; but it can at least be restricted by considering only flowers that grow wild or can be cultivated out of doors in Britain.

Each of the flowers named is like nothing else, and it is no use attempting to compare one with another. The writer is well aware that his own individual preferences have played a large part in the choice of those mentioned, but those preferences do not signify. Some readers may wish to delete, and some to add, but that also does not signify, provided that any plant named manifests a beauty all its own, beyond compare, or, as we so significantly say, "out of this world".

There are also many less conspicuous flowers that would qualify for inclusion if they were looked at carefully enough, not least the grasses and sedges, in which beauty of form is emphasized by a relative uniformity of color. And again there are many others which are indispensable as foils or backgrounds to set off the beauty of their brighter fellows, such as the Umbelliferae, the clovers, the bedstraws, and so on. The picture is one of an endless variety of degrees and kinds of perfection, some really incomparable—that is to say, limited only by the fact that they exclude other perfections—and others of lower degree and limited in other ways. It is not wrong to use the word "perfection" in this way, although, according to the strict meaning of the word, it is an absolute and as such cannot be limited. But we are speaking of the world, and that is exactly what the world is; perfection manifested in imperfection, the absolute in the relative, the infinite in the finite; every part of the world mirrors the whole. The paradoxical or mysterious or miraculous character of the world is reflected in the gaiety, the subtlety, and the extravagance of its flowers at least as clearly as in any other way.

A gardener or botanist may have noticed that all the flowers so far mentioned are species, that is to say that they occur as wild plants in this or in some other country. They are not among the innumerable hybrids or varieties that occur only in cultivation and are now conveniently described as "cultivars". These cultivars are the result of a conscious endeavor to enhance the pleasure given by flowers by selecting forms that are larger or brighter in color or more striking in form than the wild species from which they are derived; also by providing the gardener or the buyer of flowers with a much wider choice than he could obtain if he had to rely on species alone.

These cultivars are commonly referred to as "improved" varieties; perhaps the commonest and the oldest kind of "improvement" consists in a multiplication of the petals, resulting in what we call a "double" flower. Double flowers, and flowers showing unusual size or brilliance as well as other departures from the normal occur occasionally in nature, and the development of most cultivars has started by the selection of such "sports". Their peculiarities can often be accentuated under the conditions of intensive cultivation. It is this possibility of artificial selection, often resulting in great changes in the outward forms of plants, which provided Darwin with the basis of his theory of natural selection.

Whatever may be the explanation of the beauty of wild flowers, there can be no doubt that there is a conscious purpose behind the changes brought about by cultivation; it is of course the satisfaction of the desires of mankind. As those desires have never before been so ambitious as they are today, nor the means of satisfying them so easy to come by, so it is with flowers. The contemporary desire for novelty, for sensationalism, for quantity (which includes size as well as number) is catered for by new methods of inducing variations and of speedy propagation.

To what extent and in what sense can the results of the work of flower breeders past and present properly be designated "improvement"? That work has produced many long-established favorites, the double roses and pinks, the enlarged lily-of-the-valley, the endless variety of pansies, primroses, and auriculas, the double peonies, the chrysanthemums and dahlias, fuchsias and geraniums, tulips, irises, and so on. Some of these are seen in almost every garden, and no wonder, because they have endless brilliance and charm. They are however in danger of being superseded by more recent introductions, the bewildering multiplicity of which is presented to us in innumerable catalogues in which the resources of language are strained to the utmost to describe their striking colors, gigantic size, and sensational effect.

Without attempting to deny that some of these sensational novelties are beautiful, occasionally very beautiful, it may yet be permissible to suggest that in too many cases more has been lost than has been gained. The new floribunda roses do not belie their name, but most of them are shapeless and often unbelievably crude in color; the total effect of a bed of modern roses is indeed startling, but it may be little else. The latest gladioli have the same faults; the new daffodils look like artificial flowers which in a sense they are; cyclamens, among the most subtly elegant of flowers, have become enormous, distorted, and even frilled, pansies have become huge and floppy, polyanthus primrose gigantic, sometimes frilled and even pink in color, losing all their characteristic decisive neatness; the regal pelargoniums had comparable qualities but are suffering exactly the same fate. One has sometimes got to look at the leaves to see whether a flower is a pelargonium or a petunia or a hibiscus or what. Delphiniums, larkspurs, clarkias, godetias have become like solid columns of colored crinkly paper, losing all their pristine elegance of form and marking. In short the general tendency is all towards the substitution of ostentation for elegance, crudity for subtlety, blatancy for beauty, quantity for quality. People do not seem to want to look at a flower, they want to be hit in the eye by it. The frequent sacrifice of scent to gaudiness is often lamented, but it seems equally often to be accepted as inevitable.

The concerns just expressed about what is happening to garden flowers are fairly widespread although those who hold them are in a minority. The "improved" varieties are on the whole much the most popular, and that is what makes it worthwhile for the nurseryman to produce them. The word "vulgar" simply means "popular", and popular is precisely what the taste of the majority inevitably is and always will be. We saw earlier that, beauty being what it is, the criteria of taste can never be wholly arbitrary, despite the fact that individual and collective peculiarities and fashions play a very large part in establishing them in any particular case. Those criteria cannot be defined only in terms of human reactions; the ultimate criteria can only be sought in the field of symbolism, for it is through their symbolism alone that the phenomena of this world bring us into contact with the absolute.

Now it can be asserted that the symbolism of the natural is always more direct than that of the artificial, although this does not necessarily imply that whatever is man-made in whole or in part must always in all circumstances be rejected in favor of the natural, for man was not given his faculties and powers for nothing.

The natural is nevertheless always nearer to its origin, and its origin is the Origin of all things. The work of man, or man's interference with the natural, when it is directed mainly to the satisfaction of his own desires and fancies, always tends towards forgetfulness of the

Origin. This forgetfulness grows as man takes more and more pride in his own supposed originality or "creativity". In fact no man ever created anything. The most any man can do is to play about with material and rearrange it for his advantage or amusement. However, for so long as man does not lose sight of the Origin of his material, nor of the fact that its Origin is also his own—and this implies among other things that he does not lose his humility—his work may be legitimate.

Up to a point, then, the deliberate rearrangement, encouragement, or suppression of potentialities present in living things—flowering plants for example—all lead to a certain enrichment at not too heavy a cost; although the enrichment tends to be quantitative and the loss to be qualitative. Inevitably there comes a point at which the balance tips, and thereafter erroneous tendencies reinforce one another, so that not only do losses outweigh gains, but even those gains themselves prove unsatisfying, and must constantly be replaced by others. All this is aggravated by the intrusion of commercialism, with its large-scale mechanized operations, standardization, and advertising. In the end commercialism may become virtually the dictator of taste.

That being so, one can see why the improved varieties produced in the earlier years of plant breeding are likely to be qualitatively superior to later productions. The old-fashioned roses, the cottage pinks and carnations, the double stocks, and many other old favorites, although very artificial in that they are very "double", are nevertheless still a little "out of this world", and so are the auriculas, pansies, and violas; their beauty is subtle and mysterious even when they are very "showy". The same could be said of many of the Japanese ornamental cherries, maples, and peonies. Nevertheless, the enrichment represented by these more or less ancient cultivars, as well as by many of the less vulgar of their successors, is nearly always in the realm of the quantitative and sensual; the corresponding impoverishment is always in the realm of the qualitative and symbolical. And so one can see how once again the prevailing tendencies of the day are reflected in the floral domain, this time in the department of floriculture. If they are reflected less intensely there than they are in some other sectors of the field of visual aesthetics—notably in painting and sculpture—it is because the material used is the living plant, which must at least remain alive, and while it does so can never lose all its natural characteristics.

Added to the ever-growing array of new cultivars available to gardeners, is a vast number of alien species, introduced into this country from all over the world in the past hundred years or so. A few of them have established themselves firmly in our gardens, as firmly as older introductions such as tulips, lilacs, peonies, and roses, and no less worthily. We should be poorer without *Viburnum fragrans*, the regal lily, the blue-poppy, and some of the new Rhododendrons, to mention only a few of those most widely cultivated. In all, hundreds, even thousands, of exotic species are cultivated by enthusiasts and admired by many more. The hybridizers are of course hard at work "improving" them, especially the lilies.

It has been said that a greater variety of plants can be grown in the British Isles than in any comparable area in the world, and this is probably not far wrong. Here indeed is a tremendous enrichment, horticulturally speaking; it may represent something like an *embarras de richesses*: but if so, it is surely of a fairly harmless kind. But it is confined to the relatively restricted and artificial domain of horticulture, and it is a poor compensation for another result of the artificiality of modern life, the depletion of our wild flowers.

The demand for land for residential, industrial, and recreational uses, chemical methods of weed control on farms and elsewhere, and the invasion of the countryside by a motorized proletariat, pathetically longing for virgin nature but threatening its continued existence, these and other factors are resulting in an appallingly rapid depletion of wild flowers both in quantity and in variety. The creation of "nature reserves", desirable though it be, like many other attempts to preserve a precious heritage, cannot restore that heritage. It can only preserve it as a museum specimen, no longer alive, though better than nothing.

Not only the longing for virgin nature, but also the cult of flowers so prevalent today, are above all signs of an unconscious reaction against the ugliness associated with so many of the products of an industrialized society; and that ugliness is itself a sign, a sign of the hatefulness of all that brings it about.

If a modern town were in conformity with the real needs and destiny of its inhabitants, they would love it and seek it, instead of getting out of it into the country or to the seaside at every available opportunity, often at the cost of discomfort and inconvenience. But when they do they cannot help bringing the town out with them; the car, the radio, the newspapers, the cartons; and in doing so they gradually destroy the very thing they are seeking. That thing is in the last analysis, did they but know it, not so much natural beauty as communion with God. It is this, too, that the lover of flowers is really seeking, and if he knew it, he would not be so keen as he is on their supposed "improvement"; he would be more ready to accept and to marvel, and perhaps to understand.

It is mainly field botanists and Nature Conservation societies who are aware of and lament the elimination, except in a few carefully guarded sites, of many of our rarer plants, such as the Pasque flower, the fritillary, and numerous orchids. Obvious to all is the reduction in buttercups, ox-eye daisies, harebell, primrose, cowslip, meadow saxifrage, wild daffodil, in short, of almost everything that formerly made our meadows flowery. There is also the more equivocal case of the weeds of arable land. Charlock may be dismissed as both vicious and ugly, but the poppy, the corn-cockle, the corn marigold, the bindweed, and the cornflower have been deservedly admired, though harmful to the crops with which they compete. Under the older farming methods they could usually be kept more or less in check but they could not be eliminated; modern methods are more comprehensive. These weeds, together with their no less numerous and troublesome but less visually attractive companions in the field, are not defeated yet; but if modern chemical methods are pursued and developed for a few more decades they may well be virtually eliminated.

The most recent development consists in the invention of plastic flowers. By the use of modern techniques the most conspicuous features of the forms and colors of natural or cultivated flowers can be imitated very closely; this applies particularly to lilies. If the broad decorative effect of floral arrangements were the sole criterion of the value of flowers, it would be difficult to find any plausible objection to the use of plastic flowers in appropriate circumstances. They last for ever, they need no messy water to keep them going, they are washable and can be packed away when not in use, and they eliminate all the recurrent trouble and expense associated with real flowers.

The artificial flowers of the past were usually recognizable as such and did not pretend to be anything else; they were indeed often products of a real art; one could instance the charming "flowers" made out of shells in the Far East, which are the products of a gentle and unassuming form of decorative art that charms without deceiving. It is precisely their deceptiveness that condemns plastic flowers. They represent an attempt at a complete and conclusive replacement of the works of God by the works of man, a more and more complete obscuring of the reality by the appearance, a further substitution of the spurious but plausible for the genuine and guileless; death masquerading more and more successfully as life. They are like a frozen smile on the face of a corpse. Their use in churches in substitution for real flowers is nothing less than a desecration; their use elsewhere is a manifestation of bad taste pure and simple, and is correspondingly significant.

In conspicuous contrast to the durability of plastic flowers is the evanescence of real flowers. Among the innumerable types of beauty in this world, that of flowers is both the most widespread and the most untarnished, and at the same time it is one of the least durable. The ephemerality of natural flowers is only that of the material forms through which their beauty is manifested, and does not appertain to beauty as such. Those forms are continually and rhythmically renewed. This year's dog-rose is not the same as last year's, but its beauty is the same; the quality is eternal, only its manifestation in a material form is ephemeral.

The theme of the perishability of all forms and of their rhythmical renewal is frequent in the sacred Scriptures of the world. Existence is joined to eternity not only through the qualities manifested in it, but also through its rhythms, which, as it were, compensate the irreversible and devouring character of time. We can sense this directly when the repeated and identical vibrations of a string produce a single musical note. Through flowers as through music we can perhaps learn to hear something of the "music of the spheres", wherein the rhythms of the whole creation are unified in one great song of praise.

Reginald Farrer, a great gardener and plant collector who introduced many plants from the Far East, wrote from a high alpine meadow in China in 1918:

> And if, amid the cataclysms of anguish that clamor round us everywhere nowadays, you declare that all this babble about beauty and flowers is a vain impertinence, then I must tell you that you err, and that your perspectives are false. Mortal dooms and dynasties are brief things, but beauty is indestructible and eternal, if its tabernacle be only a petal that is shed tomorrow. Wars and agonies are shadows only cast across the path of man: each successive one seems the end

of all things, but man perpetually emerges and goes forward, lured always and cheered and inspired by the immortal beauty-thought that finds form in all the hopes and enjoyments of his life. *Inter arma silent flores*[3] is no truth; on the contrary, amid the crash of doom our sanity and survival more than ever depend on the strength with which we can listen to the still small voice that towers above the cannons, and cling to the little quiet things of life, the things that come and go and yet are always there, the inextinguishable lamps of God amid the disaster that man has made of his life.[4]

The evanescence of flowers is not a matter for regret. It is an ever-present reminder of what we are. Their recurrence is at the same time a guarantee of the immutability of the qualities that so delight us in them.

The reality that can be discerned through the symbolism of flowers is itself something that can only be apprehended directly, just as their beauty is apprehended; it cannot be attained by the analytical or imaginative powers of the mind alone, and it cannot be contained by any formula. An understanding of symbolism and reflection thereon is very far from being useless, but it cannot by itself either take the place of, or bring about, the direct apprehension of reality that is prefigured in our natural and unaffected delight in flowers.

One day the disciples of the Buddha were assembled to hear him preach a sermon. But he said not a word. Instead, he stooped down and plucked a flower and held it up for them to see. Of all that assembly, only one showed by his smile that he understood.

---

[3] Whatever may be the truth of Cicero's famous judgment that *inter arma enim silent leges* ("laws are silent amidst arms"), it cannot be true that *inter arma silent flores* ("flowers are silent amidst arms"). —Editors

[4] *The Rainbow Bridge* (London: E. Arnold & Co., 1919), p. 225.

17. A Cross Awry[1]

In a modern rearrangement of the interior of a church, a large wooden cross was on the point of being hung over the altar at an angle of forty-five degrees or thereabouts, presumably for some reason claiming an "artistic" justification. The error was averted, but it may be of interest to consider why the original intention can properly be called an "error".

The cross as a symbol of the sacrifice of Christ is traditionally placed in an upright position, with the "stem" vertical and the "arms" horizontal. When it is represented on a flat stone or on paper there is always a clear indication, by lettering or otherwise, as to which side of the surface represents the top, and the cross is placed accordingly; its symbolical orientation is then independent of the position of the stone or paper. Sometimes also Christ is depicted as carrying it, but then it is in a temporary position, which has of course its special significance, but is not the position in which its principal religious significance resides. That significance is centered on the circumstances of the historical event of Christ's death, which itself is central to Christianity. Therefore the upright position is an essential part of the Christian symbolism of the cross, and must not be departed from whenever the cross is used as a Christian symbol.

A Christian need go no farther than that, nevertheless he can if he wants to, because the cross has a cosmic and metaphysical significance which includes and universalizes its historical and religious significance, without in any way invalidating or detracting from the latter. On the contrary, it universalizes and makes timeless the historical event on which Christianity is centered. The universality of the cross as a religious or "esoteric" symbol needs no emphasis: it is perhaps the most world-wide of all symbols in one form or another, not always graphic. This aspect of the matter will be returned to later. Meanwhile, the scope of the cosmic aspect of the symbolism of the cross can be hinted at, but scarcely more is possible without writing a book, or even several books.

[1] This article is previously unpublished in book form. —Editors

The cosmic significance of the cross can be considered from many points of view, of which the most relevant to the upright position of the cross is one which relates that position to the law of gravitation, the most ubiquitous and inescapable of the laws governing the universe of our experience. It is our direct experience of the operation of that law that is relevant, and not any supposed mathematical explanation of that experience. It may also be remarked in parenthesis that, if there are situations in which this law is apparently inoperative, as for instance, in an orbiting satellite, it is because the force (or tendency) of gravitation is neutralized locally and temporarily by an equal and opposite force (or tendency). The law is nowhere abolished. Our experience of gravitation is such that, wherever one may be, there is always a "down", an "up", and a "sideways". This is conspicuously the case with our situation on earth which, although it is only a particular case of a general situation, is the one that affects us directly and is therefore most relevant to our habits of thinking and best used as an example to illustrate principles.

We can only look at things effectively from what is ineluctably our human situation; and we can only look at them at all, and more particularly take any sort of synthetic view of them, insofar as the cosmos as a whole—the "macrocosm"—is reflected in man—the "microcosm". It has often been said that man is "a little universe", and it is this analogy between man and the universe that alone makes it possible for man, in one way or another and to a greater or less degree, to "comprehend" the universe, whereas no other creature can do so.

In our present situation, "down" or earthwards and "up" or skywards are specific directions wherever we may be on the earth at any given moment, if, as is natural to us, we take ourselves as point of reference. "Sideways" is at right angles to the vertical axis defined by "up" and "down", and it is represented by a surface, the surface on which life is manifested. The surface of the earth is spheroidal, as we know, but not as we feel. The manifestation of life is a resultant of the meeting at that surface of that which is above it with that which is beneath it; the radiation of the sun vivifies the earth which otherwise would contain only the potentiality of life. The cosmic cross is everywhere; its center is wherever we may be.

This, very briefly, is the macrocosmic aspect of the matter, as it affects each of us directly, and it is outward with respect to ourselves. There must be something analogous in the microcosm, and therefore in ourselves as such; but being only analogous it will not be identical. There must be a "down" in which resides the potentiality of life, and an "up" which realizes that potentiality, and an "area" in which that potentiality is manifested. The "down" corresponds to the heart, the physical center of our being, without which there is no possibility of life, and it is the psychic center as well, the two being inseparable in life; the "up" corresponds to the head, the center of intellection and control; the area in which the two meet, and which is so to speak the instrument of their joint activity, corresponds to the rest of the body. This is only one example of how the "cosmic cross" is manifested within the microcosm as well as in the macrocosm. From a different point of view the human figure, upright with feet together and arms outstretched, is also analogous to the cross in a more evident but less profound sense. These two analogies taken together can confer on the traditional figure of Christ nailed to—and thus as it were forming part of—the cross, a profundity and a universality far transcending those of the ordinary conception, but not thereby invalidating it.

Such analogies as these and those that follow are in no sense accidental. They exist simply because everything in the universe, great or small, physical or psychic, obeys the same cosmic law, each in its own way and according to its own constitution. It will be noticed that the analogy between the geometrical symbol of the cross and the constitution of the human being is connected with the "uprightness" of both. (Man occupies an upright or "axial" position; the animals are horizontal; the plants are upside down: but this suggests a digression which need not be pursued). The word "uprightness" as applied to human character gains greatly in impact from these considerations. Is it less used in that sense than formerly? If so, is that because the qualities it implies are less regarded?

Thus the cross reflects the constitution both of the cosmos and of man; the involvement of man proves (if proof were necessary) that its symbolism is not solely "material"—although Descartes did his best to limit it in that sense—but includes the psychic aspect of all that is "natural". The separation of the two aspects is in any case quite artificial.

Now, if the horizontal part represents a plane, the simple cross in most of its many forms is a two-dimensional projection of a three-dimensional figure. The horizontal plane represents existence in all its expansion, and we are on that plane, and indeed of it. Here our direct experience, which is always more real than any of its elaborations, comes in again. Wherever we may be, there is always not only an "up" and a "down" and a "sideways", but the surface of that "sideways" is defined by another cross, that is to say, by two lines at right angles, corresponding in our case to a "polar" line and an "equatorial" line, the former North-South and the latter East-West. In other words, for us there is always, not only an "up" and a "down", but also a "forwards", "backwards", "right", and "left", or a North, South, East, and West, according to whether we adopt a "dynamic" or a "static" point of view. Thus there are six directions, representing each of the three dimensions followed in two opposite senses, and each of those directions is qualitatively distinct from the other five. In the case of "up" and "down" this is obvious, in the case of the other four perhaps less so. They are most easily considered in their "static" aspects, as North, South, East, and West. In the direct experience of inhabitants of the Northern hemisphere, North is cool, South is warm, East is dry, and West is moist. In the Southern hemisphere North and South would of course be reversed, but the picture is the same. These natural characteristics also correspond to qualities or tendencies in the human soul, manifested on the plane of existence but not transcending it.

Such, very briefly, are some of what may be called the "human" aspects of the symbolism of the cross. In its cosmic and purely geometrical aspects that symbolism is of a daunting complexity. It is dealt with fully in *The Symbolism of the Cross*, by René Guénon; an English translation has been published by Luzac.[2] It includes the symbolisms of the points of the compass, the winds, the seasons, the wheel, weaving, the swastika, and many other things. Incidentally, the swastika is a vertical projection of the three-dimensional cross, in which the plane of expansion is conceived as rotating. Its use as a badge has brought it into disrepute; nevertheless, like all the other forms of the cross, its essential significance is "sacred", that is to say, it is relatable to the *philosophia perennis*, the undying wisdom that unifies all the sacred traditions, but is necessarily "mysterious", "secret", or "esoteric" because it transcends the conditions of terrestrial existence, and is therefore not accessible to a science or a philosophy based on observation. In general, the simpler the form of the symbol the less particularized it

---

[2] Republished by Sophia Perennis (Ghent, NY, 2004). —Editors

is, and therefore the wider is the range of its application. This applies fully to the cross in its simpler forms.

As an example of the complexity of these matters, an ambiguity in the interpretation of the cosmic symbolism of the cross may be mentioned, affecting the downward or earthward significance of the stem. The symbolism of "earth" can be either beneficent or the reverse, according to how it is envisaged. As pure potentiality, earth is innocent and virgin, only awaiting irradiation from above to become maternal and productive; in this aspect it is the maternal principle, also symbolized (one has to be bold to add this in the present atmosphere) by the Virgin Mary. Was not her maternity "from above", and did she not stand at the foot of the cross? On the other hand, as pure indistinction, earth is darkness and chaos; in this aspect it is the abyss, the place of obscuration and destruction. Such double meanings are frequent in symbols, but they always correspond to a reality on the plane of existence as well as on a higher plane. In the present case, earth is in fact at one and the same time the substratum of life and the destination of death. The cross itself can be a symbol of discord: two lines at right angles represent naturally two incompatible tendencies. Did not Christ himself say "I came to bring, not peace, but a sword"? These matters are not easy; but how could it be easy to understand the mysteries underlying all existence? Symbolism has to be absorbed rather than learnt; its comprehension demands an orientation of the whole being rather than a mental acuity or erudition.

The cross in its Christian version alone has many different forms. It is often multiplied by additional cross-lines added to the basic four, and so on several times over. Many Coptic crosses are of this character. It is also often combined with the circle—a symbol no less universal in many Celtic crosses. There are also special forms such as that of the "Chi-Rho" where the two Greek letters "chi" and "rho"—the first two letters of the name "Christ" in Greek—are combined to form a sign which closely suggests a perspective representation of the three-dimensional cross with an added loop. The last-mentioned form has a curious affinity with the Ankh, the "looped cross" of ancient Egypt. The simple cross appears again on the Chinese "Trigram" where two horizontal lines represent heaven and earth, and a cross between them represents man—the "mediator". In non-graphic form, the three *gunas* or "tendencies" of Hinduism, respectively upward, expansive, and downward, are regarded as inherent in the cosmos, and the qualities of every being are governed by their balance on that being. The rosary is met with all over the world in various forms; it is a multiple cross in which the cord is the axis and the beads the expansions. Their multiplicity suggests the rhythms through which the eternal act of creation is manifested in the universe.

Such instances are quoted simply as evidence of the antiquity as well as the universality of the symbolism of the cross, which is always an image of the principles on which the reality of the universe is founded. It is nothing less in Christianity, despite the fact that it is so commonly regarded as more limited in scope, as little more than a memorial of a historical event of particular significance in Christianity. The Christian interpretations of its significance are peculiar to Christianity, but the sign itself is not. To some people this fact may detract from the validity of the cross as a specifically Christian symbol; to others it may appear on the contrary that, if Christianity were to attach such fundamental importance to a symbol which was in any sense arbitrary and not founded on the deepest realities of the human situation, that indeed would constitute a serious detraction, not only from the validity of the symbol, but also from that of Christianity itself. That being the case, surely the sign as such ought to be taken to signify the universality of the essentials of Christianity rather than their specificity; that is to say, the universality, not of the outward forms of Christianity, but of the all-comprehending mystery, in itself indefinable, that inspires and validates those forms. And if that be so, there seems to be no justification for supposing that the essential significance of the sign is different in the case of the other religions that make use of it in one form or another, even though they formulate that significance in different ways. The cross is woven into the very texture of our existence outward and inward, Christian and non-Christian. The word "woven" is the right word, for there is a symbolism of weaving closely connected with the symbolism of the cross.

The cross could even be taken as the symbol *par excellence* of the transcendent unity of religions. God is One; the universe is multiple; it came from God and to God it must return. The One became many—this is the cross envisaged centrifugally—in order that the many might return to the One, this is the cross envisaged centripetally. In the Christian perspective this becomes: God became man in order that man might become God. Since man represents the universe before

God, this perspective is sufficient in itself, though it may not be the only valid perspective.

That which has no name—the non-identifiable (because both ubiquitous and dimensionless) center—deploys itself, first along the vertical (ontological-intellectual) axis, and then on the horizontal (existential) plane. Central to that plane, and therefore at its point of intersection with the vertical axis which gives access to what is above the plane and to what is beneath it, is man. All other beings are relatively peripheral and are denied that direct access. Man may look only outwards and get lost in the outer darkness of the periphery; or he may look inwards and find himself as he really is.

There remains the question of "artistic" justification. Art is symbolical and didactic; it is a means of communication more direct and less analytical than verbal communication, and far more powerful for good or for evil than is generally recognized. Formerly—for example in Europe before the Renaissance—the arts were directed mainly towards the adornment and preservation of religion and tradition. Their apparent simplicity and conventionality is in conformity with a realization, perhaps not always fully conscious, of the fact that the symbol can never be fully equated to its celestial model, and that therefore traditional rules alone can preserve it from subversive innovation. The resulting beauty is something more than purely aesthetic.

Nowadays the arts admit no such directing principle and no such discipline and have lapsed into chaos and often ugliness. The natural world is seen, not as a symbol, but as a model; first in its visible aspects which are more or less neutral, but more recently and increasingly in its inferior psychic aspects which are anything but neutral. The didactic function of art is thus being exercised more and more in an anti-religious, anti-traditional, and finally actively subversive direction, usually without any such conscious intention on the part of the artist.

The only purpose of these observations, in themselves so incomplete and leaving so many questions open, is simply to suggest the range of the implications of what at first sight may seem to be a trivial error; the misorientation of a cross.

18. A Reflection on Christmas[1]

The feast of Christmas celebrates a birth which augmented a new phase in the history of mankind.

Jesus revealed a new way of seeking the reality underlying our earthly existence; a reality that is far more profound than any conception derived from a scientific or philosophical approach can ever be; and a way which, if it is followed faithfully in thought, word, and deed, leads to the salvation of souls; nothing less is the true goal of human life.

No other imaginative event could be more worthy of commemorative rejoicings. It is not however for that reason inappropriate, especially in critical times like the present, that rejoicings should be accompanied by some thought about what the Christian way really is, lest we be unduly confident that we are on the right lines.

It is surely beyond dispute that the goal of Christianity is the attainment of the "Kingdom of Heaven", and that all Christ's teaching is directed to pointing out the way to that goal. He tells us unequivocally that His Kingdom is "not of this world", and that it is "within you".[2] For some time past it has become increasingly apparent that many professing Christians seem to be seeking a "kingdom" that is of their own imagining and more or less indistinguishable from that of their non religious contemporaries—and certainly *is* of this world and for that very reason *outside* themselves. They often speak of establishing a Kingdom of Heaven on earth, or an earthly Paradise, or of their purpose being to "build a better world on Christian principles". But if Christian principles are really as described at the beginning of this paragraph, what a bad start they are making! And what presumption! As if we were sole proprietors of this world, entitled by our superior mental powers to mold it to our own notions of what the

---

[1] This article is previously unpublished in book form. —Editors

[2] The words just quoted must be taken literally and at their face value, and so must the other Biblical quotations that follow. Too many attempts have been made to water down the words of the Bible, or to make them out to mean something different from what they say, so as to make them fit in to preconceived notions.

world ought to be like; the result would probably in most cases be more like a sort of glorified welfare state than an earthly Paradise.

An earthly Paradise or a Kingdom of Heaven on earth can only become a reality when men have abandoned their world-building ambitions and learnt that it is their own inward and spiritual state and nothing else that conditions, not only all human relationships, but also all the relationships of humanity to the outside world. When that has been learnt and acted upon, and only then, will everything fall into place. God will no doubt see to it that in the end everything does fall into place, but it will be in His time and not in ours.

Meanwhile He has not left us without guidance. It comes, for instance, and with special clarity, in the story of Martha and Mary—a vivid parable far more meaningful than any elaborate dissertation could be. The "better part" that Mary chose was (and still is) "the one thing needful". Martha's work was blameless and even necessary, nevertheless it was that which caused her to miss the indispensable thing, while Mary chose to be absorbed in the contemplation of her Master. How like Martha we are!

Contemplation is a silent, motionless, and purely receptive state, open to heavenly influences and closed to earthly ones. As humans we cannot command the heavenly influences; all we can do is to lay ourselves open to them without struggle or thought and without pre-conception; we can but listen for the "still small voice" which Elijah heard on Mount Horeb when the wind and the earthquake and the fire had passed by; the heavenly voice which is always waiting to be heard when the din and confusion of the world are stilled.

We cannot see Jesus as Mary did; but we know that he is always present and waiting to be heard whenever we can shut the world out and listen, though it be only for a few moments at a time. All this of course is no new idea; it is simply a reminder of ideas and practices that are as old as religion itself. We think that we have simply not the time, but (as my mother used to say)—"you have got all the time there is". Our outward reactions to the present situation will be governed by our inward state; but God knows best; the one sure thing is that He will not be deaf to anyone who seeks His guidance in humility and sincerity, and is prepared to wait for His reply.

The contemplative approach to worship in all its forms is simple and direct. And so, fundamentally, is the approach to Christmas, which is not an affair of difficult mental conceptions but goes straight to the heart. We know (or have we forgotten?) that "whosoever shall not receive the Kingdom or Heaven as a little child, he shall not enter therein". Certainly the shepherds and the three Kings knew what that means; they did not go to Bethlehem to talk or to think, but to lose themselves in worship.

V

LESSONS FROM LIFE

For those who are granted a long life death is not abrupt. Their final departure from the world is but the culmination of a long process; their detachment from the world is gradual, both physically and psychically, and in the course of it they become less and less "of this world". The very young are not yet fully of this world, the aged are in process of becoming less so. From God we came, and to God we must return. May those who are granted a gradual return be granted also the grace to turn it to good account.

From "Old Age"

19. Old Age[1]

Anyone who has lived for three score years and ten is old in years. He may try to think and to behave as if the greater part of his life did not lie unalterably in the past, but to do so is a refusal to face the truth. That truth will eventually be forced on him by an undeniable deterioration in his physical and mental powers.

If the whole worth of man resides in his physical and mental powers, old age is no more than a regression culminating in their total extinction. In that case the best that the individual can do for himself is to defer for as long as possible any admission of the inevitable, even to himself. The best that society can do for him is to postpone the inevitable for as long as possible and meanwhile to do all it can to make the decline as little uncomfortable as possible.

Let it be said at once that, since human physical and mental powers have their place and their value in the world, so also have the individual and social attitudes and reactions mentioned above. They are not the only possible reactions, but they are the modern reactions, almost to the exclusion of any others. They are not to be despised, but they are incomplete, for they contribute nothing towards the resolution of the perennial problem of life and death, indeed they do not pretend to do so. It is for that reason that by themselves they are unsatisfying.

Birth, life, and death are inseparable. The significance of birth and life cannot sensibly be considered apart from that of death. To consider life as a sequence of events while thrusting aside as far as possible the only absolutely predictable and absolutely conclusive event associated with it as firmly as birth is unrealistic. It is impossible to understand life without understanding death. Old age stands as it were between the two, to be understood or misunderstood accordingly. It must be accepted if it comes, and, when it is understood that acceptance is positive and can be fruitful; but when it is not understood acceptance is negative and resentful and cannot be fruitful.

---

[1] From *Looking Back on Progress* (1970). —Editors

In these days old age and death seem to be regarded as nothing more than the greatest and the most ineluctable of all the many misfortunes that mar the enjoyability of human life. Their acceptance is therefore negative and resentful. A considerable proportion of the material and scientific resources of society is devoted to the alleviation of the incapacities of old age and to the postponement of death. An indefinite postponement is even mentioned as an ideal not at present attainable, but as a not impossible final triumph of science.[2] This aversion from old age and death, together with the substitution of pity for respect towards the aged, is closely connected with the over-valuation of youth now so prevalent. Youth represents promise, but rarely does it represent anything that can be called attainment. It ought to be valued and treated accordingly.

If a completed individual life does not amount to something that can be called attainment, that life has been lived in vain. If the world as such is considered to be the supreme or the only reality, and if therefore death is a total extinction, the attainment of the individual can only be assessed in terms of the tangible residual effects on the world of his actions. Of him it can perhaps be said that he has made his mark in the world, or has made a name for himself, or has "made two blades of grass grow where one grew before". An aspiration towards an attainment of that kind is not unworthy in itself, but when there is no higher aspiration it cannot satisfy the deepest needs of the soul, because everyone knows in his heart, whether it be through the teaching of religion or of science or of common sense, that all the works of man will sooner or later be overwhelmed and lost in some kind of "end of the world", much as the works of all extinct civilizations have been lost. A few people may try to console themselves by imagining that modern civilization represents such a "break-through" as to be immune from disasters of that order, but its present state does not afford much encouragement to that belief. Instinctively we know that all that is temporal really is temporal. Even the tangible residual

---

[2] Incidentally, it is inconsistent to combine this attitude and these aims with an acute worry about over-population and at the same time the attachment of a high value to the qualities of young children. (How many people would say that without a proper proportion of young children life would not be worth having?) But that is only one of many inconsistencies characteristic of modern society, or one of the many apparent impasses with which it is faced.

effects of all actions must therefore perish, be they great or small, good or bad. Instinctively we know this, and instinctively we react, for we are not satisfied with an aim directed solely to what is known to be perishable, even though it may be relatively desirable. We seek the imperishable, the eternal, the absolute, because it is our nature to do so; the urge to do so is universal and cannot be without foundation.

According to the traditional view of the situation of man in the Universe the universality of this urge needs no explanation. Scientific man, with his different view of that situation, usually tries to explain it as the outcome of an unrealistic wishful thinking.

Anyone who accepts the traditional view in its entirety must also accept the prospect of an end of the world in the form of a "judgment"[3]. That prospect is at least as terrifying as a prospect of extinction. Indeed to anyone with any imagination it is more terrifying, and a belief in total extinction may then provide an easy way out. One suspects that not a few people prefer to believe in extinction for that reason; they are too lazy-minded to face eternity, despite their instinctive dissatisfaction with temporality.

The traditionally-minded must face eternity, and accept the implications of doing so. Those implications include an acceptance of the inevitability of a judgment which, in relation to our terrestrial life, is situated in the future. They must also include some sort of vision of the universe and of man's place in it *sub specie aeternitatis*.[4] That vision is not accessible directly to a vast majority, for whom eternity is not the ever-present reality it in fact is. By that majority eternity is usually confused with perpetuity, which is simply an indefinite period of time. Eternity transcends time. Anyone who is sufficiently traditionally minded knows that a participation in this "point of view of eternity" is what distinguishes the prophets, saints, and sages of the past from other people. In this lies the secret of their powers to move the hearts of men, not so much by argument as by way of a direct contact with the urge that lies more or less hidden or suppressed in all men, and shows itself in an ingrained dissatisfaction with temporality and a thirst for the changeless. And so, for the ordinary man, that is

[3] For an explanation of the non-arbitrary nature of God's perfect justice, see p. 67 and note 6 on the same page. —Editors

[4] Which may be roughly translated "from the point of view of eternity".

to say, for almost every one of us, "facing eternity" implies above all accepting the guidance of those prophets, saints, and sages. Thus we get back to tradition. Tradition, at least in its origins, covers every aspect of life. Our present concern is only with the aspect represented by old age.

→═◇→※←◇═←

Traditionally old age is a benediction, and the excellence of its special potentialities is recognized. Anyone to whom old age has been granted has been granted a period when less of the work of the world is demanded of him, when he has fewer responsibilities (real or imagined); it is a time when passions are less insistent, when calm, patience, and detachment are less difficult to achieve; a time in which withdrawal from the world and contemplation are natural, so that attainment can be stripped of superfluities, integrated and concentrated, and, by the Grace of God, sanctified.

Spiritual attainment alone is here in question; the time for worldly attainment is past. Spiritual attainment cannot be measured by any human standard, nor is it dependent on the particular nature of the activities of youth or of maturity, provided that those activities have been necessary and have been accomplished as well as they could be. If the soul has in it any spiritual potentiality, old age is the time for the strengthening and firm establishment of that potentiality, so that the soul may be ready for the impending transformation; ready for that passage out of the world of forms which we call death.

By turning this period to good account the aged person is not benefiting himself alone, he is also exercising the function in the world that is most appropriate to his condition. No human function is more indispensable. It is the providential function of the old, who in exercising it find their place in a traditional society, where the excellence of their function is recognized. In a modern progressive society the essential function of the old is not recognized and accordingly they have no real place.

From the "point of view of eternity", and therefore that of tradition, nothing counts in the end but the quality of the soul. That quality has been manifested in the terrestrial life of the individual; it has been as it were projected into the forms, both corporeal and psychic, which constitute the living being. Alone those forms are transitory, as are all forms, but the qualities that animate them are not so; there is no reason why they should be, for a quality is what it is and remains so, independently of its manifestation. The form of the individual perishes, but what may be called his "qualitative constitution" remains, no doubt to be projected again into a world of forms subject to conditions other than those that characterize our world, and therefore not imaginable by us.

But these are all only words. Sometimes a truth is communicated more fully and more vividly by its enactment than by words. Such, for instance, is no doubt the significance of the traditional "transformation scene" in a pantomime,[5] itself a survival of a very ancient form of dramatic art. But the transformation scene has lost its significance, concurrently with the widespread obscuration of the truth it embodies, so no wonder it is dropping out and being replaced by mere fantasies, just as are the traditional fairy stories. The passage into a different world symbolized in the transformation scene is, from the point of view of that world, a birth.

From the "point of view of eternity" birth and death are one. The fact that old age is from a terrestrial point of view a decline is neither here nor there. What, then, of that clinging to the pleasures of life so commonly regarded nowadays as the only available compensation for the incapacities of old age? In such an atmosphere nothing but pity is left for the aged, and they, like anyone else, do not want to be pitied. The fault lies with a society that fails to see that those who are granted the opportunity afforded by age to prepare for their transformation are blessed, and that their benediction could be reflected back on to the society as a whole. Not, of course, that the aged are the only people who are blessed; others may be no less so, for instance by a high spiritual attainment (in youth or maturity) or by being granted a death that is in a real sense sacrificial; but a discussion of that aspect of the matter here would take us too far from our subject.

The important thing is that the opportunities afforded by old age should not be missed. That is why, for instance, in traditional civilizations, particularly in the East, the care of aged parents is an overriding

[5] Transformation scenes such as: Cinderella—slave to princess; Snow White—dead to alive; Sleeping Beauty—asleep to awake. —Editors

duty that must be undertaken whatever the sacrifice involved may be. To neglect it is a matter for the deepest shame; the idea of allowing an aged parent to be cared for by anyone else, and particularly by the State, is horrifying. The natural ties between parent and child make the latter more suited than anyone else could be to undertake this care, but in addition their mutual affinity favors the reflection on the child of the blessedness of the parent's state. Often no doubt these ideals are not realized to the full, or even at all, in every case, but the principle is there, and the machinery for its implementation in a traditional society is there.

How remote such ideas are from those prevalent today! It would be tedious to point out the contrast in detail. Nowadays people are retiring from work or business earlier and earlier, largely thanks to public and private pension schemes, while death is postponed, thanks to new medical techniques. So-called advanced civilizations are faced with old age as a problem; there is even a new branch of medical science called "gerontology". If an increasing percentage of the population are superannuated, what are they going to do with themselves? How can boredom and futility be kept at bay?

The modern outlook on old age is based on assumptions concerning the purpose of life and the destiny of man totally different from those prevalent in traditional societies. The aged are now valued, if at all, for what they have done or are believed to have done, and not for what they are; their potentiality is supposed to have been exhausted; the potentiality they possess by virtue of their age itself is not recognized as such, and is therefore not valued. Even if it were recognized as a potentiality of sanctification—that being the shortest way of stating what it is—one cannot help wondering to what extent it would be valued. For "sanctity" is a very unscientific term. Its nature cannot be precisely specified for the reason that it is not of this world (or not wholly of this world, since it has a human aspect).

For those who are granted a long life death is not abrupt. Their final departure from the world is but the culmination of a long process; their detachment from the world is gradual, both physically and psychically, and in the course of it they become less and less "of this world". The very young are not yet fully of this world, the aged are in process of becoming less so. From God we came, and to God we must return. May those who are granted a gradual return be granted also the grace to turn it to good account.

20. The Problem of Pain[1]

The existence of pain, as well as of its correlative pleasure, or more broadly the existence of the disagreeable and the agreeable, is one of the most obvious facts of our terrestrial life. Most people probably feel that the abolition of pain appears at present too remote to be within the range of possibility, and what worries many people is not so much its existence as its distribution, which appears to be unfair as between individuals, and therefore difficult to reconcile with the conception of Divine Mercy, Justice, and Omnipotence.

Although the existence of pain or its distribution may seem to present a problem from a certain very limited point of view, it does not do so from a more comprehensive point of view. I will try to explain that very briefly. The possible ramifications of the question being endless, I cannot do more.

First, on the general question of fairness and unfairness, it is evidently no more "unfair" that one person should suffer more pain than another than it is that he should be less clever or less beautiful or less rich or less favored in any way than another. Anyone can see for himself that no two human beings are alike either in constitution or in experience, or, in other words, in form (both physical and psychic), in situation, and in destiny. This applies not only to man and to every living creature, but also to every identifiable object in the universe, otherwise those objects would not be identifiable. There can be no repetition in the universe, since any two beings or things which were alike in all respects would be not two but one. This is a "metaphysical" proposition, and that is much the same as to say that it is self-evident and that, if it is not accepted with all its consequences, it can only be ignored or misapplied, but not refuted.

The distinction between two very simple objects, like peas and grains of sand or the elementary constituents of matter (insofar as the latter are something more than mere mathematical constructions) may, as far as we can see, be only one of situation; but the possibilities inherent in an entity as complex as a human being are of a different

---

[1] This article is previously unpublished in book form. —Editors

order; human beings are therefore immeasurably more different than peas in constitution and in destiny, and always will be. This formal refutation of the possibility of any equality of nature or of destiny as between individuals may be a glimpse of the obvious, but we often forget the obvious. Inequality is the very stuff of which existence is made; it is the operative factor in the cosmic process of individuation. To refuse to accept any of the consequences of this principle of differentiation is to flout reality; it is to allow emotion to outweigh intelligence, thus depriving oneself of the possibility of understanding the universe, and that is the indispensable prerequisite for effective action of any kind.

If the problem of pain is very much to the fore at present, the main reason is simply that peoples' hopes and interests are more than ever centered on their terrestrial experience as such, and not on its ultimate significance; or, as St. Paul says, on "the things that are temporal" and not on "the things that are eternal". The pain suffered by creatures on this earth is ephemeral and not eternal—and so incidentally is the pleasure they enjoy. What matters most? The ephemeral experience or the eternal significance? If existence as a whole has an eternal significance, so has pain, for they are inseparable. And it is the eternal significance that matters, and not the actual experience, for there is no common measure between time and eternity.

Atheists and agnostics deny that existence has any eternal significance, but I am talking exclusively from the point of view of those who are sure that it has. But even they are not unaffected by the present centering of hopes and interests, in which man and his ephemeral experience become in effect the measure of all things, so that the idea of God has either to be rejected or, if it is retained, it has more and more to be modified to conform to current ideas.

Current ideas are dominated by faith in the scientific approach to truth, which is confined in principle to the domain of phenomena, that is to say, to that of terrestrial experience. In fact modern science is precisely the "intellectual" expression par excellence of that concentration of attention on "things temporal" to the exclusion of "things eternal" which gives rise, among other things, to the existence of a "problem" of pain. Being blind to the limitations of science, most people today swallow its dogmas whole, although, as any honest scientist would admit they are never more than hypotheses.[2]

The result of all this is that, involuntarily and imperceptibly, God becomes less and less the one underlying certainty, the one fixed center to which everything must be referred directly or indirectly, and more and more a hypothesis, the object of an investigation in which man is the fixed point of reference; paradise and hell become less and less "concrete" realities and more and more mere ideas; God becomes less and less absolute and more and more relative, less and less divine and more and more human. Man and not God becomes the measure of all things—even of God Himself.

In short we tend, now more than ever before, to invent a god within our own image, and to be surprised that apparently he will not join us in our well-meant endeavors to "make the world a better place", by which we mean, in the last analysis, "a more comfortable place" and nothing else. We are equally surprised at our own lack of success in that direction, and the last thing we do is to blame it on our own unwillingness to accept the realities of our situation, of which no feature is more conspicuous than its inherent inequalities in all fields and in all directions. We fail to see that God could not arbitrarily redistribute the incidence of pain or pleasure without abrogating the laws—His own laws—that make the world what it is.

All creatures are subject to those laws, absolutely and inexorably, including ourselves; the uniqueness of our present state resides in the fact that we alone can be conscious of our subjection, and by the manner of our acceptance of it can rise above ourselves towards a higher state; but this freedom necessarily implies a freedom to do the opposite. This applies as much to the manner of our acceptance of pain as to anything else; but pain in particular can be a help towards that detachment from "the things that are temporal" without which it is very difficult to become attached to "the things that are eternal", whereas pleasure is more likely to be a hindrance. That, in one sense

---

[2] This applies particularly to the dogma of progressive evolution, which poisons much thought which might otherwise be intelligent, and makes us think that we must be wiser or better or both than our predecessors, and therefore that their acceptance was less admirable than our rebelliousness.

at least, is the "eternal significance" of pain; and that is why St. Paul could thank God that he was "accounted worthy to suffer".

One is reminded of the story of the man born blind (John 9:1), whose affliction conforms fully to our broad definition of pain. The disciples asked Jesus whether it was a punishment for his sins or for those of his parents. Jesus said that it was neither, but rather than it was "that the works of God should be made manifest in him". And He gave the man his sight. May God so deal with our blindness.

21. The Ineluctable Alternative:
A Letter to My Descendants[1]

For some time I have wanted to bequeath to my descendants something to think about, and this is it. It is based on a long and fairly varied though not particularly adventurous experience, an important feature of which has been a thoroughly happy family life, enlivened and diversified by twenty-one direct descendants.

The reasons for selecting the title of this discourse will soon become apparent. Its purpose is to relate the present situation of mankind to what I believe to be the essentials underlying it. I may have tried to cram too much into too small a space, but those "essentials" are spiritual. They could never be rigidly and unequivocally defined however much space were to be devoted to them. They can only be suggested by analogies or by illustrations drawn from familiar things—or by parables. Everything is a parable—if only we could see it so!

Part I
First Principles

Whence did we come, what are we here for, and whither are we going?

It is—or at least it used to be—the function of religion to teach us about our origin, our terrestrial situation, and our end. There are of course still many people who have not wholly forgotten the teachings of religion in this respect; but there can be no doubt that most people behave, for most of the time, as if they had. Our planning and policies, decisions and actions, seem to be based on a tacit assumption that mankind is independent of any principle or power that is beyond its control and beyond its comprehension. We seem to believe that the nature and origin and end of mankind is a matter of opinion—pending

---

[1] The following is an edited version of Lord Northbourne's "bequest" to his descendants, written c. 1980. —Editors

full scientific investigation—and that meanwhile our main function is to look after our own terrestrial welfare.

Many people in the past have thought and acted more or less on this assumption; but until very recently a large majority has had no doubt that the world is in reality governed by a principle or power that is greater than itself. If that is true, then the greatest good must reside in a conscious conformity to the nature of that principle or power, insofar as human nature is able. Human nature is evidently limited in its capacity to arrive at a full understanding of that which is greater than itself.

In the past, and among most peoples, a conviction that the world is governed by a principle or power greater than itself has been axiomatic, and has been acted upon in many and various ways, never perfectly and often very badly; but the underlying idea, however it may have been expressed and acted upon, has rarely been wholly lost sight of. It has dominated all the great traditional civilizations, including of course the Christian—until (to cut a long story very short), after many ups and downs, the so-called "age of reason" appeared rather suddenly in the West. The influence of this new ideology grew steadily, but only very recently have the ideas associated with it become dominant all over the world. This age can also be called the "age of humanism", and could equally well be called the age of the self-glorification of man.

Man has increasingly usurped the place of God as supreme authority and administrator of this world, and has become the principal object of all his own endeavor and service. This development coincided with the rise of the modern scientific outlook, with its exclusively quantitative, utilitarian, and progressive aims, and with its all-pervading technological applications. A point has now been reached at which anything that cannot be fitted into the scientific and technological framework, religion and art for instance, have been relegated to the status of optional extras, luxuries, recreations, or fads.

The position is now that the point of view of humanity has changed from one that can appropriately be called "traditional" to one that can appropriately be called "evolutionist".[2] These two points of

---

[2] The author uses the term "evolutionist" to describe the now commonly held view that through a process of societal "evolution" we must be "wiser or better or both than our predecessors". —Editors

view differ fundamentally in their assessment of the primary realities underlying the existence of the universe and of man. In that respect they could be said to be diametrically opposed, and therefore irreconcilable.[3]

Since the evolutionist point of view is predominant at the moment and is therefore sufficiently familiar to us, whereas the influence of the traditional point of view has become residual and is always diminishing, it may be useful first to recall some of the essential features of the traditional point of view as it is exemplified most familiarly to us in the Christian tradition. Other traditions will be mentioned, when such mention may be useful in illustrating the universality of religion and tradition.

The word "tradition" and its derivatives are now commonly used to cover anything, however recent or trivial, that is not new and has been superseded or is likely to be so. We have no distinctive word for the sacred traditions which were characteristic of all great human civilizations.

A sacred tradition is the means whereby the doctrines, the symbols, the moral precepts, and the practices characteristic of a religion and its accompanying civilization are transmitted from generation to generation. That particular religion and its associated traditions are the vehicle of the divine revelation that inaugurated the civilization in question and made it acceptable to God. They are spiritual in their essence, but their terrestrial manifestations are temporal—and are therefore liable to change—and, like all things temporal, liable to an eventual disintegration. Meanwhile, it is the duty and in the best interests of all peoples to maintain the integrity of their sacred tradition in the face of all difficulty and all opposition. The difference between civilizations is the difference between their respective sacred traditions. The history of mankind is the history of its traditions, of their rise, their flourishing, and their eventual disintegration.

There is a word for the human attitude that is indispensable for the maintenance of the chain of tradition. That word is "orthodoxy". It means by derivation "opinion rightly directed". When society begins to believe that one man's opinion is as good as another's the

---

[3] If they are, as is now often the case, kept in separate compartments, one or the other must give way.

word drops out of use or is maligned because it suggests the control of opinion by authority. And so it does, but in a true orthodoxy the source of authority is divine and is then not open to question.

Since God is one and all true religion has its origin in a divine revelation, then there must be an overriding, imperishable, and primordial orthodoxy common to all revealed religions and traditions, uniting them all in one Spirit despite differences in their outward forms that are often apparently irreconcilable. Could it be otherwise in a world that is multiple and mutable, while the God who made it and rules over it is One and changeless?

The term "orthodox" must therefore be applicable to all revealed religions in an extended sense, and not confined as it often is to the internal affairs of a single religion. Its meaning is then equivalent to the words "in an unbroken line of descent from a major divine revelation", and it will hereafter be used in that sense. The religions that can properly be considered "orthodox" in the sense just defined are broadly those that are commonly called the "great religions". They differ widely one from another in their outward forms, doctrinal, ritual, and moral or legislative.

The plurality of religions in the world presents a real difficulty to some people even if they are not in principle unfavorable to religion. The forms of religion, they say, differ so widely as to be mutually incompatible, and they cannot all be right. This is of course a shallow view, but nevertheless for some people it serves to confirm a tendency toward the rejection of all religion, while for others it favors the acceptance of one religion on condition that all others are denied any real redemptive value.

This last view (which was perhaps more widely held in the past than it is now) is not consistent with the broader view that it is difficult to believe in an all-powerful and all-merciful Creator who may be supposed to have condemned all but an insignificant handful of humanity, past and present, to live without hope of redemption. This broader view implies the adoption of a respectful and charitable—and not merely tolerant and still less patronizing—attitude to religions other than one's own.

It is natural and legitimate to claim that one's own religion is the best, since it is in fact the best for those for whom it was destined; but that does not justify the denigration on principle of all other religions, lest we be in fact setting ourselves up against what God has blessed.

Human groupings differ in mentality, temperament, and background. Just as there is no knowledge, so there is no religion, save in the mode of the knower. The spiritual needs of different human groupings are fundamentally the same; but those needs cannot be met by identical formulations. There is an analogy with beauty, in which a mysterious element is combined with a physical form. A human body, a melody, a flower, and a cathedral can all manifest beauty, but who can say that the beauty of one is greater or less than the beauty of another? And who dares to say that beauty itself is but an accident existing only in the mind of the human subject, or that it is not a quality of divinity itself and a manifestation of the "eternal" in the temporal? So it is with the things of the Spirit; and so it is too with the "great religions".

What is the traditional view of the function of mankind? The basic answer to that question is expressed in different ways in different traditions. I will choose here the expression likely to be most familiar to my readers. The book of Genesis says: "In the beginning God created the heavens and the earth." Here God is the supreme cause, and as such He is Absolute, Infinite, and Eternal. Only His creations are limited, and they are so without exception, from the universe as a whole to a man or an atom. In other words, they are relative and not absolute, and moreover, since they had a beginning they must also have an end.

Among those creations is man, who was created last and in God's own image and likeness, and was given dominion over all creatures. This implies that man has a unique position. In fact, man alone is fully conscious, and so can be conscious of his own situation, not only in relation to all other creatures, but also in relation to God himself. Nevertheless, because of man's limitations, he cannot comprehend God's limitlessness in all its fullness, but he can have a sense of God's supremacy and inescapability, and of his own total dependence.

This clearly implies that man has a very special function, which is no less than that of representative of God in the world. That function is to keep the world in touch with God, in order that when the world comes to an end it may be fit to be reabsorbed into the Substance of its

Creator. Such is the end of all things created. Whatever is compatible with that Substance will live for ever, and whatever is incompatible with it must be purified in the fire either in this life, or in the next.

The all too obvious existence of evil makes it difficult for some people to believe in a God who is absolute Goodness and Mercy. Yet if we allow, as we must, that God is One, Absolute, and Infinite as well as All-merciful, and that He created the world, the rest follows. This world and all it contains, and all other worlds as well, owe their existence to God's Infinity. Infinity is not infinite unless it comprises not only all that is, but also all that is possible. There are possibilities of unity and of harmony, and also of multiplicity and differentiation; the latter lead to incompatibilities and oppositions. With these last comes the possibility of evil. Thus even evil as such is a necessary element in the complete fulfillment of God's purpose, though seen as a whole that purpose is wholly good. "And God saw everything that he had made, and, behold, it was very good" (Gen. 1:31).

But if evil is a manifestation of God's ultimate purpose, it is so by way of negation and not by way of affirmation. That is what Meister Eckhart was thinking of when he said of someone who was accused of blasphemy, "The more he blasphemes, the more he praises God." So evil must be purified, but thereafter God takes all things back to Himself.

Humanity has an essential part to play in this return to God; let us not therefore refuse to accept the part allotted to us. For humanity as a whole represents the spiritual center of the world; its function is akin to that of a priesthood or an aristocracy, and it carries all the obligations of that status. Those obligations comprise, in the first place to praise God, to pray to Him and to thank Him on behalf of the world (one might say to be articulate on behalf of a world that can only worship mutely), and then, in his dealings with the world to practice nobility (not of rank but of soul), generosity, mercy, justice, sacrifice, and humility before God and the beauty of His works.

Man's true worth does not reside in his temporal achievements, nor in his accumulation of material wealth or of a factual knowledge that is mainly quantitative and impossible to unify, nor in his ingenuity, nor in a purely aesthetic culture, nor in all these things put together. Man's true worth lies in the effectiveness of his mediatorship between God and the world. Insofar as he submits himself to his worldly desires instead of to God, he reduces himself to an insignificance comparable to the insignificance of his physical existence in time and space in relation to the unimaginable extent and duration of the physical universe.

Such, in a very synthetic and summary form, is the traditional view of the collective function of mankind. The function of the individual is of course closely related to it. Each individual is free, within the limits of what is possible for him, to choose his own path. He must do so in a manner that contributes to the fulfillment of the collective function.

In relation to his own soul, and in that respect alone, everyone is in a unique position in which he alone has the last word. It has often been suggested that an aspiration for the salvation of one's own soul is "selfish", because our aspirations ought to be directed to the good of others rather than our own. But that aspiration is anything but selfish, for three reasons. The first reason is that to seek to purify the ego is something very different from seeking the worldly satisfaction of the ego which alone constitutes selfishness. The second reason is that you cannot do your neighbor any good unless you yourself are a sincere seeker after that which alone is wholly good, and thus have some experience of the way that leads to it. The third reason is simply that the salvation of your own soul is the part that is specially assigned to you, and to you alone, in the fulfillment of the true function of all humanity. It is precisely "your business" as nothing else ever can be.

Thus the salvation of your own soul is the best thing and the most charitable thing you can aspire to, not only for your own sake but for the sake of your fellow human beings; and not only for them but also for all creatures, great and small, high and low, which by themselves do not have the freedom of choice that you enjoy, and which are much more dependent on us than we usually think.[4]

---

[4] Not for nothing, and least of all for our own satisfaction alone, were we given dominion over all creatures. It was given to us in order that we might exercise our true collective function of mediatorship between heaven and earth with authority and without hindrance. When we neglect that function our relationship with other creatures becomes equivocal, a mere balance between predation and sentiment, while at the same time our right to exercise dominion over them is forfeited.

The alternative to accepting in its essentials the traditional view is to accept the evolutionist view that the human race is the culminating point in a global process of evolution from a "lower" to a "higher" state. The origin of humanity is attributed to a chance interaction of physical forces. The function of humanity is to look after itself by the operation of the superior mental powers that have evolved within it. The goal of humanity, as well as its foreseeable end, is a temporal and terrestrial utopia. The end of each individual is extinction.

The word "progressive" is often used, and almost always implied in connection with the word "evolution". This shows that evolution is considered to be a movement from something less good towards something better. Whatever that may be taken to mean, the idea is wishful rather than objective. That is why many scientists are anxious to find "proofs" of its validity by the study of natural phenomena.

The objectivity of the scientific outlook is real enough when it is confined to the study of natural phenomena, but not otherwise.[5] When this outlook is dilated with a subjective optimism, the phenomena that seem to confirm that optimism are subconsciously selected for study, so that the resulting "proof" is biased.

The unbiased scientific picture of the universe is terrifying and purposeless; popular opinion instinctively—and rightly—revolts against it, since people cannot live without hope. Evolutionism seems to offer a hope, though it be centered on nothing more than a variety of purely imaginary utopias, more and more distant and more and more improbable, all confined to space and time and to the other conditions of our terrestrial existence, and therefore all fugitive.

Science is still hunting in this physical universe for primary causes, inevitably in vain. The findings of science are not wrong as far as they go; they are true within the limit which science imposes on itself as a matter of principle, and that is why they work—but only up to a point. The result of the limitation of relevance to whatever is measur-

---

[5] The modern scientific outlook claims for its findings a validity superior to findings arrived at in any other way. It has in effect become the final arbiter of truth. Modern science used to be called "natural" science, and still is so sometimes, but the limitative significance of the word "natural" has been lost sight of. In fact the supernatural has been excluded on principle, because it is neither observable nor measurable. The result is a questioning of the reality of the supernatural, or at least of its relevance.

able is that science cannot rightly claim to have anything whatever to say about, for instance, beauty or love or sanctity, or religion.

Most reputable scientists would indeed admit that a final solution to the problem of existence is nowhere near to being within the reach of the methods of science, and perhaps may never become so. And they would be right. The primary mystery, the real problem, and the real wonder does not reside in what things look like and how things behave in different circumstances, but in the fact that there is anything at all—anything observable and still more anyone to observe it.

The outlook on which the development and popularization of modern science is based has temporarily deprived humanity of a living sense of the transcendence and the unity of truth and of the mystery of its own existence. Nevertheless, that sense—call it a knowledge or a wisdom or a humility or all three—has always existed in the hearts of men, however hidden it may have become in some periods of history or in some places. It is indestructible and will reveal itself again and again for as long as there is a humanity to receive it, as indeed it has done in the past. Meanwhile it is latent in every human being born into the world. It will become real only to one whose heart is in a fit state to receive it. For such a person it will do so however unfavorable outward circumstances may be.

How wonderful it is, then, to have been born into the human state, and to be among the only creatures that can have a sense of the mystery of their own existence and the existence of all that is other than themselves!

But a mystery remains a mystery; as such it cannot be fully resolved and must be accepted as it is or not at all. Since it reveals itself to human societies or individuals who differ widely in qualities and in capacities, it necessarily does so in endless different forms, and in the shape of symbols adapted to each recipient of the revelation. Humanity can do no more than cherish the symbols, knowing that they point the way to a full realization of the truth, even though it may only come to the vast majority at death.

Small wonder that our favored position imposes obligations on us, and that it involves us in the making of a choice.

⟶⟾◇→※←◇⟽⟵

At some time in our lives each of us has to make a choice. Under present conditions that choice presents itself to us most clearly as one between the traditional and the evolutionist points of view. It has something absolute about it, for we shall not get a second chance. We can neither stand still nor move in two contrary directions at once. We must choose one way or the other, since the flux of time keeps us moving inexorably forward. We are compelled to choose between the "Kingdom of Heaven" and the "world"; between the service of God and the service of Mammon.

Nearly every contemporary influence is directed towards the choice of Mammon. That is what makes it so difficult for anyone living today to make the right choice. The normal corrective influence, that of an established and unquestioned religion and tradition, is obscured; religion is in the melting pot, tradition is mostly in abeyance and what remains of it is regarded chiefly as something to be improved on. False guides, mostly claiming some religious or traditional authority, are rampant. Some are plain frauds, some are deceiving themselves as well as others; some have an enormous following.

Despite all these difficulties—of which God is well aware—everyone who is born into this world faces an ineluctable alternative which affects his fate for good or for ill.

The natural question arising out of all this is "What ought I to be doing about it?"

There is one thing that ought to be said before going any farther, namely, that it is impossible to put the clock back. We are living here and now and cannot live in the past, however hard we may try to do so. Nor can anyone live in the future, though that seems to be very much what this generation, animated as it is by the notion of progress and obsessed with long-term planning, is trying to do. Here is here and now is now, and we cannot get away from that.

It should already be clear that there is at least one thing that is necessary and possible for almost anyone, whatever his individual gifts or situation may be. That is to confirm and strengthen an existing affiliation to an orthodox religion—or, of course, if no such affiliation exists, to seek one.

Affiliation involves an initiatory rite (e.g., baptism), a whole-hearted acceptance of a doctrine, accomplishment of a ritual, and conformity to a code of behavior. Such an attachment is far from being an affair of the mind alone with all the mutability of an ideology; it is a mystical incorporation into a spiritual chain of tradition, and as such it attaches the whole being, body, mind, and spirit. Its effect is not to guarantee salvation, but to confer a potentiality of salvation. That potentiality must be developed by the individual's own efforts and above all by his sincerity and perseverance in prayer, in order to make the affiliation effective. Those efforts are the measure of the strength of his faith.

Religion is not an easy way out; it demands dedication and sacrifice. The word "sacrifice" means properly "to make sacred" and not merely "to give up", though it may involve the latter, even to the extent of giving up life itself.

All this was easier when the authority of religion, and indeed its very nature, were less questioned. Nevertheless, despite the existing confusion of ideas, the symbols wherein the essentials of religion are enshrined are still in the main accessible. Such symbols may be verbal (as in the Scriptures) or ritual (as in the Eucharist) or in some other form (as in the cathedrals). Neglect or misunderstanding, however widespread, does not impair their intrinsic significance, which is real and not merely fanciful, and remains always accessible.

There is an important reservation to be made here, and it is one that always applies when matters of spiritual import are in question. We are told that "the wind bloweth where it listeth and thou hearest the sound thereof but canst not tell whence it cometh or whither it goeth" (John 3:8). The "wind" is the spirit, and we cannot foresee its impact. God is the Judge (and there will be many surprises in the day of judgment). Nevertheless, man was not given his discriminatory faculties for nothing; God has pointed out a way that is broadly definable. Therefore it is not presumptuous to assert that anyone who has a valid attachment to a traditional orthodoxy is at least very much more likely to find salvation than one who has no such attachment, although "with God all things are possible" (Matt. 19:26).

Part II
Principles in Practice

What I have said so far may seem to be related more to principles than to practice. The element in religion primarily concerned with principles is the doctrinal. It is fundamental, but ineffectual unless it is translated into practice by the other two elements, the ritual and the moral.

The ritual element covers the specifically ordained and regular observances that are essential for a full and effective participation. It is more positive in its operation than the moral element, which is concerned with general behavior at all times, and particularly with the avoidance of errors—or sins—that are harmful to the soul as well as to other people. The moral element has a purifying rather than a constructive function, and that is why it is insufficient by itself, though each element reacts on the others.

Although every man is in the last analysis alone with God, he is at the same time a social being. His relationship to God must therefore find a collective expression, and it can do so only in some form of "organized" religion, the purpose of which is to support and to direct the individual's personal—and necessarily lonely—relationship to God.

The word "religion" is often loosely used. I use it here so as to cover only such religions as I believe can rightly be considered as originating in a direct divine revelation of which they are subsequently the vehicle. Nothing less can effectively be a meeting-place between the divine and the human, which is what religion is. Such a religion is a unique and coherent whole, much as a living being is. Like a living human being, it can be considered as comprising a divine component and a human component although it is in principle one and indivisible. The divine component is invisible, mysterious, changeless, and impregnable. The human component is visible, comprehensible, changeable, and vulnerable, and it alone is perishable.

Neither Christianity nor any other revealed religion brings a new truth. Each brings truth itself, the truth that does not change with time and place, but is eternal and universal, the truth that is the origin, sustainer, and end of all worlds.

What each religion does is to clothe that truth in a new garment, the form of which is unique and providential, and fulfils the needs of its destined followers as nothing else could. Every orthodox religion plays a necessary part in the working out of God's over-riding plan, and in its essence, though not in its form, it always has been and always will be, "Before Abraham was, I AM" (John 8:58). To see Christianity in this light does not detract from its validity or its completeness; on the contrary, it enhances them by emphasizing its universality and all-sufficiency and by clarifying the nature of its very real and providential uniqueness.

It is only the human and formal component of religion that can decline and perish, and must do so. It will be replaced by a successor as and when God may decide; but the essence of religion is imperishable and while there is a humanity in this world, that humanity must be its guardian. This is true even when most of humanity may seem to have abandoned or distorted almost all religion. At such times the task of its preservation rests with a minority whose names are known to God alone.

In most religions there is an "exoteric" or popular branch and an "esoteric" or more intensive and specialized branch. The latter is generally more directly concerned than the former with the preservation of the essential and universal truths of religion and with what may be called its metaphysical content; but everyone whose faith is impregnable and who lives accordingly has a part to play.

The word "metaphysical" is etymologically equivalent to the word "supernatural". Among the "supernatural" and therefore mysterious elements in this world are certain qualities in which God manifests Himself more directly than in others. We call them "sanctity" in human beings, "sacredness" in the non-human, and "holiness" in either. Reverence and awe rather than inquisitiveness are the appropriate human attitudes towards the beings or objects that embody these qualities. In these days, however, those qualities, when their reality is admitted at all, are usually belittled or distorted under the microscope of scientific—or pseudo-scientific—enquiry. Human sanctity becomes a psychological phenomenon in principle explicable, whereas it is in fact essentially a divine intervention and as such it is inexplicable.

The word "saint" is usually applied to someone who is no more than very virtuous, and for that reason alone. Of course a real saint is virtuous, but he is so because he is a saint and not the other way round. His sanctity presupposes virtue, but is on a higher plane; it is infinitely precious, for its radiance, even when it is not perceived or recognized for what it is, keeps mankind in touch with God and, through mankind, the rest of the world as well. Saints do not speculate about the hereafter, they see it.

The greatest lack in the world today is its lack of saints. A few there are no doubt; but they may be anywhere and in any walk of life, and they are rarely if at all recognized or valued for what they are. They are the very embodiments of religion and all that it stands for, and they normally adhere to its forms more firmly than other people. Meanwhile the saints of the past are accessible to us, not only through their own writings and those of their devotees, but no doubt also more mysteriously through our own attitude to them.

Miracles also are direct divine interventions. They are phenomena, but are supernatural rather than natural. For that reason their occurrence cannot be accounted for in terms of experience based on observation alone. Phenomena that appear to be miraculous, or can be made out to be so, can however arise from a variety of causes, even from causes that are diametrically opposed, as are the divine and the satanic. There are plenty of people ready to be deceived; but this does not invalidate the real miracle that comes from God.

Existence itself is a miracle. Since everything came from God, everything exists by Him, and everything returns to Him; therefore in principle everything is sacred. And so it was in the beginning, and so it remains, except where man is concerned. Man alone can rebel against God and through man comes corruption.

The most familiar aspect of the uncorrupted work of God is what we call virgin—or more commonly "unspoilt" Nature, and its corruption is what we now call "pollution", which includes the destruction of natural beauty and its replacement by ugliness, in addition to poisoning by chemicals and over-exploitation of all kinds. The sacredness of virgin Nature is reflected in its beauty and its innocence, which shine through even its more rigorous aspects—the storm, the desert, the heat and the cold, the ubiquity of hardship and death. It can remind us that all is not yet lost and can never be wholly lost.

Virgin Nature is under attack by us as never before. We cannot live without her; but I cannot help wondering whether she, and with her humanity, can be preserved otherwise than by the abandonment, or more likely the collapse, of our present competitive and industrialized civilization.

To live in harmony with Nature is an ideal that cannot be realized for as long as our demands on her remain anywhere near what they are now. If Nature was made for man, man also was made for Nature. We cannot neutralize our failure to exercise our cosmic function of mediatorship between Heaven and earth while we continue to pillage and pollute Nature, nor yet by treating her as a museum for scientific study, nor as a reserve of genetic potentiality, nor as a recreation ground; for in a very real sense Nature is our "Mother" even as God is our "Father". That is one reason, and an important one, why a decline in religion involves a decline in everything else. We are not involved in an unfortunate concurrence of numerous unrelated phenomena, but rather in one single comprehensive phenomenon.

I must now deal briefly with some features of the present decline in religion and some of their consequences. Christianity alone will be considered here, although most other religions have undergone a decline that is in many ways comparable. In all cases that decline is more important for its qualitative than its quantitative aspects.

Religion everywhere is fiercely attacked by enemies from without. The open attack, such as that of Communism, is probably less dangerous than the insinuations of a secular philosophy, or the parodies of truth that emanate from the innumerable new cults that are now so fashionable. The decline that originates internally is more dangerous than any attack from outside.

The earlier symptoms of decline included a subdivision into numerous denominations or sects, each claiming to represent the revelation more truly than others. The situation in that respect is sufficiently familiar to everyone. This phenomenon has been accompanied by a growing emphasis on the moral element in religion, as against the doctrinal and the ritual elements. The latter have been replaced in varying degrees by a moralistic ideology based on sentiment.

Sentiment, or "feeling", is a universal characteristic of humanity, and together with intelligence and will it has a necessary part to play in the salvation of souls. These three elements must however be sufficiently well balanced if the integrity of a religion—or of society—is to be maintained. By themselves, intelligence is cold, will is violent, and sentiment is unstable. When, as now, sentiment gets the upper hand its instability becomes dominant. This change has led to a preoccupation with social reform, and thence to incursions into the field of politics, sometimes culminating in the active support of purely political movements that are anything but religious in their origins or tendencies. This development has been rightly described as the "secularization" of religion. It could also be described as a systematic reduction of religion to the commonplace. Among its more conspicuous symptoms are an obsession with liturgical and ritual innovations and with new versions of the Scriptures, and the adoption of more or less democratic forms of Church government, which tend inevitably to mediocrity of judgment, even in matters of the highest spiritual import.

These changes are justified by their sponsors as being adaptations to the modern world; and that is exactly what they are. So much the worse for them. The secular dogmas of progressive evolution and of egalitarianism have replaced many traditional dogmas, and have at the same time whittled away the authority of the religious leadership, the main function of which is to act as custodian of the integrity of the chain of tradition that leads from the revelation to the present day.

Adaptations have been considered necessary in the past in order to compensate as far as possible the inevitable consequences of a growing remoteness from the original revelation, but never before has adaptation been accompanied to the same extent by an abandonment of tradition and an abdication of ecclesiastical authority. Yet never before has it been more necessary to cling at all costs to the strictly traditional elements in religion, and, incidentally, to their reflection in the organization of society. A stable organization cannot come about by any purely human planning, but only by way of the prevalence in society of a realistic sense of the origin, function, and end of mankind, which it is the special function of organized religion to inculcate and to preserve.

"Religion has failed" say its critics. They do not understand that it is not religion but those who analyze, criticize, and neglect it who have failed in the first duty of humanity which is precisely to be religious (since no other creature can be) and that humanity has through its fault lost its sense of direction.

The formal aspects of religion—doctrinal, ritual, organizational, and legislative—are crumbling like other human institutions. Its inward or spiritual or mysterious aspects are what they always were and always will be. The latter can never be wholly hidden for as long as a world and a humanity exist. If they were wholly lost the world would cease to exist, since it would then be completely cut off from both its cause and its fulfillment. If the world were to lose contact with its Cause it would instantly evaporate into nothingness. Humanity is, through religion, a necessary link in the maintenance of that contact.

While there is a world and a humanity the "undying wisdom" or *philosophia perennis*, which constitutes the heart of all true religion cannot be wholly lost, though it may be hidden from a majority of mankind at certain periods. That is why the words "seek and ye shall find, knock and it shall be opened unto you" are as true today as they always were and always will be. Seek with humility and patience; knock with perseverance and confidence. You cannot know what you will find until you have found it; you cannot tell what the opening of the door will reveal until you have seen it. Such is the great adventure of faith.

Like all adventures it is risky (for if it were impossible for it to go wrong it would not be an adventure) and it involves concentration on a goal and the sacrifice of anything that could impede the attainment of that goal; and this implies a discipline. (Note that in this connection the word "sacrifice" is used in its original sense, that of "making sacred"). In these days such a discipline must be mainly self-imposed because so little support for it can be found among the distractions and deceptions of the modern world. The saving power of all revealed religion survives and can never be destroyed, though its accessibility may be diminished by attempts to adapt doctrine, ritual, and forms of worship to contemporary heresies, prejudices, and fantasies. Something always remains. Even the dominance of church buildings in the landscape is of real significance as a symbol and a reminder of a truer hierarchy of values than that now exemplified in the tower block and the power station.

Membership of a Church is useful as a discipline, a support to individual effort, and a witness to the indispensability of faith. The scriptures and liturgy especially in the older forms reflect something of the beauty, the solemnity, and the mystery of the relationship between man and God.

Then there is reading. In these days it is not easy to choose wisely, because we are faced with a mass of literature on an unprecedented scale, most of which is, from our present point of view, at best unprofitable and at worst pernicious. The choice arrived at must depend very much on the kind of approach that appeals to the individual: for example, the metaphysical approach is very useful to some people while to others it is merely confusing. It is important to find if possible an approach that is congenial and to follow it. The Bible, of course, is in a different category. It must be read, but not critically nor analytically nor impatiently. The version chosen must be one in which the words themselves are memorable, quotable, and beautiful. It must be allowed to reveal itself according to the capacity of the reader and it will do so according to his familiarity with it.

I have already referred to the essential virtues. They can be summarized as being: detachment and humility, courage and perseverance, patience and thankfulness, hope and trustfulness.[6] The most direct approach of the soul to God is, however, through prayer. All other approaches, including the practice of the virtues, are indirect, however necessary they may be. Prayer in all its forms—and they are many—is the very essence of man's relationship to God; it alone keeps the world in touch with God, thus fulfilling the purpose for which man was created. Prayer in any form is a conscious acknowledgment of the Presence of God. Its neglect is a forgetfulness of God, and therefore a forgetfulness of what we really are and why we are here. Prayer is the remembrance of God, and the remembrance of God is prayer. The greatest need of the world (non-human as well as human) is prayer—and man alone can pray.

There is nothing better that anyone can do than to cultivate the practice of prayer as far as his gifts make it possible for him to do so; and since all prayer is in the last analysis wholly inward, nothing and nobody can stand in his way. However legitimate and necessary any activity may seem to be, still the remembrance of God is best—and the two need not in fact be incompatible.

In the past most occupations were far more compatible with prayers than they are now. Many of the older ones would now be classed as "drudgery"; but they were at least simple and directly

---

[6] Love, wisdom, and sanctity are goals rather than virtues, though the practice of the virtues is indispensable for their attainment. It purifies the soul in order that it may be fit to receive the influx of the Divine Grace which is always waiting to enter into it.

related to basic human needs, as well as to Nature. Ecclesiasticus says of people thus occupied: "the handiwork of their craft is their prayer." Not so the service of a machine devoted to quantity production, and ministering largely to the superfluities and the artificialities of the modern world, depriving the worker of the opportunity of a vocation to which he can dedicate his gifts as he was able to do in a world which, whatever its faults, had got its priorities more nearly right than we have.

Anyone who is moved in these days to try to integrate prayer with daily life, or at least to give it a more important place than it has held in the past, must therefore be prepared for difficulty. A profound conviction backed by much determination and patience is indispensable, as well as a traditional starting-point and permanent support. Fortunately such a starting-point is not lacking in anyone to whom these words are addressed, for a Christian baptism is valid for life. Baptism is our initiation into the orthodoxy of Christianity. As such it does not guarantee salvation, the attainment of which depends on baptism being effectively followed up; it does however validate the use of all the traditional rites, practices, and teachings of Christianity (except the central rite which demands a second initiation called "confirmation"). A valid way is therefore open to you all.

A correlative necessity is a discipline. Discipline means not only the control of behavior and of thought, but also the establishment of a regular program. In this last respect regular attendance at church services has a part to play, and so has a regular period allotted to reading; but even more important in these difficult days is regularity in the practice of private prayer. Regularity needs as a foundation two or more periods a day of at least ten minutes in tranquility and solitude. To these other periods, long or short, can be added according to individual aspirations and opportunities.

A state of perpetual prayer (the "prayer without ceasing" of St. Paul—1 Thess. 5:17) has been attained by a few—not necessarily recluses—but there are very few who are qualified to aspire to such heights. There must be many who could, if they would, aspire to take at least a few short steps in that direction, and there is nothing to prevent anyone so moved from doing so. Any such aspiration involves not only making good use of times not otherwise usefully occupied, but also interrupting or accompanying, be it only occasionally and for a few moments, most daily occupations with a short and simple prayer—a few words or silent thoughts of praise or gratitude or supplication.

The establishment of such a habit under present conditions of rush and worry and conflicting counter-attractions may prove at first so difficult as to be virtually impossible, and so no doubt it is for some people; but it must not be forgotten that what is impossible to man is possible to God, and that therefore help and guidance must above all be sought directly from Him. God does not try a soul beyond its powers. Even so, periods of lassitude and discouragement are sure to be met with and must be faced.

Nothing of what I have just suggested is incompatible in principle with the sort of life any one of you is leading or may legitimately hope to lead, or with a life that may be imposed on you by future circumstances not under your control; for all real prayer springs from the inmost recesses of the heart, where it is a secret shared only between the individual and God. Nothing is hidden from God. He hears every sincere prayer addressed to Him by anyone, whatever may be his situation, and no such prayer is ever wasted. The question we so often ask ourselves—"What am I to do?" is always best answered by first turning to God.

Truth is unchanging and it is the same for all. Comprising as it does all unity and all multiplicity it cannot be isolated and grasped by a single mind which, however exceptional its capacity may be, is but a fragment of a fragment of the whole. Nevertheless, God—who is Truth itself—has decreed that man alone of all His creatures can sense the direction in which truth lies. God has provided a rope to cling to as man struggles upwards towards the invisible summit to which the rope is attached. That rope is woven of religion and tradition, and only if we cling to it in faith, perseverance, and prayer can we play the part assigned to us as human beings in the scheme of things, thus becoming worthy of our calling.

Was Jesus a social reformer? Surely it is evident that he takes for granted obedience to the temporal power and rejects social reform or political revolution as such. It is Judas Iscariot who was the disappointed revolutionary. Could anything be more specific than: "Render unto Caesar the things that are Caesar's, and unto God the things that are God's"? (Matt. 22:21). What Jesus offered was redemption and salvation, to be attained by way of a purely inward change of heart, a "rebirth" transcending all outward circumstances and of infinitely greater value than anything outward circumstances can supply.

At the same time, He tells us that if we seek first the Kingdom of Heaven, all we need on earth will be added unto us. To seek the satisfactions and pleasures of this life first is to relegate the Kingdom of Heaven to second place. Not only must it be sought first, but also for its own sake alone, and not with a view to procuring any terrestrial advantage. And the Kingdom of Heaven must be sought where it can be found; that is, "within you", in the secret and inmost heart which is known only to each one of us and to God. Only when men's hearts are filled with His Presence will everything else fall into place; for God works in this world through the hearts of men, if only they will allow room in their hearts for Him.

Once, nearly two thousand years ago, there was no room in an inn. The inn, the busy and crowded place, is the image of men's hearts. So Joseph and Mary had to take refuge among the animals in a stable. I recall a little poem, quoted in a sermon by the late Bishop Rose, of which he could not give me the source. It runs as follows.

I saw a stable, rude and very bare, / And a little child in a manger, / The cattle knew him, had him in their care, / To man he was a stranger. / The safety of the world was lying there, / And the world's danger.

One hears a lot of talk about the need for us to "build a better world" and we are pestered with conflicting policies, reforms, reorganizations, and long-term plans meant to create this terrestrial utopia. But if the word "better" does not mean "nearer to God", all those maneuverings will lead to nothing but growing confusion and, in the end, to utter darkness.

A better world will come no doubt, and it will be a world that is nearer to God; but it will come in God's time and not in ours, and by His means and not by ours, and not until we have abandoned our pride in our own achievements, nor until everything that is incompatible with a Kingdom of Heaven on earth has been swept away.

We must choose our ultimate goal, for the tendency of all plans is conditioned by it. All I have tried to do is to indicate the nature of the two goals between which a choice must be made, the one eternal, the other temporal. For the present the second way has been chosen, and the resulting confusion has led to the individual having been to a great extent deprived of the collective support that is normal in human society. Let him therefore remember, when he feels lost, that he is in fact alone with God. Then, God willing, he may find peace in that very loneliness, in the peace of God that passeth all understanding. And with it may come the light of the Truth that underlies our situation here on earth; for we are strangers here and we seek a way home. That Truth is the only "treasure" worth possessing, for where it is "there shall your heart be also". How marvelous that it should be within our reach!

So let us not squander this precious life in the exclusive pursuit of the things that are temporal, but rather let all our thoughts and actions be illuminated by the truth that conquers all things; for in this life all can be won and all can be lost.

There is a Chinese proverb I like very much: "It is better to light one candle than to curse the darkness." St. Paul says (in Rom. 12:21) "Be not overcome of evil, but overcome evil with good." Job says (in Job 13:15) "Though He slay me, yet will I worship Him."

This short survey of what I believe to be the realities underlying our terrestrial existence could be expanded indefinitely in many directions. However long it might become, the last word could never be said. I had better stop here.

If anything I have said seems questionable or obscure, have patience with it, or ask me about it if I am still available.

APPENDIX

One could go on indefinitely. Have I said too much, or just enough, or not enough? The middle course has been my aim.

From A Letter to Thomas Merton

Correspondence with Thomas Merton

To Lord Northbourne, Easter 1965

I have just finished reading your book *Religion in the Modern World*. Since I did not want to send you a mere formal note of thanks, but wanted also to share my impressions with you, I have delayed writing about it until now.[1]

After a careful reading, spread out over some time (I have read the book a bit at a time), I believe that your book is exceptionally good. Certainly I am most grateful for the opportunity to read it, and needless to say I am very glad that Marco Pallis suggested that you send it to me. Not only is the book interesting, but I have found it quite salutary and helpful in my own case. It has helped me to organize my ideas at a time when we in the Catholic Church, and in the monastic Orders, are being pulled this way and that. Traditions of great importance and vitality are being questioned along with more trivial customs, and I do not think that those who are doing the questioning are always distinguished for their wisdom or even their information. I could not agree more fully with your principles and with your application of them. In particular, I am grateful for your last chapter. For one thing it clears up a doubt that had persisted in my mind, about the thinking of the Schuon-Guénon "school" (if one can use such a term), as well as about the rather slapdash ecumenism that is springing up in some quarters. It is most important first of all to understand deeply and live one's own tradition, not confusing it with what is foreign to it, if one is to seriously appreciate other traditions and distinguish in them what is close to one's own and what is, perhaps, irreconcilable with one's own. The great danger at the moment is a huge muddling and confusing of

---

[1] At the suggestion of Marco Pallis, Lord Northbourne had sent Merton a copy of *Religion in the Modern World*. Merton in turn sent Lord Northbourne a copy of his analysis of Vatican II's Constitution on the Church in the Modern World (*Gaudium et Spes*). Called "The Church and the 'Godless World'", this essay became Part I of Merton's *Redeeming the Time* (published in England by Burns & Oates in 1966). Merton's side of the correspondence reproduced here was first published in *Witness to Freedom: The Letters of Thomas Merton in Times of Crisis*, selected and edited by William H. Shannon (New York: Farrar, Straus & Giroux, 1994). —Editors

the spiritual traditions that still survive. As you so well point out, this would be crowning the devil's work.

The great problem that faces me in this regard, is twofold. The Council has determined to confront the modern world and in some way to decide what ought to be its attitude, and where it ought to stand. Now I must say in this area I am very disturbed by both those who are termed conservative and some who are called liberal in the Council, and out of it too. I am afraid that on both sides too superficial a view of "the world" is being taken—whether that view be optimistic or pessimistic. I don't think that the implications of the technological revolution have even begun to be grasped by either side. Then there is the unfortunate fact that Catholic tradition has become in many ways ambiguous and confused. Not in itself, but in the way in which it is regarded by Catholics. Since people have got into the unfortunate habit of thinking of Tradition as a specialized department of theology, and since spiritual disciplines have undergone considerable shrinking and drying out by being too legalized, and since the traditional styles of life, worship, and so on have become, for us, merely courtly and baroque to such a great extent, the question of renewal does become urgent.

Here is where we run into the greatest difficulties and confusions, especially in America. Personally I can see the wisdom of simply trying to purify and preserve the ancient medieval and earlier traditions which we have in monasticism, and can easily be recovered. Thanks to the work of Solesmes and other monasteries, the material we need is all at hand. Unfortunately it becomes clear that in America at least, and even to some extent in Europe, this will no longer get through to the new generations. And the misfortune is that they seem happy with the most appalling trivialities and the silliest of innovations. In my own work I do my best to keep the novices in touch with monastic sources and convey to them something of the real spirit of monastic discipline and interior prayer. I find that they respond to this, and that the sense of living tradition is not totally dead. But on the other hand, if one is to get into polemics and start battling for tradition, and for right interpretations, one tends oneself to lose the spirit of tradition. And of course perspective and the sense of value disappear along with one's real spirit. If one must choose, I suppose it is best to try oneself to live one's tradition and obey the Holy Spirit within one's tradition as completely as possible, and not worry about results.

More and more I become aware of the gravity of the present situation, not only in matters of tradition and discipline and the spiritual life, but even as regarding man and his civilization. The forces that have been at work to bring us to this critical point have now apparently completely escaped our control (if they were ever under it) and I do not see how we can avoid a very great disaster, by which I do not mean a sudden extermination of the whole race by H-bombs, but nevertheless a general collapse into anarchy and sickness together. In a certain sense, the profound alterations in the world and in man that have resulted from the last hundred years of "progress" are already a disaster, and the effects will be unavoidable. In such a situation, to speak with bland optimism of the future of man and of the Church blessing a new technological paradise becomes not only absurd but blasphemous. Yet at the same time, this technological society still has to be redeemed and sanctified in some way, not simply cursed and abhorred.

The great problem underlying it also, as you so well see, is idolatry. And here the great question is: can the society we have now constructed possibly be anything else than idolatrous? I suppose one must still hope and believe that it can. But in practice I cannot feel too sanguine about it. In any case, I think we have our hands full seeking and helping the victims of this society, and we cannot yet begin to "save" and spiritualize the society itself. I am certainly not one of those who, with Teilhard de Chardin, see the whole thing in rosy and messianic colors.

In any case I am very grateful for your important and thoughtful book, and I am sure you can see I am in the deepest possible sympathy with your views. It is not possible for me, and doubtless for you, to get into lengthy correspondence about these things, yet they are so important that I do hope we will be able to share at times ideas and suggestions that might be profitable. I will try to send you some books and writings of my own that you might like. In the book of poems I shall send there is a long letter which you might find interesting, together with a prose poem, "Hagia Sophia". I should be most interested in your own writings or statements that might come out from time to time.

Précis of Lord Northbourne's Reply

Thanks . . . welcome exchange of ideas . . .

Is not the confusion prevalent even in the ecclesiastical hierarchy largely attributable to preoccupation with outward and quantitative results as against inward and qualitative perfection? The Council fails to grasp the implications of technological revolution because preoccupied with it and not with "trying to purify and preserve . . . tradition".

There could be no worry about the Council's attitude and where it ought to stand if there were no uncertainty about what it, or the Church, really *is*. One fears wrong choice of priorities between outward relations and inward perfection.

A right choice implies that renewal must come about secretly . . . even "unintentionally", no particular result being envisaged. If it comes through any organization it will be monastic in spirit even if not in form.

[Allusion to Frithjof Schuon's article and forthcoming book. Promise to send.]

I question whether "this technological society still has to be redeemed and sanctified". God has destroyed societies for their abominations. But never refused Himself to a soul that has remained faithful. Therefore society in His eyes is a framework or testing ground; not it, but souls are precious. It can be sanctified (i.e., when traditional) or not (when otherwise); but souls and not society are saved or dammed. Living now is easy for the body and hard for the soul, in other times it was often the other way round; God will take this into account and not judge us too severely.

The idea that anything "positive" can emerge from modern civilization seems heretical, because it postulates that good can come out of evil. Evil posing as good adds to confusion.

Am I muddling redemption, sanctification, and salvation and failing to see the sense in which your words are applicable?

Some must battle outwardly, others only inwardly: the latter is the essential—perhaps because it takes no account of results. "Covet earnestly the best gifts."

Renewed thanks . . .

To Lord Northbourne, February 23, 1966

Thank you for your kind letter and for the copy of your lecture, which I read with great interest, finding it clear, objective, and firm. Many thanks also for the first copy of *Tomorrow* in the attractive new format (I very much like the design on the cover). I like this magazine and will be happy to receive it. Last evening I read your article on "Flowers", which I enjoyed very much. The purely utilitarian explanation of the attractiveness of flowers is always annoying, it is so superficial.

I have written a commentary of the Council's Constitution on the Church in the Modern World. This was done, not because I particularly wanted to do it, but because it was needed as asked for by [the London publisher] Burns & Oates. I am very much afraid that the job is unsatisfactory in many ways. At least I am not at all satisfied with it. The basic purpose of the Constitution is one that I obviously agree with: the maintaining of reasonable communication between the Church and the world of modern technology. If communication breaks down entirely, and there is no hope of exchanging ideas, then the situation becomes impossible. However, the naive optimism with which some of the Council Fathers seem to have wanted a Church entirely identified with the modern scientific mentality is equally impossible. I have said this in the end as conclusively as I could, with respect to one issue in particular. But in any case if I can get some copies made of the text I will send you one. There might be a few points of interest in it. I am of course very much concerned with one issue which is symptomatic of all the rest: nuclear warfare. It is true that one should not focus on one issue so as to distract attention from the entire scene in all its gravity. I think I have touched on a few other things as well, but have certainly not done a complete job, and have tried to be conciliatory in some ways. In a word, I am not satisfied with it and perhaps few others will be.

Meanwhile, as I do have a copy of this meditation on "events" ["Events and Pseudo-Events", published in *Faith and Violence*, 1968], I am sending it along. I hope I am not burdening you with too many things, but obviously I realize that you will not feel obligated to read them, and will do so only if you are really interested.

To Fr. Thomas Merton, August 5, 1966

I have read your commentary on the Vatican Council's Constitution on the Church in the Modern World with great care, and I hope profitably, and am most grateful to you for sending it. You provide a very useful explanatory summary and you clarify many issues. Those issues, I cannot help feeling, important though they may be, are however subsidiary to something else. I have hesitated long as to whether I should try to say what it seems to me to be. I do not see how I can acknowledge your kindness suitably without attempting to do so. So here goes, as shortly as possible, and therefore perhaps rather violently. What I have to say relates mainly to the Constitution itself, and only indirectly to your commentary.

We live in a "Godless" world. What does this mean? It is indisputably a religionless world, unless one stretches the meaning of the word "religion" to cover anything one believes to be true, or even expedient. What I mean is that most people nowadays reject or ignore the great Revelations and the observances in which they have been crystallized. They substitute some kind of ideology, related either to a "God" of their own invention or to an open agnosticism. On this view, the world rejects the one true God, and so can properly be said to be Godless, exactly to the extent to which it substitutes a man-made ideology for revealed religion and its crystallizations, or more simply to the extent that it substitutes humanism for religion.

What does the word "humanism" mean, unless it be the subordination of the essentials of religion to human ideologies? And even if that is not so, I feel sure of one thing, namely, that the distinction between the Christian humanism advocated by the Council and the various other brands of humanism is much too subtle to be grasped by a vast majority of those who take any interest in the matter at all. It is, as you point out, the distinction between treating the individual as "object" and as "person", but the metaphysical perception of "personality" is either absent or is regarded as having been superseded by more recent notions. A scientific and agnostic humanist would argue that exactly what he is out for is the treatment of human beings as "persons" and not as "objects", and he will never be able to take the other point of view because it is meaningless to him, as well as to most of his hearers. I wonder if humanism is not always humanism, whatever its label.

What does the Church expect the fate of a Godless world to be? Apparently some kind of humanitarian demi-paradise. Is that what the saints were seeking, or do we know better than they do? The Council may be held to be speaking in the first place to Catholics, who are supposed to know what the true priorities are and to live accordingly—but do they? In any case, is it really prudent (to put it gently) to *appear* not to be putting first things first, despite the danger that religion can always decline into religiosity.

What is a "better world"? I am perfectly clear as to what it is in the view of a vast majority: it is a more comfortable world, and nothing else. Certainly not a more saintly world—unless humanitarianism is confused with sanctity, as it so often is. A world that is "better" in any sense of the word, even merely humanitarian, cannot in any case be built out of the material of a Godless world, though it can, and doubtless will, arise out of its ashes. To anyone who can read the signs of the times, the temporal optimism of the Council is hard to justify. I hazard the guess that you have found it so.

There is a statement, quoted by you on page fifty-eight, which, if it means what it says, reveals so profound a misconception of the real state of affairs that I can hardly believe my eyes. It says: "It is now possible to free most of humanity from the misery of ignorance." The assumption, I suppose, is that modern science has at last revealed the truth and provided the means for its dissemination, or that it has offered hope where before there was none. I am reduced to silence.

I hope you see why such considerations as these seem to me to put all others in the shade, and why I cannot help fearing that this adaptation of Christianity to the contemporary mentality has not been carried much farther than is necessary in order to safeguard the very existence of Christianity. As in the past, nothing else can justify a major adaptation, especially coming as it does now with the fullest possible authority of the Church. Or have I completely misinterpreted the tendency of the Constitution?

With one small point in your commentary I cannot agree. You say on page seventy-two that "inhumanity is accepted without protest by the vast majority simply because they believe this is the way things have to be". No, it is because they simply cannot think what to do about it, and no wonder. This feeling of helpless despair counts for much. It is in fact a despair at the failure of humanism, whether they see it as such or not.

One could go on indefinitely. Have I said too much, or just enough, or not enough? The middle course has been my aim.

To Lord Northbourne, August 30, 1966

I am really very grateful for your thoughtful letter [on Merton's "The Church and the 'Godless World'"], and of course you know that I am basically in agreement with you, temperamentally and by taste and background, when it comes to appreciating the values of the ancient cultural and spiritual traditions which today are not only in many ways threatened but even to some extent undermined. And you know, too, that in writing my book on the Constitution on the Church in the [Modern] World, I was not so much trying to clarify a personal philosophy as to interpret what the Council was trying to say, and do so objectively. I have come to the conclusion that the effort was unsatisfactory and have decided not to publish this material in book form in the U.S.A. With this in mind I will take up the points you raise, not with the intention of "answering" arguments but simply of clarifying my own position—if possible. And it is not easy.

First there was a deliberately permitted ambiguity in the title of the book. There is much discussion now of what it means to be "godless" and one of the ambiguities about it is that certain Christian values have in fact been smuggled over to the "godless" side at times. But this too is ambiguous insofar as they tend to become merely "humanitarian" and so on. But behind the whole question is the fact that the Church has had to admit the futility of an embattled, negative, ghetto-like resistance to everything modern, a "stance", as they say, which was rather unfortunate in the 19th and early 20th century, not because it was conservative but because it was also quite arbitrary, narrow, uncomprehending, and tended to preserve not necessarily the best of the Catholic tradition but a kind of baroque absolutism in theology, worship, and so on. Now, since the Church obviously has to outgrow this, and since in doing so it has to become for better or for worse "contemporary", there has been an inevitable reaction, with an insistence on "openness" and so on which I think is necessary though I do not accept without reservation some of the naive optimism about "the world" that goes along with this. The general idea is that man has to be understood in his actual present situation, and not with reference to some situation which we would prefer to have him in.

The situation of man today is one of dreadful crisis. We are in full revolution, but it is not the simple, straightforward old-fashioned political revolution. It is a far-reaching, uncontrolled, largely unconscious revolution pervading every sphere of his existence and often developing new critical tendencies before anyone realizes what is happening. Now, I think that the Constitution, though it does vaguely recognize this, does not say enough to underline the real seriousness of the situation, and it does, as you say, tend to accept the surface optimism of some secular outlooks on progress without much hesitation. It does seem to say that if we just go along with technology we will have a happier and better world. This is by no means guaranteed. On the other hand, I do not feel, as some do, that the Constitution should simply have admitted frankly that the future promises little more than apocalyptic horror. Though this possibility is very real and was perhaps not brought out very clearly. In other words I think the attitude taken by the Council is basically reasonable, and it seems to be this:

Much as we appreciate the great value of ancient and traditional cultures, the coming of the industrial and technological revolution has undermined them and in fact doomed them. Everywhere in the world these cultures have now been more or less affected—corrupted—by modern Western man and his rather unfortunate systems. It is simply not possible to return to the cultural stability and harmony of these ancient structures. But it is hoped that one can maintain some sort of continuity and preserve at least some of their living reality in a new kind of society. For my part I am frankly dubious: I foresee a rather pitiful bastardized culture, vulgarized, uniform, and full of elements of parody and caricature, and perhaps frightening new developments of its own which may be in a certain way "interesting" and even exciting. And terrible. The Council assumes that we just go on peacefully progressing and reasonably negotiating obstacles, making life more and more "human".

I certainly think that we need a much "better" world than the one we have at the moment, and I make no bones about insisting that this means feeding, clothing, housing, and educating a lot of people who are living in the most dreadful destitution. Remember that in South America, Africa, Asia, we are no longer comparing the ancient tribal cultures with modern culture but the rural and urban slum culture of destitution and degradation that has ruined and succeeded the old cultures. This *must* be dealt with, and in facing the fact the Church has simply done her plain duty: and a great deal more needs to be done on the spot. It is a well-known fact that if in South America the people who call themselves Catholics would get down to work and do something about the situation, it could be immensely improved. Hence I see nothing wrong with the Council demanding work for a "better world" in this sense. It is not a question of comfort, but of the basic necessities of life and decency. In this respect, "humanism" is a matter of simple respect for man as man, and Christian humanism is based on the belief in the Incarnation and on a relationship to others which supposed that "whatsoever you do to the least of my brethren you do it to me" (i.e., to Christ). Here I have no difficulty. Except of course in the way in which some of this might be interpreted or applied. Literacy is not a cure-all, and there are plenty of absurd modern social myths. Nevertheless there are realities that must be faced in the terms of our actual possibilities, and return to the ancient cultures is simply not possible. Though we should certainly try to see that their values are preserved insofar as they can be.

Since the purpose of this Constitution was that of giving largely practical directives for the way in which Catholics should participate in the work of trying to help man through his present crisis, the "first things" were simply stated in a few obvious broad principles in the place where this was most relevant: beginning of the Constitution, beginning of various sections, and so on. It must be remembered that the Constitution is part of a whole, and the work of the Council fills a volume of nearly eight hundred pages in the edition I have. The "first things" are treated much more extensively in places like the Constitution on the Church and on Revelation. But in practice, with man in a position literally to destroy himself and his culture, I do not think that concern about saving him temporally and giving him a chance to set his house in order is merely secondary.

It is for this reason that I cannot take a merely conservative position, though I see a great deal wrong and suspect about the progressive view and I do not find myself always able to speak its language. But I wonder if the traditional spiritual language of charity and mercy does not in fact demand to be put into action in these social forms in our new situation. But of course here we are in a realm where I cannot competently speak. I am not an economist or a politician.

In any case I really appreciate your letter. Doubtless it was my own fault if the book was not clear and gave the impression that this was just a matter of the "social gospel" over again. It is much more a problem than that.

Stated in the baldest terms, in my own situation, I meet the problem daily in this form: I can completely turn my back on the whole "world" and simply try to devote myself to meditation and contemplation, silence, withdrawal, renunciation, and so on. I spent at least twelve years of my monastic life with no further object than this. At the end of that time I began to see that this was insufficient and indeed deceptive. It was unreal. It could indeed create in me the impression that I was putting first things first and striving for sanctity. But I also learned in many ways that it was false and that the whole thing rested on a rather imaginary basis. I still devote most of my time to meditation, contemplation, reading—in fact I now give much more of my time to these things since I am living in solitude: but also I read a great deal more about what is happening and the common problems of the world I live in, not so much on the level of newspapers (I do not get the paper) or of magazines, still less radio or TV (I have barely seen TV once or twice in my life). But I do feel that if I am not in some way able to identify myself with my contemporaries and if I isolate myself so entirely from them that I imagine that I am a different kind of being, I am simply perpetrating a kind of religious fraud. I quite simply believe that I have to hear the voice of God not only in the Bible and other writings, but in the crisis of this age, and I have to commit myself to a certain level of responsibility: in my case being a writer I have to be able to speak out and say certain things that may need saying, to the best of my knowledge and according to my conscience and to what seems to be the inspiration of the Holy Spirit. I realize the enormous difficulty of this, and I have no illusion that it is easy to be a prophet, or that I must necessarily try to be one. But there are things I think I must say. In the case of the book about the Council Constitution, however, I am, I think, quite aware that what I was saying did not need to be said, at least by me, and I have decided that there is no point in having the book published here. It is not the kind of thing I am supposed to be doing.

In the long run, I think that is what you were trying to tell me in your letter, and I quite agree.

Thus you see that in the end we do meet, though I think there are genuine accidental differences in our viewpoint. I think you are simply more straightforwardly conservative than I am and that for you the conservative position does not present the difficulties that it does for me. You are fortunate, because your position is thus much simpler than mine can be, and it is easier for you to be quite definite on every point where I might have to hesitate and qualify. In fact there are many points that are to me uncertain, and I cannot say what I think about them.

To Fr. Thomas Merton, October 9, 1966

Thank you very much for your letter of 30th August. It has been helpful to me in clearing my own head, and in giving me a broader view of the nature and intentions of the Constitution on the Church in the Modern World. In one respect my position is indeed "simple" and as "conservative" as you like—but only in one. If I have given the impression of being definite on every point (your penultimate remark) it is my fault, for that is the last thing I would profess to be. It is not the same thing as being definite on *one* point, as I am (if it can be called a single point), and then trying to relate other points to it. That is where complexity and uncertainty come in, for me as for you, and they tend all too often to obscure the main issue. So may I try to clarify?

In the present context, my one point could be expressed, among endless other possible ways, as follows. You cannot give yourself to mankind in charity unless you have first given yourself to God. If you try to do so your gift will be valueless—it will be giving a stone for bread—or worse, giving for a fish a serpent. (There is a more positive corollary to this: if you give yourself to God, you are thereby giving yourself to mankind.) Surely this is the essence of the teaching of the Gospels (summarized in the two commandments). If that is not so, I am beating the air. But because I believe it to be so, I cannot but feel that the Council could have insisted on this essential point, again and again and again, without being any less specific about the application of this principle to the particular problem in view. Some such insistence would seem to be specially important in this particular section of the whole work of the Council, simply because the principle in question is the very one that scientific humanism seeks above all to eliminate, knowing that victory depends on its elimination; scientific humanism parodies Christian charity by substituting terrestrial welfare for salvation. Hitherto the Roman Catholic Church has been the arch-opponent of this heresy. She has not only put first things first,

but has also appeared to do so. If she ceases to maintain an uncompromising position in this one respect, what may not the end be? *Quis
custodiet ipsos custodes?*[2]

The Constitution on the Church in the Modern World, besides
receiving much more publicity than any other part of the Council's
work, has been widely accepted as a pronouncement which stands on
its own. There is no indication to the contrary in the English translation published by Burns & Oates for the Catholic Truth Society
(which is the one I have).

That seems to me to be the starting-point, which admits of no
compromise, to which all else must be made to conform, whatever
the immediate cost of conformity may appear to be. That is my case.
I do not suppose for a moment that yours is any different. If we differ
it is only in details of its application to this or that problem.

I was much interested in what you say about your own situation.
I suppose that the art of living could be said to consist largely in rec-
ognizing one's own vocation, and acting accordingly. I feel sure that
my vocation is not that of a monk or hermit. (If it is, I have missed
it!) I did not begin to see things consciously as I do now till nearly
fifty (I am now seventy). By that time my five children had already
arrived (and have since proliferated into an additional twelve) and I
was thoroughly involved in the affairs of a hereditary landowner and
farmer. Such has been my destiny and I should be the last to quarrel
with it. One must do what one can within the framework of one's
destiny. Are you not by vocation a preacher? Preaching covers writing,
especially in these days. If so, you seem to have followed it to some
effect. Others are pure contemplatives, and I would on no account
depreciate the importance of the part they are called upon to play.
In these days destiny is disregarded and vocation is suppressed. We
imagine that we control not only our own future, but also our own
nature. No delusion could be more unfortunate. We are terribly like
the Laodiceans in Revelations, chap. 3, especially verse 17.[3] It is easy
enough at the moment to see the temporal and tenebrous aspect of

---

[2] "Who will guard the guards themselves?", a phrase from the Roman poet Juvenal.
—Editors

[3] "For you say, I am rich, I have prospered, and I need nothing; not knowing that you
are wretched, pitiable, poor, blind, and naked." —Editors

existence; less easy to see its eternal and luminous aspect. Yet the latter is the reality.

To Lord Northbourne, June 4, 1967

To begin with, I am more and more convinced that *Redeeming the Time* is a superficial and inadequate book. I do, of course, believe still in the urgency of social change in places like South America, where, frankly, too many people are living in appalling conditions, brought on in many cases by "progress". In any event, this book is not being published anywhere else.

What really prompted me to write to you today: I am reading a curious book called *Evolution and Christian Hope* by one Ernst Benz. Curious is not the word for parts of it. He has a chapter which justifies technological progress by the Bible and by ideas like God the potter framing his creatures on a potter's wheel. And he finds in Catholic medieval tradition (where the Victorines for instance speak of the "arts" in terms like Marco Pallis) warrant for the idea that "technology is a means of overcoming original sin". I thought that gem of modern thought should be shared with you. Fantastic, isn't it? Really, you are so very right. That is what we are facing now. I do not suggest that you read this book, it would shock you. But that particular chapter is so funny, in its own bizarre way, that you might dip into it there if the book ever comes your way. But I do not suppose it will, and do not encourage you to go looking for it.

I just thought I would send you these few badly typed lines as a sign of life and a reminder that I do very much appreciate all that you have to say, and that I am very aware of the ambiguities of the current Catholic position. I am frankly quite alienated from much of the thinking going on in my Church, on both sides, both conservative and "progressive".

Lord Northbourne in his garden at Northbourne Court

INDEX

Index

For a glossary of all key foreign words used in books published by World Wisdom, including metaphysical terms in English, consult:
www.DictionaryofSpiritualTerms.org.
This on-line Dictionary of Spiritual Terms provides extensive definitions, examples, and related terms in other languages.

BIOGRAPHICAL NOTES

CHRISTOPHER GEORGE WALTER JAMES, 5TH BARON NORTHBOURNE, was born 18 February, 1926. He is a British farmer and businessman. The son of the 4th Baron Northbourne and Katharine Louise Nickerson, he succeeded to his father's title in 1982. He was educated at Eton College in Berkshire and Magdalen College, Oxford, where he graduated with a Master of Arts in 1959. Lord Northbourne is one of the ninety hereditary peers elected to remain in the House of Lords after the passing of the House of Lords Act in 1999. Northbourne is Chairman of the Stepney Children's Fund, the Parenting Support Forum and Kent Salads, and a Governor of Wye Agricultural College In 1959, he married Marie Sygne Claudel, daughter of Henri Claudel. They have three sons, including his heir Charles Walter Henry James, and a daughter.

JOSEPH A. FITZGERALD studied Comparative Religion at Indiana University, where he also earned a Doctor of Jurisprudence degree. He is a professional editor whose previous publications include *Honen the Buddhist Saint: Essential Writings and Official Biography*, *The Essential Sri Anandamayi Ma: Life and Teachings of a 20th Century Saint from India*, and *The Cheyenne Indians: Their History and Lifeways*. He lives with his wife and daughter in Bloomington, Indiana.

WENDELL BERRY is a conservationist, farmer, essayist, novelist, professor of English, and poet. He was born August 5, 1934 in Henry Country, Kentucky, and is the author of 32 books of essays, poetry, and novels. The *New York Times* has called Berry the "prophet of rural America". A former professor of English at the University of Kentucky and a past fellow of both the Guggenheim Foundation and the Rockefeller Foundation, Berry now lives and works on a farm near Port Royal, Kentucky. He has received numerous awards for his work, including an award from the National Institute and Academy of Arts and Letters in 1971, and the T. S. Eliot Award in 1994.

Titles in the Perennial Philosophy Series by World Wisdom

Journeys East: 20th Century Western Encounters with Eastern Religious Traditions, by Harry Oldmeadow, 2004

Light From the East: Eastern Wisdom for the Modern West, edited by Harry Oldmeadow, 2007

Living in Amida's Universal Vow: Essays in Shin Buddhism, edited by Alfred Bloom, 2004

Of the Land and the Spirit: The Essential Lord Northbourne on Ecology and Religion, edited by Christopher James and Joseph A. Fitzgerald, 2008

Paths to the Heart: Sufism and the Christian East, edited by James S. Cutsinger, 2002

Remembering in a World of Forgetting: Thoughts on Tradition and Postmodernism, by William Stoddart, 2008

Returning to the Essential: Selected Writings of Jean Biès, translated by Deborah Weiss-Dutilh, 2004

Science and the Myth of Progress, edited by Mehrdad M. Zarandi, 2003

Seeing God Everywhere: Essays on Nature and the Sacred, edited by Barry McDonald, 2003

Singing the Way: Insights in Poetry and Spiritual Transformation, by Patrick Laude, 2005

The Spiritual Legacy of the North American Indian: Commemorative Edition, by Joseph E. Brown, 2007

Sufism: Love & Wisdom, edited by Jean-Louis Michon and Roger Gaetani, 2006

The Underlying Religion: An Introduction to the Perennial Philosophy, edited by Martin Lings and Clinton Minnaar, 2007

Ye Shall Know the Truth: Christianity and the Perennial Philosophy, edited by Mateus Soares de Azevedo, 2005